*DISCIPLINES AND INTERDISCIPLINARITY
IN FOREIGN LANGUAGE STUDIES*

# Disciplines and Interdisciplinarity

## in

## Foreign Language Studies

edited by

Hans Lauge Hansen

University of Copenhagen

Museum Tusculanum Press

2004

Hans Lauge Hansen (ed.)
*Disciplines and Interdisciplinarity
in Foreign Language Studies*

© Museum Tusculanum Press and the Authors 2004
Layout: Nils Soelberg
Cover design: Pernille Sys Hansen
Printed in Denmark by Narayana Press
ISBN: 87 7289 940 9

The editors gratefully acknowledge the financial support from
The Language and Culture Network
and The Faculty of Humanities, University of Copenhagen

Museum Tusculanum Press
University of Copenhagen
Njalsgade 94
DK-2300 København S
Denmark
www.mtp.dk

# Contents

Hans Lauge Hansen: Foreign Language Studies and Interdisciplinarity ... 7

## Discussions on the Theoretical Foundation of Foreign Language Studies

Karen Risager: A Social and Cultural View of Language .............. 21

Helge Jordheim: Philology of the Future, Futures of Philology.
Interdisciplinarity, Intertemporality, and *Begriffsgeschichte* ......... 35

Mette Steenberg: Cognitive Models. Language and Thought in Cultural Studies ................................................... 51

## A Novel Look at Traditional Disciplines of Foreign Language Studies

Hanne Leth Andersen, Merete Birkelund & Thora Vinther: Traditional and New Approaches to Theoretical Grammar Teaching .......... 65

Jørn Boisen & Pia Schwarz Lausten: The study of literature – Does it matter, and if so, why? ...................................... 77

Sofie Nielsen: Cultural Orientation and Interdisciplinarity. The German debate on *Literaturwissenschaft als Kulturwissenschaft* ............. 91

Francesco Caviglia : 'Advanced literacy'. Bridging traditions in the study of language and culture ...................................... 105

## Interdisciplinary Approaches to Foreign Language Studies

Edmond Cros: Towards a Sociocritical Theory of the Text ........... 121

Inge Degn, Lisbeth Verstraete Hansen, Anne Magnussen, Jens Rahbek Rasmussen: The Construction and Deconstruction of Nation and Identity in Modern Belgium ................................. 131

Johan Pedersen & Teresa Cadierno: Construction Grammar and Second Language Acquisition: A Cognitive Understanding of Language in a Contrastive Perspective ..................................... 151

Nina Nørgaard: Challenging the Boundaries: Exploring the Interface of Linguistics and Literature .................................... 169

Jan Gustafsson: Narratives of Natives: The construction of the Other as object of aid. ............................................... 183

## The Deconstruction of the Eurocentric Perspective of Foreign Language Studies

Heidi Bojsen & Ingemai Larsen: Narrating Postcolonial Nations: Reading Homi Bhabha's Notions ..................................... 197

Anne Marie Jeppesen & Ken Henriksen : Studies of postcolonialism and the Latin American tradition: National Identities and Indigenous struggles. ................................................... 211

Bernard Mouralis & Heidi Bojsen: African Literature Today: The Stakes in Teaching and Research ...................................... 229

List of Authors ................................................ 242

# Foreign Language Studies and Interdisciplinarity

by
Hans Lauge Hansen

Foreign Language Studies, both in Denmark and internationally, find themselves in a difficult situation: although contemporary society has a great need for linguistic and cultural competences, Foreign Language Departments at the universities are going through a slump. Student entries are declining, the academic prestige of the departments is waning and they are subjected to cutbacks in funding. This situation prompted the foundation, in September 2002, of *The Language and Culture Network*, with the aim of establishing and encouraging interdisciplinary collaboration between the traditional branches of Foreign Language Studies (linguistics, literary studies and history). The network brings together more than 100 scholars from different departments of Foreign Language Studies throughout Denmark, the purpose of this interdisciplinary enterprise being to comprehend each individual discipline in the light of a unitary object of study, the text. The present collection of articles reflects the activity of the *Language and Culture Network* between September 2002 and September 2003.

But how can interdisciplinarity be regarded as a solution to the kind of problems that haunt Foreign Language Studies? In order to address this question, it will be necessary to look both at the present situation of these studies and at the recent history of these departments.

### The Object of Study of Foreign Languages Studies
The academic study of foreign languages was first implemented early in the 20th century with the purpose of providing society with high school teachers of foreign languages such as English, German and French, and it was created in the image of national philology. The tradition of Classical Philology goes back at least to the Renaissance, where the universal ideals

associated with the emergence of Humanism led to the rediscovery and reintroduction of the Classical texts. The national philologies (Romance, Germanic, Nordic, etc.), on the other hand, emerged during the 19th century as a fusion between early positivist tendencies in the description of national languages and the historicist movement of national Romanticism. Within national philology, the Romantic concept of the *Volksgeist* gave unity to the philological enterprise in the sense that language and literature were considered forms of expression that gave privileged access to the study of this essence of the national spirit (Grabes 1996).

The 20th century saw the emergence of the comparative disciplines of the human sciences such as history, linguistics, comparative literature and anthropology, and the object of study of the philologies was compartmentalized. Each discipline was established with its own methodology and generated its own tradition, and philology lost its position as the scientific paradigm that provided the overall structure of the human sciences. One could claim that traditional philology outlived itself in the last half of the 20th century, not as a specific practice in the professional handling of texts, but as a scientific paradigm governing the organization of the Human Sciences. This overall change of paradigm within the human sciences also changed the character and position of Foreign Language Studies. The centre of theoretical innovation and research was displaced from the philological departments to the comparative disciplines, and the academic prestige of Foreign Language Studies was damaged. The old philological departments found themselves in an increasingly paradoxical situation: although no other paradigm took over philology's position as a unifying principle capable of holding together the various disciplines of Foreign Language Studies, the overall character of these departments did not change substantially.

The compartmentalization of the formerly unified object of the philological enterprise into general linguistics, comparative literature, social history and anthropology resulted in a setback for Foreign Language Studies in different ways. The study of foreign languages was divided into different disciplines with hardly any connection, seen from the students' point of view, and within each of the disciplines this situation generated a kind of frustration as it became evident to both teachers and students that foreign language students could not reach the same theoretical level as students in the comparative departments. The lack of a unified object of study in the formerly philological departments thus resulted in a situation where the students felt less theoretically qualified than their colleagues in the specialised departments, and where the academic staff often thought of themselves as representatives of their different disciplines within these departments. In some cases this has had the consequence that the development of the professional profile of the departments has depended just as much on the power balance between disciplines as on the actual requirements of society. It has therefore been of great importance for the network to scrutinise the curriculum of our traditional disciplines and to discuss whether and to what extent the empirical focus does meet the social request for professional competences, and whether and to what extent the theoretical approach does reflect the state of the art of the discipline.

If we understand the general object of study of the Humanities as an investigation into the relation between self and other, i.e. the comprehension of our own cultural specificity through the acquisition of knowledge of the cultural 'Other', the main challenge of the human sciences at the change of the millennium could be understood as the cultural impact caused by the increased processes of economic and political globalization and the mediation of this cultural encounter by information technology. The processes of increased political domination and economic transactions on a global scale imply the increase of cultural encounters at all levels of society, and it is necessary for the human sciences to adjust to this reality. As argued in *Changing Philologies*, Foreign Language Studies must learn to conceive of culture as an open, multi-voiced and dialogical interaction full of contradictions, rather than as the deterministic, homogeneous and closed structure that belonged to the era of the nation state (Hansen 2002). Within the literary and cultural disciplines Foreign Language Studies might wish to break down the Eurocentric canons of national philology and engage with the study of dialogues across linguistic, discursive and cultural boundaries (Gumbrecht 1995, Navajas 2002), and the recent development within the field of visual media might oblige us to reconsider the position of literature within the broader field of artistic and cultural expressions. And within the discipline of linguistics, Foreign Language Studies might consider whether our studies really teach students of grammar a theoretically reflected concept of language that makes it possible to establish the relations between languages, history and cultures.

**Theory and interdisciplinarity**
Although we must maintain that the different disciplines of Foreign Language Studies have a unitary object of study, the text, the recent development of the empirical focus implies that in the future the character of the texts studied will be diversified and multifaceted. This is why conscious reflection on the theoretical approach today is more important than ever as a means of interdisciplinary practice across both disciplines and languages. This should not be understood as meaning that one theory, or even a limited canon of chosen theories, can be specified as the solution or salvation of Foreign Language Studies, but as a welcoming gesture encouraging the interaction and collaboration of a broad variety of different approaches (Jordheim 2001). Recently, i.e. within the last 15 or 20 years, a

change of paradigm within the human sciences has allowed for three 'turns' within three of the core disciplines of foreign language studies, making possible the reestablishment of a unitary object of study for the former philological departments: the pragmatic turn within linguistics, the linguistic turn within historical and cultural studies, and the cultural turn within literary studies.

I have argued that these three disciplinary 'turns' are related to a general change of paradigm in the human sciences that I called dialogism (Hansen 2002). According to the traditional modernist paradigm of science that dominated the major part of the $20^{th}$ century, the interest governing scientific investigation was directed towards the structures underlying phenomena, and the answer to the scientific quest was expected to reveal the systems of relations beyond the reach of immediate human cognition. The dialogical change of paradigm has reoriented the human sciences towards living processes, towards discourse, and it has become increasingly clear that the scientist is not only himself a part of the studied object, but that the very process of investigation is one of the most important aspects of the construction of the object. The interest of the human sciences is no longer exclusively oriented towards the anti-subjective and closed systems that rule our actions and ideas behind our backs as in, for instance, economics, psychodynamics or grammar (Foucault 1966). The human sciences of the $21^{st}$ century will have to engage with the study of human agency within cultural processes. And this requires a return to the study of living discourse within language studies. Not to the authoritative discourse that, according to Foucault, characterized the encyclopedic project of enlightened despotism and delivered the rational grid for the monological representation of truth, but rather to an open, dialogized and non-finalized discourse through which we not only represent the world but also construct our own presence within it.

### Education, instrumentalization and language studies

Another important consideration when accounting for the crisis in Foreign Language Studies is related to a general change in the way concepts like 'knowledge' and 'education' are conceived of by society and the consequences of this change for educational institutions, consequences that seriously affect the whole sector of the humanities. According to Andreas Kazamias, the education systems, including the universities, have changed on a global level from institutions dedicated to the creation of culturally capable citizens into centers for the production of instrumental knowledge:

> [The idea of the university] is changing from one whose main ingredient has been the English and US concept of 'liberal education', the German *Bildung*...

to one where the main ingredients are 'instrumental rationality' and what the postmodernist French thinker Lyotard has called *performativity*. (Kazamias 2001, 2)

This shift of ideal from general education, or *Bildung*, to instrumental rationality implies that the values traditionally related to entities such as understanding and knowledge are increasingly being converted into the internalisation of useful techniques. And it can be claimed that this change in the overall conception of knowledge and scholarship, and the changed role that this gives the universities in a globalized knowledge society, have had an enormous impact on the way we regard language, and consequently on the way language studies are situated within the totality of the human sciences. Within language studies, 'instrumental rationality' might be understood as a concept of language as a neutral tool in the communication process, with focus on the acquisition of certain communicative skills understood as writing practices (Godzich 1998).

The conception of language as a pure and transparent instrument assumes that the transmission of the same content is possible through translation. It is therefore the supposed transparency and symmetry of different languages that allow instrumentalists to comprehend global English as the tool that can supply the obvious need for increased intercultural understanding in the era of globalization. In other words, to the instrumentalists global English is becoming the cultural pocket calculator of the era of globalization. In Denmark this concept of language is advocated by, for instance, representatives of the Industrial Complex and the Association of Trade and Commerce, but it is regrettably also an attitude which is increasingly present in academia, and not only in, for instance, the social and natural sciences, but also within the Humanities, where it reproduces the blind spot of economic and political globalization theory. This has come about, I believe, because the instrumentalist theory had a point to make in the critique of the traditional Romanticist concept of language that haunted Foreign Language Studies for far too long.

Today the essentialist concepts of language and culture that belonged to the heyday of national Romanticism in the late 19th Century are outdated, but they have survived as ideology. National ideologies *naturalize* national languages, presenting them as emerging by natural growth, and encourage the Romantic notion of 'language' as equivalent to 'culture'. Nationalism presupposes national identity to be more important, more deeply rooted, or even superior to other aspects of cultural identity such as gender, class, occupation, political orientation etc. But national languages are just as much a result of the construction of nation states as are the social and political institutions. As stated by Karl W. Deutch, the number of national languages increased at a faster rate between 1800 and 1900 under the influence of national Romanticism than in any of the preceding ten centuries, and between 1900 and 1937 the number of Europe's standard languages increased more than in the foregoing millennium (Wilken 2001, 177). And even today nationalist movements use national languages and national frontiers as ideological arguments against such consequences of globalization as emigration and the subsequent ethnic and cultural 'pollution' of their supposedly pure languages and cultures.

Although neither the Romanticist nor the instrumentalist concept of language is considered to be scientifically valid today, they remain as important ideological presuppositions for the public debate and for political decision-making. It is therefore the duty of professionals engaged with the study of language and culture to advance alternative ways of understanding this relationship, whether based on functional, pragmatic, semiotic, cognitive or any other theory. Facing the challenge of globalization and the subsequent increased cross-cultural encounters, it would be as fatal to submit to nationalist ideology and protectionism as to ignore the strong relations between linguistic practices and the construction of cultural identities. Nobody can escape the social and cultural consequences of globalization: we just have to adjust to them, and this being the case, it would be an error to try to separate language and life, culture and history. The meaning of our words cannot be reduced to their dictionary definitions, but has to be understood in their specific concrete dialogue with the social and cultural context at the moment of their occurrence. It is therefore necessary for Foreign Language Studies to conceive of language as social practice, and of cultural identity, whether of the individual, of the minority group or of society as a whole, as constructed through discursive practices.

Texts, in the very broadest sense of the word, are philology's object of study, and this tradition creates opportunities for modern Foreign Language Studies since texts, understood as discursive practices, offer themselves as the ideal object of interdisciplinary investigation. Instead of inquiring into the formal character of literary texts, we might ask what these texts *do*. Like any other texts, literary texts have social, political and aesthetic functions, and the study of these functions might help us to clarify the social and political purpose of the whole scholarly enterprise within the field of the Humanities. Discussing the social function of literary studies, Hans Ulrich Gumbrecht points to the obvious loss of weight of this discipline in the 20$^{th}$ century, compared to the importance of literature in the previous century (Gumbrecht 1995). According to Gumbrecht, the role of literary criticism in the 19$^{th}$ century must be understood as related to the bourgeois ideal of education or *Bildung*, where literature and literary criticism mediated between the "institutionalized normative expectations about society and recurrent forms of experience in everyday social life" (Gumbrecht 1995, 7). In other words, literary criticism contributed to the elaboration of normative schemata and images of 'the good life' by extracting ethical values from literary texts and relating them to the experiences of individual persons (op. cit. 8). On this background Gumbrecht points out that literary criticism might reintegrate the social function of *Bildung* in the 21th century, by making "part of our active experience those cultures and literatures that had been kept in the background under the traditional hegemony of Eurocentric values and paradigms" (ibid. 24 and 25). In this way, Gumbrecht argues, we might transport the 19$^{th}$ century bourgeois ideal of education or *Bildung* into the 21$^{st}$-century globalized society as a demand for intercultural knowledge and competences. It is therefore, in my wording, the responsibility of the human sciences to provide the globalized knowledge society with graduates trained in foreign languages and with the profound knowledge of the cultural 'Other' that endows the individual with genuine intercultural competence.

**Disciplines and Interdisciplinarity in Foreign Language Studies**
The simultaneous presence of linguists, literary critics, historians and scholars of media and social sciences within university departments of Foreign Language Studies offers a unique opportunity to engage in an interesting and challenging interdisciplinary collaboration that focuses on the relation between language, culture and history in the study of texts. Many foreign language departments are rather small and divided into even smaller sections dedicated to the study of different languages and/or disciplines, and this structure, together with the centuries-old tradition promoting the stereotype of the solitary scholar, has meant that collective work and collaboration have not been the usual procedures. This is why the network focuses on interdisciplinary collaboration between experts within each of the established disciplines. The specialisation of the disciplines has already gone too far for us to hope that the individual teacher or researcher will be able to survey the whole field covered by Foreign Language Studies, so we have begun to discuss our disciplines from within, trying to relate each of the established disciplines to the perspective of a unitary object of study.

A real and profound change of paradigm in any field of knowledge must have the character of an interdisciplinary enterprise. Ties with existing scientific traditions and communities must be loosened in order to concentrate on the actual object of study from the perspective of other methods and other traditions, and new methods and new traditions must be developed. If Foreign Language Studies mean to take seriously the challenge presented by globalization and the electronic knowledge society, and to deliver graduates trained in foreign languages and with genuine intercultural competences, we must engage in this kind of interdisciplinary collaboration. Real intercultural communication, understood as a dialogue between equal parties, presupposes highly developed linguistic competences and a profound knowledge of culture and history enabling 'translation' from one context to another. Foreign Language Studies have today an opportunity to develop a whole new branch of cultural studies that combines highly developed linguistic competences with an interdisciplinary collaboration between scholars trained and deeply rooted in a series of different disciplines within the Human Sciences.

### Introduction to the articles

The *Language and Culture Network* held its second national assembly in Aarhus in September 2003 under the heading *Disciplines and Interdisciplinarity in Foreign Language Studies,* and the majority of the articles are rewritings of the original papers presented at this conference. But the book also contains several contributions from network members who did not make their way to the conference, and papers presented by international guests invited by the network at other occasions. The articles are divided into four sections that reflect some of the most important issues introduced above:

- Discussions on the theoretical foundation of Foreign Language Studies
- A novel look at traditional disciplines of Foreign Language Studies
- Interdisciplinary approaches to Foreign Language Studies
- The deconstruction of the Eurocentric world view

It must be stressed that the purpose of the book is not to advocate one theoretical perspective or one methodological approach for Foreign Language Studies, but to present a variety of different perspectives and approaches. Consequently, the ambition is not to establish a theoretically coherent line of argument linking the different contributions to each section, or a methodological coherence between sections in which the theoretical section has consequences for educational practice and for the interdisciplinary enterprise, etc. Rather, we have aimed at allowing a variety of qualified voices to speak from their different points of view, and leaving it to the reader to draw conclusions.

*Discussions on the Theoretical Foundation of Foreign Language Studies.*
It seems evident that some of the articles, or rather all the articles to some extent, must concern themselves with the fundamental question of how to conceive of Foreign Language Studies in its present situation between tradition and the new challenges imposed by a globalized world. In this section we have selected three contributions that make this discussion their main topic.

The point of departure for the first contribution, "A Social and Cultural View of Language" by Karen Risager, is that a new theoretical foundation is needed for Foreign Language Studies, one that comprehends them as sites of linguistic and cultural encounters in an increasingly globalized world. According to Risager, the most important concept to rethink and clarify in this respect is that of language itself, and she sets out to define language as a social and cultural phenomenon. The social view of language is based on Ulf Hannerz' social network theory, while in her account of the cultural view Risager develops the concept of the 'languaculture', a concept that is discussed at greater length in the recent thesis by the same author. The concept of languaculture covers the cultural dimensions of language and is designed to analyse different kinds of variability in (oral and written) linguistic practice and thus to function as a bridge between the structure of language and the socially constituted personal idiolects related to the personal identity of the individual. Like 'languaculture', the concept of 'discourse' is an intermediary between language and culture, and the cultural view of language must be seen as comprising two levels: languacultures and discourses. According to Risager, this revision of the concept of language implies a series of consequences regarding the organization and overall focus of Foreign Language Studies: language is not only to be understood as first language but must be investigated in all its practices leading to interdisciplinary studies of multilingualism and multiculturality, etc.

In the next article, "Philology of the Future, Futures of Philology – Interdisciplinarity and Intertemporality in Foreign Language Studies", Helge Jordheim raises the question of how Foreign Language Studies may return to a philological, i.e. a historical or diachronic, approach to language, to counter the domination of Ferdinand de Saussure's synchronic and systematic approach and the subsequent structuralist paradigm of language studies. Jordheim takes his point of departure for this interdisciplinary challenge in the concept of 'intertemporality', which is understood as a simultaneous presence of different historic layers of signification in language, mediating between synchronic and diachronic perspectives. As alternatives to the Saussurian approach Jordheim mentions Bakhtin and Coseriu, but elects to base the study of history, language and culture on his own reading of Reinhardt Koselleck's *Begriffsgeschichte*.

In the last contribution to this section, "Cognitive Models – Language and Thought in Culture Studies", Mette Steenberg argues that cognitive theory in general and cognitive linguistics in particular point the way to bridging the gap between linguistics and cultural studies on a scientific basis. Contrary to the accepted truisms of national ideology, we do not carve up reality differently due to the constraints that language puts upon our conceptualisation. Instead, Steenberg argues, it is reality that constrains our conceptualisation. We are thus not locked up in the prison house of language, but defined by our own experiences. Through analysis of general cognitive models, cognitive theory paves the way for an understanding of the cognitive models of the cultural 'Other' and alternative ways of conceptualising the world.

*A Novel Look at Traditional Disciplines and Education in Foreign Language Studies.*
In the past year one of the main issues for discussion on the network has been the relationship between the disciplines that traditionally support Foreign Language Studies. In this section the present problems and future perspectives of the disciplines of grammar and literary studies are discussed by members of two of the network's working groups, while Sofie Nielsen summarizes the debate on the relation between literary and cultural studies in Germany, and Francesco Caviglia presents his perspective of 'advanced literacy' as a means for the study of language and culture.

In the first article, "Traditional and New Approaches to Theoretical Grammar Teaching", the teaching of grammar in Foreign Language Studies at university level is discussed by Thora Vinther, Hanne Leth Andersen and Merete Birkelund. According to these authors, there are historical reasons for the decisive influence of structuralist theory on grammar teaching in Denmark, and although a variety of other approaches to language have been introduced in Foreign Language Studies, e.g. pragmatics, text linguistics, sociolinguistics and language acquisition, grammar as a university subject remains a formal discipline, mainly engaged in the discussion of criteria for classification etc., from a language-inherent point of view. Therefore, they argue, it is necessary to develop a kind of grammar teaching that might incorporate other aspects of knowledge than the form-based approach to the construction of correct, written sentences.

In the next contribution "The Study of Literature – What Does It Matter and Why?", Jørn Boisen and Pia Schwartz Lausten discuss the consequences for literary studies of globalization, neo-liberalist ideology and the development of the mass media and the consumer market. The article is divided in two parts, each dominated by a stereotyped voice, one a pessimistic Adorno-like voice and the other an optimistic, more postmodernist voice. The pessimistic voice asks whether it is not already too late to save literature and literary studies, seeing that the philistines of postmodernist culture relativism have planted their standard of TV-programs and themed shopping bags in the sanctuaries of literature and high culture. The optimistic voice, on the other hand, answers that literature in general, and literature in foreign languages in particular, gives a privileged access to the experience of otherness, and thus has the capacity to extend one's horizon and lead to the recognition of one's own cultural specificity – i.e. it has a contrastive or intercultural dimension that is more needed than ever.

The discussion of the relation between disciplines and interdiciplinarity in Foreign Language Studies is evidently not only a Danish phenomenon: in an article entitled "Cultural Orientation and Interdisciplinarity – The German debate on *Literaturwissenschaft als Kulturwissenschaft*", Sofie Nielsen briefly summarizes the discussions concerning the relation between literary and cultural studies in Germany over the last decade. The German discussion raises the question of the political and social function of literary studies, and in the last part of the paper the author herself advocates a historical and pragmatic approach to literature that considers literature as a social practice.

The last paper of this section, "Advanced literacy – Bridging traditions in the study of language and culture" by Francesco Caviglia, is dedicated to the issue of the cultivation of reading and writing competences for graduates in Foreign Language Studies. Caviglia advocates an understanding of 'advanced literacy' that implies a view of reading and writing as a means for creating and transforming knowledge, for understanding and influencing others, for constructing identities and relationships and thus as a goal for the study of language *and* culture. Caviglia's contribution might also have found a place for itself in the next section, focussing as it does on language learning as a practice in an interdisciplinary setting.

*Interdisciplinary approaches to Foreign Language Studies.*
The interdisciplinary enterprise of Foreign Language Studies is represented by five very different papers, some written by individuals who integrate knowledge and skills from different disciplines, others written in collaboration between two or more scholars. One of the individual authors has devised his own theory and methodology, while others adapt known theory to new material. One of the collective works is broad in scope (comprising history, literature, cultural studies and discourse analysis), while the other is narrow in that both of the authors are cognitive linguists. Thus the five articles represent a wide range of the heterogeneity that must characterise interdisciplinarity in its experimental approach to opening up new perspectives and creating new knowledge.

In the short first text of this section, "Towards a Sociocritical Theory of the Text", Edmond Cros explains the theoretical presuppositions of what he terms 'Sociocriticism', an interdisciplinary approach to the study of the historical, socio-ideological and cultural nature of literary texts. Unlike most sociological approaches, Sociocriticism assumes that the sociological and cultural specificity of the literary work of art must be located within the text, and Edmond Cros, who is himself considered to be the founder of Sociocriticim, sets out to show how the collective subject of emerging capitalism is traceable in the specific discourses that permeate *Guzmán de Alfarache*, a Spanish picaresque novel from the 16th century.

The discursive construction of a collective subject as bearer of a cultural identity is also the point of departure for Inge Degn, Lisbeth Verstrate Hansen, Anne Magnussen and Jens Rahbek Rasmussen, who in their article "The Construction and Deconstruction of Nation and Identity in Modern Belgium" engage in the interdisciplinary study of notions like nation, state and identity in relation to modern Belgium. Different analytical perspectives, such as history, discourse analysis, literary history and cultural semiotics, are applied to a number of different texts, e.g. historiographical treatises, political manifestos, histories of literature and comics, all concerned with the construction and deconstruction of national identity in this particular European country, and in the process the authors test a variety of tools that can help to elucidate some of the challenges to the field of Foreign Language Studies deriving from current social, political and cultural changes.

In the article "Construction Grammar and Second Language Acquisition: A Cognitive Understanding of Language in a Contrastive Perspective", Johan Pedersen and Teresa Cadierno examine the concepts of language and culture in the theoretical framework of Cognitive Linguistics with a view to discussing the possible interdependence and mutual inspiration between the disciplines of general linguistics and second language acquisition from this determinate theoretical point of view. In the second part of the article the authors present a series of research cases as a basis for discussing the contribution of usage-based cognitive theories to the study of second language acquisition.

The interdisciplinary approach to literature and linguistics, or literary linguistics, is the topic of Nina Nørgaard's contribution "Challenging the Boundaries: Exploring the Interface of Linguistics and Literature". After a brief introduction to M.A.K. Halliday's Systemic Functional Linguistics, Nørgaard engages in an analysis of a short story by James Joyce, illustrating how the Hallidayan model of language, with its focus on the experiential, interpersonal and textual meanings produced by the text, can be seen as a richly equipped tool kit that literary critics may draw on for linguistic substantiation of their interpretation of the text.

In the last paper of this section, "Narratives of Natives: The construction of the Other as object of aid", Jan Gustafsson engages with the analysis of official documents related to Danish development aid programmes, a kind of text that we have seldom used as an object of study in traditional foreign language education, but which is of great value for the creation of intercultural awareness. Applying models originally created by structuralist narratology, Gustafsson studies the construction of cultural identity as a relation between self and 'other' in the texts, and shows how the cultural representation of these entities implies a *mise en scene* based on discursive constructions that tend towards narrative structures. Just as Caviglia's paper, in the previous section, could also have been located in this section, it would also have been possible to print Gustafsson's paper in the next section, focussing as it does on the relation of self and 'other' in the intercultural encounter.

*The deconstruction of the Eurocentric world view.*
In this section we have grouped together three papers dealing with the Postcolonial deconstruction of the Eurocentric world view, i.e. how Foreign Language Studies today must be able to work with texts, literary as well as non-literary, from areas outside the European countries that have traditionally given form to the established Canon.

In the first article, "Narrating Postcolonial Nations: Reading Homi Bhabha's Notions", Heidi Bojsen and Ingemai Larsen discusses the representation of 'nation' and 'nationhood' in the work of two different postcolonial authors, Garcin Malsa from the French Caribbean island of Martinique and Mia Couto from Mozambique. As indicated by the title, the conceptual framework of the analysis is inspired by the theory of Homi Bhabha, whose concept of 'temporality' is applied to establish a relation between the texts and the social and cultural context of their utterances. The authors consider their contribution an interdisciplinary work that includes material and knowledge from disciplines like linguistics, history, philosophy, and literary and cultural studies.

In the second contribution, "Studies of Postcolonialism and the Latin American tradition: National Identities and Indigenous struggles", Anne Marie Jeppesen and Ken Henriksen inquire why the various Postcolonial theories that have largely influenced studies of former British colonies have not been employed in the case of Latin America to a greater extent than they actually have. The authors find the answers in the specific history of Latin America, where the indigenous 'Other' has been excluded from imagined communities, both during the period of colonial submission and in the subsequent processes of liberation and the construction of independent nation states in the 19$^{th}$ century. Finally, the Miskitu Indians on the Nicaraguan East Coast are used as a case study of the use of ethnicity in the 20$^{th}$ century to confront state repression and exclusion.

In the final contribution, "African literature today. The stakes in its Teaching and Research", Bernard Mouralis and Heidi Bojsen give a presentation of 'literature in Africa' as an object of literary study, thus making a contribution to the discussion of the diversification and fragmentation of the empirical object of Foreign Language Studies. According to Mouralis and Bojsen, African literature demands a reading that acknowledges the importance of intertextuality, the presence of universal themes of human concern and the autonomy of the writer. The bibliographical selection is of great importance, since the subject matter does not exist in itself but depends upon the questions asked. The explicit focus on 'literature in Africa' and not 'African literature' is thus significant in as much as it reflects the influence of Pierre Bourdieu's sociological notion of the literary field as a key to reading the texts in dialogue with the ever-shifting historical and cultural contexts.

**References**

Altmayer, Claus: 1997. "Zum Kulturbegriff des Faches Deutsch als Fremdsprache". *Zeitschrift für Interkulturellen Fremdsprachenunterricht*, 2, 2.

Foucault, Michel: 1966. *Les mots et les choses*. Paris, Galimard. English translation: *The Order of Things*. New York, Vintage, 1994.

Godzich, Wlad: 1998. *Teoría literaria y crítica de la cultura*. Frónesis/Cátedra, Madrid.

Grabes, Herbert: 1996. "Litteraturwissenschaft, Kulturwissenschaft, Anglistik". *Anglia* 114, 3.

Gumbrecht, Hans Ulrich: 1995. "The Future of Literary Studies?" *New Literary History* 26,3.

Hansen, Hans Lauge: 2002. *Changing Philologies*. Copenhagen, Museum Tusculanum Press.

Hansen, Hans Lauge: In press/a. "Towards a New Philology of Culture". In: H. J. Jensen (ed.), *The Object of Study of the Humanities*. Copenhagen, Museum Tusculanum Press.

Hansen, Hans Lauge: In press/b. "Globalization of the Semiosphere". In: Ashley & Finke (eds.), *Geolinguistics*, New York.

Jordheim, Helge: 2001. *Lesningens vitenskap*. Oslo, Universitetsforlaget.

Kazamias, Andreas: 2001. "Globalization and educational cultures in late modernity: the Agamemnon syndrome". Cairns, Lawton and Gardner (eds.), *Values, Culture and Education*. World Yearbook of Education 2001. Kogan Page, London.

Navajas, Gonzalo: 2002. *La narrativa española en la era global*, Barcelona, EUB.

Wilken, Lisanne: 2001. *Enhed i Mangfoldighed?* Århus Universitetsforlag.

# A Social and Cultural View of Language

by
Karen Risager

Introduction
A fundamental element in the further development of Foreign Language Studies (the philologies) is a rethinking of the view of language and of the relationship between language and culture (including literature).
  In what follows I will present some reflections on this issue, based on my conviction that we need to develop Foreign Language Studies that are characterized by a truly integrative view of language, and by a conceptualization of the relationship between language and culture that clearly transcends the traditional national paradigm. A new foundation is needed for Foreign Language Studies, one that theorizes them as sites of linguistic and cultural encounters in a world that is becoming increasingly globalised[1]. We need to see language as both a social and a cultural phenomenon.

A social view of language
The teaching and learning of languages have been influenced since the 1970s by the pragmatic turn in linguistics. Today it is unexceptional to assert that language use should be analysed in relation to the context of communication, and that language teaching and learning should focus on the appropriate use of the target language, oral and written, according to the situational and wider social contexts. This communicative approach is often characterized as sociolinguistic as it rests upon a concept of language that foregrounds it as a means of communication in social interaction. However, whilst recognizing the importance of a communicative approach, I want to develop a more dynamic view of language in a global perspective.

---

[1] The following is based on my book *The National Dilemma in Language and Culture Pedagogy. A Study of the Relationship between Language and Culture* (Risager 2003), in Danish, so far.

In doing so, I will refer to the concept of a social network, which is widely used in the social sciences (for instance Hannerz 1992). Social network theory makes it possible to examine social relations and chains of social interaction at various levels of social practice, from the micro-level of interpersonal interaction to macro-levels of mass-communication and communication between organisations and other collective actors.

As regards language, these approaches encourage the study of how a specific (national) language is used and how it spreads via social networks of various ranges. The French language, for example, is used in many kinds of social networks at various levels in francophone countries. But it is also used in other parts of the world. In fact French is a world language in the sense that there are French speakers in practically every country and region of the world – as tourists, students, business people, diplomats, doctors, journalists, scientists etc. etc. So languages such as French (i.e. people using French) spread all over the world, across cultural contexts and discourse communities. This mobility (which is by no means accessible to all) is made possible by modern technologies of transportation.

Thanks to modern telecommunication and the World Wide Web, people throughout the world are connected in patterns of social networks. For instance, I can correspond in French by e-mail with a colleague in Australia; I can read on-line newspapers produced in the German-speaking community in Argentina; I can talk in Danish on my mobile phone to a relative who is travelling in Poland. We are witnessing the development of more or less global linguistic networks. Many languages take part in this process, not just the major ones that are taught as foreign languages.

The various language-specific networks meet locally, thus creating local multilingual situations of great complexity. Almost every country (state) in the world is multilingual in some sense. In a small country like Denmark, for instance, maybe over 100 languages are spoken by various groups of immigrants.

**Foreign Language Studies in a global context**
Learning and teaching a language contribute to the spread of the target language to new learners and new contexts. So every language department is an actor in the continuous formation and reformation of the target language's global network. Foreign Language Studies should therefore not confine themselves to the national scenes of the so-called target language countries, but should recognize that all states are multilingual in some sense, including the countries where the target language is taught, and the countries in which it is the dominant first language. The target language is always in a state of competition with other languages that have perhaps a minority position.

# A Social and Cultural View of Language

That is why the notion of a linguistic area (the French-speaking area, the Russian-speaking area etc.) is problematic. Languages are not territorially bound; of course the specific network of, for instance, Danish is especially dense in the Danish territory, but the Danish language network has a global range, as Danish speakers can be found in many parts of the world. States have boundaries, languages haven't.

When I refer to language users, I mean everyone who speaks the language, whether as first, second or foreign language. In this context, a *second language* is one learnt in childhood or later, and which is the dominant language in the country where the speaker lives, so its acquisition is a necessary condition for participating as a citizen in the life of the society. A *foreign language*, on the other hand, is one that is studied mainly at a distance, in another country. Of course, one can think of many examples where these two prototypical cases overlap.

This inclusive concept of language is essential. Students participating in Foreign Language Studies come from many different linguistic backgrounds: the target language may be their first language (native speakers studying their first language abroad); they may be minority language speakers who speak the dominant language as a second language (for instance Danish in Denmark) – and their teachers may be equally varied[2]. Because of the strong monolingual focus on the target language, foreign language departments may in fact be multilingual without anybody really noticing or exploiting this situation.

As far as target-language countries are concerned, parts of the population speak the language in question not as a first language but as a second language, so an important part of the social and cultural life of the target language country will be missed if attention is restricted to those who speak and write the language as a first language (mother tongue).

I would therefore suggest that one way of transcending the national and monolingual focus of Foreign Language Studies would be to further an awareness of the target language as just one in the whole ecology of languages. As one of its objectives Foreign Language Studies might contribute to multilingual awareness in a global perspective, for instance via course work or project work on sociolinguistic issues such as bilingualism, intercultural communication and code-switching (in everyday interaction or as represented in literature, film etc.) (see also Risager 1998).

## Linguistic practice, linguistic resources and the language system

Until now, I have focussed on language use, or linguistic practice. This focus enables us to develop the image of language use spreading in social

---

[2] Teachers of French in Danish universities have had, among others, Danish, French, Belgian, and Icelandic backgrounds.

networks. But this is only one of the existential loci (or ontologies) of language. It is necessary to distinguish between three loci of language:

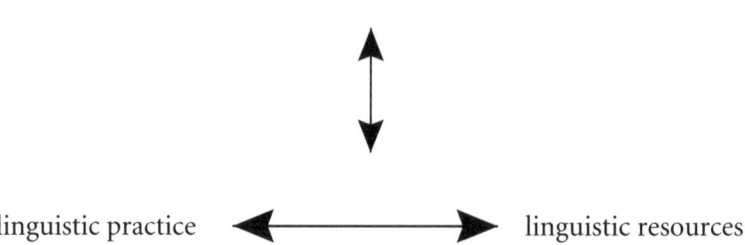

Linguistic practice denotes oral and written interaction in social networks, including the production and reception of literature and other cultural products. Linguistic resources are in the domain of the individual, the socially constituted knowledge of language developed as part of a person's life history. These two loci of language presuppose each other: linguistic practice cannot be produced and received without the linguistic resources of individuals, and the linguistic resources of the individual cannot be developed without the experience of linguistic practice.

Whereas these two loci of language are both natural and necessary, the idea of the 'language system' is not. It is necessary to deconstruct the idea that there is a language 'out there' that can be used and studied as a natural object. The 'language system' is a construct or, in other words, a family of historically and discursively constructed notions ('English', 'French' etc.). At the same time it is important to note that this construct has consequences for linguistic practice and linguistic resources. The idea of the language system interacts with both linguistic practice and linguistic resources, being a kind of – more or less conscious – normative factor.

I emphasize these three loci in order to point out that there are many kinds of language study beside the sociolinguistic one. Foreign Language Studies should encompass both sociologically oriented studies of language use, psychologically oriented studies of cognition and competence, and system-oriented studies of phonology, grammar and the lexicon. But these activities should be accomplished with an overall understanding of language as a social phenomenon not limited to the national scene of the target language countries.

### A cultural view of language
There are many ways of theorizing the relationship between the social and the cultural. In this limited context, I want to stress that all societal life

may be considered as both social and cultural. Analysis of social life typically deals with relational, temporal and spatial aspects of activities, institutions and structures, whereas analysis of cultural life typically deals with the production and reproduction of meaning and representations of various realities. These two areas cannot be separated. All social life carries meaning, and all exchanges and negotiations of meaning are embedded in more or less shifting social structures and relations of power.

When we focus on language as a means of forming meaning, we enter an intellectual tradition very different from the sociolinguistic approach I have just outlined. The intimate connections between (specific) languages and (specific) cultures have been a fundamental theme in the nation-building process in Europe since the late 18th century, not least in the German form of national Romanticism. Since the 19th century Foreign Language Studies have been profoundly influenced by this figure of thought, and are just starting to question the national paradigm and seek alternative ways of conceptualizing the study of language, literature and culture[3].

**Inseparability or separability?**
Nowadays, the usual and easiest way of dealing with the relationship between language and culture is to state that it is a complex relationship, thus verbalizing the difficulty of coming to grips with this thorny question. Those who do formulate an opinion may largely be characterized as holding one of two opposing positions:

- language and culture are inseparable
- language and culture are separable

The first view is associated with the cultural turn in linguistics since the 1980s, and is maintained in various forms in research disciplines such as linguistic anthropology, translation studies, and studies of intercultural communication. It is of course also a popular belief, not least in Europe during the present process of political integration of nation states into a larger union. The second view is principally associated with the study of English as an international language. In this case it is maintained that languages – and especially English – should be seen as flexible instruments of communication that may in principle be used with any subject matter by anybody anywhere in the world.

---

[3] In my Dr.Phil. thesis (Risager 2003) I have made a thorough historical analysis of the discourse on language, culture and nation within the discipline of cultural pedagogy: the teaching of culture and society as part of foreign- and second-language teaching (for example: Byram 1986 and 1997, Kramsch 1993, Roberts et al. 2001, Byram and Risager 1999).

Neither of these positions is satisfying. The first emphasizes that language is culture-bound, and is not far from a conception of a closed universe of language, people, nation, culture, history, mentality and land. This position is totally at odds with the social and transnational view of language that I have just presented. The other position claims that language is culturally neutral. Language is seen as a code, and this view seems like a reconstitution of the classical structuralist conception of the autonomy of language. My response would be that no language is culturally neutral. All natural languages (i.e. their users) constantly produce and reproduce culture (i.e. meaning).

How then can we construct a model of the relationship between language and culture that neither locks language into a national Romantic universe, nor forwards the claim that language is culturally neutral?

**The generic and the differential level**
At this point I want to emphasize something important: in the analysis of the relationship between language and culture, it is necessary to distinguish between on the one hand language and culture in the generic sense, and on the other hand language and culture in the differential sense.

In the generic sense language and culture are general human phenomena. There are two variants of the generic: a psychological/cognitive and a social. In the first, language and culture are seen as psychological/cognitive phenomena with a (neuro)physiological basis. In the second variant, language and culture are seen as social phenomena that have been developed as part of the social life of the human race. At the generic level it doesn't make any sense to maintain that language and culture can be separated. Human culture always includes language, and human language cannot be envisaged without culture. Linguistic practice is always embedded in, and in interaction with, some cultural (i.e. meaningful) context.

The differential sense comprehends different languages and different cultural phenomena: specific forms of linguistic knowledge and linguistic practice relating to 'whole' languages, language varieties, loan words etc; and specific forms of cultural knowledge and practice: different meanings and meaningful forms relating to sign systems such as pictures, fashion, food, music, dance etc., different norms and values, symbols, ideas and ideologies. Topics concerning language spread and culture spread belong to the differential level.

In my view, much of the confusion concerning the relationship between language and culture may be ascribed to the fact that the generic and the differential level are often not clearly distinguished. It is at the differential level that one may ask, for instance: What forms of culture are associated with the Russian language? What forms of culture are associated with the English language?

## Languaculture

The concept of languaculture is very useful in the construction of a new understanding of the relationship between language and culture (at the differential level) in a globalised world. This concept has not been widely used until now, but it was developed by the American linguistic anthropologist Michael Agar in a book published in 1994[4]. For Agar, languaculture covers language plus culture; he is especially interested in the variability of languaculture in discourse (verbal interaction), both among native users of the same language and among people who use the language as a native and/or a foreign language. Agar focuses on the semantic and pragmatic variability of linguistic practice, and invites the reader to explore 'rich points' in intercultural communication, i.e. points where communication goes wrong.

Whereas Agar uses the concept of languaculture in order to theorize the single universe of language and culture, its attraction for me is that it may offer us the opportunity to theorize deconnections and reconnections taking place between language and culture as a result of migration and other processes of globalisation. Languages (i.e. language users) spread in social networks, across cultural contexts and discourse communities, but they carry languaculture with them (this is also suggested in the alternative wording: 'culture in language'). Some dimensions of culture are bound to a specific language (languaculture), and some are not, for instance musical traditions or architectural styles. There may of course be many historical links between such cultural phenomena and the language in question, but the point is that the phenomena are not dependent on that specific language.

## Three dimensions of languaculture

The study of languaculture is the study of the various kinds of meanings carried and produced by language. But what exactly is that? I suggest that we distinguish between three dimensions of languaculture, corresponding to three cultural perspectives on language:

- the semantic and pragmatic potential
- the poetic potential
- the identity potential

The semantic and pragmatic potential is the dimension explored by Agar, and by many other scholars interested in intercultural pragmatics and contrastive semantics. It has also been a longstanding focus of interest for

---

[4] He has borrowed this term from Friedrich (1989) who called it linguaculture (se also Risager 2003, 363).

linguistic anthropology since Boas, Sapir and Whorf[5]. This dimension is about constancy and variability in the semantics and pragmatics of specific languages: the more or less obligatory distinctions between 'sister' and 'brother', between 'he' and 'she', between 'red' and 'orange', between 'hello' and 'how are you', between 'nature' and 'culture' etc., and the social and personal variability found in concrete situations of use.

The poetic potential is the dimension related to the specific kinds of meaning created in the exploitation of the phonological and syllabic structure of the language in question, its rhymes, the relations it displays between speech and writing etc. – areas that have long interested theorists focusing on literary poetics, style, literariness and the like.

The identity potential is also called social meaning by some sociolinguists (for example Hymes). It is related to the social variation of the language in question: in using the language in a particular way, for instance with a specific accent, one identifies oneself and makes it possible for others to identify one according to their background knowledge and attitudes. Linguistic practice is a continuing series of 'acts of identity' (Le Page and Tabouret-Keller 1985) where people project their own understanding of the world onto their interlocutors and consciously or unconsciously invite them to react. This dimension has been explored by scholars within sociolinguistics who are interested in the relationship between language and identity[6].

As I have stressed above, languaculture is both structurally constrained and socially and personally variable. It is a bridge between the structure of language and the socially constituted personal idiolect. The most interesting potential of the concept may lie in a focus on individual semantic connotations and language learning as a process that is integrated in the life history of the individual subject as speaker-hearer, as reader and as writer.

**Languaculture in linguistic practice**
If we consider languaculture in linguistic practice, both oral and written, there is usually a high degree of semantic and pragmatic variability in the process. When a text is produced, languacultural intentions are laid down within it concerning how this text is going to function semantically and pragmatically in the communication situation: what speech acts are intended, what references are made to the context, what representations of the

---

[5] Whorf around 1930 (and to a certain extent Sapir, and Humboldt before them) introduced the idea that the structure of language may have a strong influence on thought and world view).

[6] Due to lack of space, I will restrict myself in the following sections to the first (semantic and pragmatic) dimension.

world are to be conjured up. These languacultural intentions are restricted or expanded during the reception of the text. The addressees/ readers perceive and interpret the text according to their personal languacultures and their knowledge of the world. A negotiation of meaning goes on.

In situations where the language is used as a foreign language, there are many opportunities of adding even more variability than is the case with native language use, for instance as described by Agar in his comments on examples of intercultural communication in English between Austrians and himself.

## Languaculture in linguistic resources

The personal languaculture of the individual cannot be separated from his/her personal life history and social and cultural identity formation. It is not possible to distinguish the denotative and connotative dimensions of a personal languaculture.

In the case where a language is the first language (mother tongue), it should be noted that the idea of an intimate relationship between language and culture primarily concerns the language in its function as first language, even if this is rarely stated explicitly. The national-Romantic idea of an inner association between the language and the people/nation (and thus the national culture) relates in fact to people who have grown up from their childhood with the mother tongue and the mother-tongue culture (in German: 'die muttersprachliche Kultur').

This idea of an association between mother tongue and mother-tongue culture at the national (or ethnic) level ignores the possibility of great variation between the linguistic and cultural upbringing of different individuals. The acquisition process is in any case socially differentiated, and all human beings develop their personal linguistic and cultural repertoires with which they express themselves and interpret the world. Therefore language and culture are always different from individual to individual, characterized by a specific emotional and cognitive constitution, a specific perspective and a specific horizon of understanding. For example, the meaning of such notions as 'work' and 'leisure' may be quite different even within the same professional group or the same family.

What is the character of the relationship between language and culture when the language is a foreign language? A Dane learning German, for instance, especially in the first stages of learning, must draw on his/her cultural and social experience related to the Danish language. There are semantic and pragmatic distinctions that are obligatory in using German, such as an appropriate distribution of 'du' and 'Sie'. But otherwise it will be natural to use the languaculture developed in relation to the first language (or other languages learnt). Personal connotations of words and phrases will be transferred, and a language mixture will result with the foreign language supplemented with languacultural material from another language (in this case Danish, and possibly other languages learnt). From the learner's perspective, the alleged intimate association between German language and culture is normative, not descriptive. It is his/her task to establish the association, and this task must be accomplished on the basis of a growing understanding of some of the associations common among native speakers. But even when learners reach a high level of competence, their languacultures will always be the result of an accumulation of experience from their whole life histories.

### Languaculture in the language system

Since the language system is a discursive construction, so too is the description of languaculture in the language system, and considerations of relevance and utility are to be expected. Descriptions of languaculture may range from a minimalist description of the semantic and pragmatic potential of relative constancy – the denotative core of the language – to a maximalist description in the form of a gigantic encyclopaedia supplemented by a gigantic handbook of patterns of linguistic practice in specific situations. It should be noted that the structuralist tradition has primarily, and implicitly, focused on language as a first language; but some studies of interlanguage (learners' language in development) have built on this tradition, giving, for instance, descriptions of Danes' German interlanguage, or Germans' school English, and the like.

### Language/languaculture and discourse in a global perspective

The concept of Languaculture is a theorization of the interface between language and the rest of culture, and is related to one or more specific languages. However, the cultural view of language should also embrace the concept of discourse, which may be used as an intermediary concept between that of language/languaculture and the more general concept of culture.

I refer to work on discourse as represented by Fairclough (1992) and other proponents of critical discourse analysis (Wodak, Jäger, van Dijk). Discourse and discourses are primarily defined relative to their content: a discourse deals with a certain subject matter from a certain perspective. It is primarily verbal, but may be accompanied by for instance visual material.

Discourses may spread across languages. For example, a discourse on Christianity is not bound to any one language, although some languages are more specialized than others with respect to the verbalisation of topics related to Christianity. Discourses move from language community to language community (or from one linguistic network to another) by translation and other transformation processes, and are incorporated into the local language over longer or shorter periods of time. Some discourses are formed as various kinds of literature, and so literary topics, genres and styles spread from language to language.

Specific languages and specific discourses do not necessarily spread along the same lines (see also Risager 2000), but they may exhibit a parallel development in an area or in a specific linguistic network. Pennycook is among the few scholars who have analysed relations between language and discourse in this way, with special reference to the adherence of colonial discourses to the English language (Pennycook 1998).

Thus the cultural view of language may be said to comprise two levels: the level of languaculture, bound to specific languages, and the level of discourse, not necessarily bound to any one language (though a discourse must be expressed in some language at any point of time).

Languages/languacultures and discourses spread in a variety of different social networks across cultural contexts, tracing a dynamic pattern of deconnections and reconnections, disembedding and reembedding, and of processes of cultural influence, domination and integration.

The general ideology of inseparability between language and culture seems to be attributable to two different but related factors. On the one hand, individuals have a tendency to project their own subjective feelings of association between their personal languages, cultures and identities onto the community, for example the nation, and thus imagine an association at the system level for which there is no empirical basis. On the other hand, this psychological tendency is used politically in national propaganda, where an image is constructed of the nation state characterized by a common national culture expressed in a common national language. Two constructs are articulated together: the idea of the language system and the idea of the culture or cultural system.

## Implications for Foreign Language Studies

The first implication for Foreign Language Studies is that the empirical field is not 'the language area' in a geographical sense but the worldwide network of the target language. Where and in what situations do people speak, read and write the target language? How is the target language used on the internet by ordinary people and interest groups? What role does the language have in transnational migration of all sorts? What role does it have in transnational companies, markets and media? In international politics? In all these situations it is important to consider that the target language carries languaculture with it. It has specific semantic, pragmatic, poetic and identity potentials, both possibilities and limitations; and this specificity – these differences from other languages – should be an important preoccupation for Foreign Language Studies.

The second implication is that the analytical object is not only (texts in) the target language as first language, but also as second and foreign language. The target language is learnt and spoken by many kinds of people and for many different reasons. So an awareness of the complex functions of the target language opens up for studies of multilingualism and multiculturality in all places where the target language is spoken. How is the target language – French for instance – used by Arabic immigrants in France? How is it used by Chinese immigrants in Canada? Questions like this raise issues of the relations between language and identity: the use and construction of linguistic identities and the role of language in the construction of cultural identities, national or ethnic, etc. They also raise issues of the role of languages in the power structures of society and the world. They may focus attention on various forms of linguistic and cultural encounters and conflicts, and on processes of translation and interpretation, both linguistic and cultural. They may lead to insights into the great languacultural variability of the language in question.

The third implication is that the study of a specific language is not confined to specific discourses or specific thematic areas (disciplinary fields). Discourses, topics and genres may spread from language to language by various kinds of translation or transformation, and so a language community is never a closed discourse community, though certain discourses may be preferred in certain local and social contexts at certain points of time. Thus it is not necessarily the case that Foreign Language Studies should always focus on the (native) literature of target language countries. The link between the study of language and the study of literature is not 'natural' but a historical construction once important in the nation-building processes. When this link is maintained today it has to be specially motivated, for Foreign Language Studies may as well focus on social studies, cultural studies, media studies, business studies, art studies etc. etc.

The fourth implication is that it is necessary to construct Foreign Language Studies that are characterized by an integrative view of both language, text, discourse and (the rest of) culture and society. For instance, the target language should be seen as a cultural phenomenon, and similarly, literature and other texts in the target language should be seen as linguistic phenomena. Although texts are usually studied as cultural products carrying some kind of global content or meaning (representing cultural reality in some way or other), they are always also instances of linguistic practice in a specific language.

It is important to try to counteract the unfortunate traditional division between language, literature and history/society in Foreign Language Studies. This does not mean that the histories of the different academic traditions should not be acknowledged. But it does mean that the problems of modern (and not-so-modern) life should be approached as complex problems demanding a range of different means of analysis and interpretation. We need interdisciplinary approaches to everyday phenomena of intercultural learning and communication, oral and written. We need to study these phenomena with combinations of theories originating both in linguistics (including sociolinguistics and cultural linguistics), in literary studies (including studies of all sorts of texts in the media), and in social and historical studies more generally.

One way of furthering this idea is to introduce problem-oriented project work as a central form of study, supplemented by course work. Looking for and defining social and cultural problems may offer opportunities for students and teachers/supervisors to develop a sense of the interdisciplinary nature and potential of Foreign Language Studies. A project (in French) on problems of intercultural understanding arising from the use, in a small rural community in Bourkina Faso, of children's books produced in France, would perhaps illustrate the necessity of applying both linguistic, cultural and historical knowledge (theories and methods) to clarify the issues involved.

In conclusion, we need redefinitions of Foreign Language Studies that transcend the national paradigm and introduce a dynamic transnational and global perspective, including multilingual awareness, centering on the study of meaning as it is produced at the interface of languaculture and discourse[7]. We need study programmes in which course work and project work are equally important as contributors to the theoretical knowledge and analytical training of students: programmes that are sites of linguistic and cultural encounters, programmes that have a global outlook.

## References

Agar, Michael: 1994. *Language Shock. Understanding the Culture of Conversation.* New York, William Morrow.

Byram, Michael: 1989. *Cultural Studies in Foreign Language Education.* Clevedon, Multilingual Matters.

Byram, Michael: 1997. *Teaching and Assessing Intercultural Communicative Competence.* Clevedon, Multilingual Matters.

Byram, Michael & Karen Risager: 1999. *Language Teachers, Politics and Cultures.* Clevedon, Multilingual Matters

Fairclough, Norman: 1992. *Discourse and Social Change.* Cambridge, Polity Press.

---

[7] Many of the ideas expressed in this paper have been developed into a Master's programme at Roskilde University. The programme is called 'Cultural Encounters', and focuses on studies of identity, ethnicity, nationality, multilingualism and multiculturalism, discourse studies, post-colonial studies and studies of cultural and linguistic globalisation. There is no specific target language so it does not aim at language learning. Thus it is not in itself a Foreign Language Study programme, but Foreign Language Studies may be inspired by it.

Friedrich, Paul: 1989. "Language, ideology, and political economy". In: *American Anthropologist*, Vol. 91, 295-312.

Hannerz, Ulf: 1992. *Cultural Complexity. Studies in the Social Organization of Meaning.* New York, Columbia University Press.

Kramsch, Claire: 1993. *Context and Culture in Language Teaching.* Oxford University Press.

Le Page, R. & A. Tabouret-Keller, 1985. *Acts of Identity: Creole-based Approaches to Language and Ethnicity.* Cambridge, Cambridge University Press.

Pennycook, Alastair: 1998. *English and the Discourses of Colonialism.* London and New York, Routledge.

Risager, Karen: 1998. "Language teaching and the process of European integration". In: M. Byram & M. Fleming (eds.), *Language Learning in Intercultural Perspective. Approaches through drama and ethnography.* Cambridge, Cambridge University Press, 242-54.

Risager, Karen: 2000. "Bedeutet Sprachverbreitung immer auch Kulturverbreitung?" In: U. Ammon (Hrsg.), *Sprachförderung. Schlüssel auswärtiger Kulturpolitik.* Frankfurt a. M. etc., Peter Lang, 9-18.

Risager, Karen: 2003. *Det nationale dilemma i sprog- og kulturpædagogikken. Et studie i forholdet mellem sprog og kultur.* København, Akademisk Forlag.

Robert, Celia et al.: 2001. *Language Learners as Ethnographers.* Clevedon, Multilingual Matters.

# Philology of the Future, Futures of Philology
Interdisciplinarity, Intertemporality, and *Begriffsgeschichte*

by
Helge Jordheim

Introduction

In this article I wish to develop some of the ideas I introduced in my book *The Science of Reading. Towards a New Philology* (Jordheim 2001). Here I used the term 'philology' to indicate a relationship between language and what I have referred to in a very general way as 'history', not as opposites but as necessarily interdependent and interrelated phenomena. It is thus not a question of language *or* history, or even of language *and* history, but of language *in* history.

In this article, however, I will try to move one step further, redefining and hopefully thus defining more clearly the notoriously ambiguous notion of 'history'. Redefining in this case actually means replacing. More specifically, it means replacing 'history' and 'historicity' with the concepts of 'time' and 'temporality', one important effect of this redefinition, this replacement, being that 'temporality' doesn't seem to have the same disciplinary constraints as 'historicity', but also points in the direction of linguistics and literary criticism. From the concept of 'temporality' I shall then move on to another concept, that of 'intertemporality'.

As I see it, there is more than a morphological affinity between this concept and the already mentioned concept of 'interdisciplinarity'[1]. The question I shall ask here is whether one way of achieving the ambition of interdisciplinarity in the study of foreign languages is by means of a the-

---

[1] In this article I shall refrain from going into a theoretical discussion of the concept of 'interdisciplinarity' as such, but stick to what I understand as the interdisciplinary ambition of the Foreign Language Studies: to integrate the linguistic, literary, historical and cultural perspectives that are always at stake when we study a foreign language.

oretical reflection upon the intertemporality of language itself. Hence, I make two presuppositions which will be discussed later in the article: firstly, that the notion of discipline is in fact interrelated with the notion of temporality; secondly, that there is a connection between interdisciplinarity as an ambition and a possibility in Foreign Language Studies, and intertemporality as an aspect of language *in* history.

This article will proceed in three steps. In the first part, I shall return to the title 'Philology of the future, futures of philology' and discuss the possible implications of this rather prophetic vision of philology, a discussion that leads on to a first and very tentative explanation of what I mean by 'intertemporality'. In the second part, I will explore how the temporality of philology is challenged by the so-called 'linguistic turn' which derives from the lectures of Ferdinand de Saussure. Finally, in the third and longest part of the article I intend to explore how the idea of intertemporality is developed by the German historian and theorist of history Reinhart Koselleck, within the framework of the so-called *Begriffsgeschichte*, the history of concepts.

### Nietzsche and the *Zukunftsphilologie*

To start with, I'd like to reconsider the term the young aspiring classicist Ulrich von Wilamowitz-Moellendorff chose for his devastating critique of Nietzsches *Geburt der Tragödie* from 1872: "Zukunftsphilologie!" – philology of the future[2]. Philology, Wilamowitz objected to his more famous colleague, should not occupy itself with the future, but exclusively with the past. Nietzsche on the other hand, in his work on Greek tragedy, had claimed that the Dionysian principle, the principle of violence, transgression and ecstasy, represented a transcendent or transhistorical truth, underlying all reality and reappearing in his own time in the form of a Germanic myth among Richard Wagner and his followers. Less known than Wilamowitz's critique, however, is the polemical reply by Nietzsche's friend Erwin Rohde, presumably ghost-written by Nietzsche himself, under the title "Afterphilologie"[3]. Even though this title is more or less untranslatable, the archaic German prefix 'after-' combining the meanings of 'false', 'anal' and 'post', an element of temporality is definitely at stake. Who is vanguard, who is rearguard? Who – Nietzsche or Wilamowitz – represents the real future of philology? It is, however, the question that

---

[2] The full title of Wilamowitz-Moellendorf's critique was "Zukunftsphilologie! Eine Erwiderung auf Friedrich Nietzsches ord. Professors der classischen Philologie zu Basel Geburt der Tragödie von Ulrich von Wilamowitz-Moellendorf Dr. Phil". Cf. Ross 1994, 298.

[3] This text is discussed in Porter 2000, 16. On Nietzsche's 'ghost-writing' of Rohde's text see p. 293, n. 34.

should interest us, not the possible answers. In this article Nietzsche is merely a symptom of, or even a metaphor for, what I am going to discuss. Philology, it seems, especially the national philologies that are our subject here, is trapped between the past and the future, between its traditional obligations to a national, linguistically defined and communicated past and the wish to create a future for the study of foreign languages, cultures and literatures.

The well-known and often quoted anecdote about Nietzsche and Wilamowitz seems to invite all philologists, at least subconsciously, to take sides with the learned and conscientious scholar against the wild ramblings of the mad philosopher. At least this is what the literary scholar William Arrowsmith seems to believe when he formulates his attack on philologists in the course of a presentation of Nietzsche's writings. Of the philologists Arrowsmith says that they "unanimously preferred to believe that Wilamowitz – who caught Nietzsche in several factual errors – had the best of it." "But," he continues, "in point of fact none of Wilamowitz' arguments disproves or even seriously damages Nietzsche's thesis" (Arrowsmith 1963, 8). He then goes on to talk about the philologists' naïve faith in method as opposed to Nietzsche's "large, intuitive, aesthetic insight" (ibid.). Arrowsmith, however, like Nietzsche, is only a symptom, this time of a very simplified notion of what is included in the concept of philology. Even though we needn't envy Nietzsche his aesthetic insight, we should, I think, envy him his almost prophetic vision of philology. As he puts it in the polemical fragment "Wir Philologen" from 1874/75: "Many think that it's over with philology; I think it has not yet begun" (Nietzsche 1977, 330).

Ironically, at the time of this visionary statement in the late 19th century, there seemed to be no real future for philology as a general science of language, culture and history. After the last attempt at a large-scale synthesis by August Boeckh in his *Enzyklopädie*, published after his death in 1886 (Boeckh 1966), the traditional philological triad of grammar, criticism and hermeneutics broke apart, leaving no evident basis for a sustained theoretical reflection upon the integration of the study of language on the one hand and the study of culture and history on the other (Jordheim 2001, 43-70) – a situation, in other words, not unlike the one that we, at least some of us, are experiencing today.

### The philological predicament
My point, however, is not – or at least not only – that we should all become visionaries or prophets on behalf of philology. On the contrary, my intentions in presenting the case of Nietzsche and Wilamowitz are primarily analytical. To me this case illustrates how and to what extent the ambition of any philological practice is stretched between the past and the future, at the same time constantly asking what to make of the present.

Even after quitting his position in Basel and giving up his academic carrier as a philologist, Nietzsche continued to reflect upon the essence and future of philology, and throughout most of his published and unpublished works we find comments and remarks related to these issues (ibid. 70-78). All these remarks, however, have a certain ambiguity in common, pointing at once backwards towards history, tradition and what Gadamer will later call *Wirkungsgeschichte*, and forwards towards the language, culture and philosophy of the future.

As I see it, this is necessarily the predicament of any philologist, or indeed anyone working within the field of Foreign Languages Studies. The question is, however, how we are coming to terms with it. In many cases, I believe, we tend to choose. Cultural and literary historians choose the past, linguists and new critics the present, whilst the future is left very much to itself – even though the future is what our students, faculties and universities are constantly worrying about. Hence, different disciplines can be said to have different temporalities. From this conclusion, however, it seems to follow that interdisciplinarity might indeed have something do to with what I in this article have referred to as 'intertemporality', the one being either the consequence or the precondition of the other. To study the uses of a language, not only in its past or its present forms but as something that is continually changing, continually *moving* from the past through the present and into the future, turns out to be a fundamentally interdisciplinary task.

One possible way for the national philologies and the Foreign Language Studies to achieve their ambition of interdisciplinarity is by taking on the challenge of the temporality of language, of describing how language is moving through historical time and how it at the same time is creating its own past, it own present, and its own future. From this perspective the future of philology – or at least one of its futures – seems to lie in philology's own ability to analyze the pasts, presents and futures of language, or in other words, its ability to engage with the linguistic phenomenon of intertemporality. However, making a commitment to this genuinely philological project also means taking on the fundamental challenge of the linguistic turn.

### Opening the gap: Saussure and the linguistic turn

At this point there is no reason for me to go into all the different aspects of the linguistic turn in its often very different Anglo-American, French and German versions[4]. All that really needs to be stated is that one of the *effects* of the linguistic turn in the humanities after World War II was the opening of a gap between language and history, affecting many or most disciplines,

---

[4] For a comparative perspective see Jordheim 2001, 79-84.

among them philosophy, linguistics, literary criticism and, as a consequence, philology. Probably the most important theoretical vehicle for this division was the ideas of the Swiss linguist Ferdinand de Saussure, more precisely his famous dichotomies of *langue* vs. *parole* and synchrony vs. diachrony. Largely in defiance of their rather heuristic function in Saussure's own thought[5], these dichotomies are at least partly responsible for the linguistic turn within the humanities, understood as a turn *towards* language, structure and discourse, and *away* from history, movement and change[6].

Saussure's ambition in his *Cours de linguistic gènèrale*, given at the University of Geneva from 1907 to 1911, was to found a *science* of language. To study language in a scientific way, Saussure claims, is to study a system or a structure, in which every part, i.e. every sign, is defined by its relations to other parts, other signs. *Langue* in the Saussurian sense is a system of differences without any actual contents. Hence, a sign can have neither meaning outside of the system nor any historical duration or temporality of its own. The linguistic counterpart to Saussure's *langue* is of course *parole*, referring to language as used by an individual, or, as Saussure puts it, as "an individual act of the will or the intellect" (Saussure 1967, 30). Today we tend to speak of 'statement' or 'speech act' or even 'enunciation', depending on which theoretical traditions are invoked. This dichotomy, *langue* and *parole*, was then taken up by thinkers in the structuralist tradition, such as Levi-Strauss, Barthes, Lacan, de Man, Derrida and to a certain extent Foucault, as a way of theoretically founding their aims of excluding the entire level of *parole* and thereby the whole field of historical and temporal dynamics and change from the study of language or society.

Thus the focus shifted: from diachrony – the movement of language and texts through and in history – to synchrony – the structural and systematic aspects of a language or a text, outside, above or beneath historical reality. Historical change was something that took place on the level of *parole* and could never be the object of scientific investigation[7]. Of course, Saussure never denied the existence of linguistic change, but he claimed that it was merely a by-product of historical, social and political transformations and should be studied as such. Or, to put it another way: if you are studying temporal and historical change, it's not language you are studying but

---

[5] The methodological status of Saussure's dichotomies is discussed for instance in Scheerer 1980, 73ff.

[6] For an example of this version of the linguistic turn see de Man 1993, 21-26.

[7] This reading of Saussure has been extensively revised by several excellent Saussure scholars, among them Paul J. Thibault (1997, esp. 53-162). The impact of the Saussurian dichotomies on the disciplines of the humanities in general and Foreign Language Studies in particular seems, however, to persist.

history. What Saussure is proposing, are in fact two totally different, though both perfectly legitimate, objects of research: either language as a synchronic system of differences between signs, as *langue*, or history as a diachronic process of political and social transformations, hermeneutically linked to the level of *parole*. As already suggested at the start of this article, the theoretical dichotomy thus reproduces itself at the level of disciplines, intertemporality as well as interdisciplinarity becoming obsolete at the same time.

**Engaging with Saussure**
To reject and revoke Saussure's conclusions, handed down since World War II by a variety of theoretical traditions from New Criticism to generative grammar, is in my opinion the great challenge of philology. At the core of this ambition, or so I claim, lies the relationship between interdisciplinarity and intertemporality. An interdisciplinary approach to language and texts will have to address both the diachronic time of historical change and the synchronic time of linguistic structures.

To avoid any misunderstandings I will explain what I mean by 'synchronic time'. If we follow Saussure, the concept of synchronic time or synchronic temporality is a contradiction in terms, synchrony, in a linguistic sense, being exactly that which eludes and transcends the sphere of temporality. However, if we want to approach a concept of intertemporality, synchrony can and should also be seen as referring to the specific temporality of contemporaneity, of the present, of the 'now'. As we shall see, this redefinition of the concept of synchrony is in fact a precondition for the entire theory of temporality which is developed in this paper.

Of course, there are many different ways of embarking upon the project of overcoming Saussure and reinstalling intertemporality and interdisciplinarity at the heart of the study of foreign languages. The *Begriffsgeschichte* and the works of Reinhart Koselleck are but one of them. However, Koselleck never explicitly engages with the theories of Saussure, and for this reason I shall start by very briefly considering three other approaches, which move in the same direction as Koselleck but take Saussure and structural linguistics as their starting point, thus giving us a clearer impression of what is really at stake.

The first position or tradition to be considered is Prague school structuralism, recently presented to a Scandinavian audience in an excellent book by the Danish scholar Karen Gammelgaard, *The Meaning of the Text* (Gammelgaard 2003, 9-20). The essential aspect of this version of a structuralist theory of language is the focus on the functional aspects, i.e. the use of language in specific historical and social contexts. According to the Czech structuralists, the primary manifestation of language is not the abstract system but the text. Linguistic structures can only be found within texts, and are thus fundamentally open and dynamic. By claiming that individual statements or texts actually affect and even change the norms according to which they are construed, the Czech structuralists explicitly revoke one of the main principles in Saussures *Cours* (ibid. 38-40).

A second useful approach is developed by the Russian linguist and literary scholar Mikhail Bakhtin. The key concept in the works of Bakhtin is *dialogue*. Every text enters into a dialogue with earlier texts and statements, and to understand it we as readers have to take part in the same dialogue (Bakhtin 1998). Concerning the engagement of Bakhtin with Saussure, on the other hand, it takes place primarily in his little book on *Marxism and the Philosophy of Language*, published in the name of one of his pupils, Valentin N. Volosjinov[8]. According to the authors, the theories of Saussure are not adequate for understanding the mode of existence of language itself. Language, they claim, exists not as an abstract and closed system, but as a continuous generative process linked with concrete historical situations (Bakhtin/ Volosjinov 1986, 98-99).

A third position comes to the fore in a major work by the Rumanian linguist Eugenio Coseriu, with the almost emblematic title *Synchrony, Diachrony and History*, in which he confronts Saussure's rigid dichotomy of *langue* and *parole* by returning to Wilhelm von Humboldt's concept of language as *energeia*, the speaker's creative activity (Coseriu 1974). Hence, for Coseriu the essential characteristic of language is not structure but change, the subtitle of his book being in fact "the problem of linguistic change". Common to all these theories is a return to the level of *parole*, the statement or the text in its historical and social context, as the fundamental aspect of language.

## Koselleck, *Begriffsgeschichte* and the layers of time

Any of these positions could serve as starting points for a discussion of both the temporality and the intertemporality of language. The reason, however, why I chose Koselleck for this article, is his sustained theoretical as well as empirical engagement with temporality as a phenomenon that is primarily *historical*, and not merely linguistic. According to Koselleck, what distinguishes his theoretical project from that of structuralist linguistics is the emphasis on "the *historicity* of the key concepts that are being discussed" (Koselleck 1972, XXI).

Essentially, both Koselleck's theoretical and empirical works are to a large extent dedicated to the project of *Begriffsgeschichte*, the 'history of concepts', culminating in the eight-volume encyclopaedia of *Geschichtliche Grundbegriffe. Historisches Lexikon zur politisch-sozialen Sprache in*

---

[8] The origin of this text is disputed among Bakhtin scholars, but in the introduction to the English edition of Bakhtin's *The Dialogic Imagination* the editor, Michael Holquist, claims that ninety percent of text in question is the work of Bakhtin himself (Holquist 1998, XXVI).

*Deutschland*, published between 1972 and 1992, of which Koselleck was one of the three editors. He also contributed with several important articles, for instance on 'progress', 'revolution' and 'prognosis'. Koselleck's engagement with political and social concepts, however, goes back even further, to his first major work *Kritik und Krise. Eine Studie zur Pathogenese der bürgerlichen Welt*, published in 1959. Although this book is dedicated to the intellectual history of the Enlightenment, it contains important discussions of such concepts as 'criticism', 'crisis', 'revolution' and 'civil war'. The more theoretical aspects of *Begriffsgeschichte*, however, are developed primarily in two later collections of articles, *Vergangene Zukunft. Zur Semantik historischer Zeiten* from 1979 and *Zeitschichten. Studien zur Historik* from 2000 – both titles being obvious manifestations of exactly the kind of temporality I am discussing in this paper (Koselleck 1992a, 1992b, and 2000a).

Concerning the first of the two titles, *Vergangene Zukunft*, the English edition from 1985 featured the both precise and poetic title "Futures past" (Koselleck 1985). It is, at least in our context, rather striking that if the English translation had followed the German word-order, not "futures past", but "past future", the title would in fact have referred to a specific tense of the verb, thus illustrating the proximity of *Begriffsgeschichte* to the linguistic and even grammatical paradigm. Furthermore, the second title, *Zeitschichten*, would in an English translation probably correspond to something like 'layers of time'. To talk about "Futures past" marks an obvious instance of intertemporality, as I understand the term, communicating that there is nothing absolute or exclusive about either the past or the future, but that the history of concepts must be studied in a continuum between different temporalities. It is, moreover, very important that this continuum is understood both in a diachronic and synchronic sense: On the one hand, past, present and future are succeeding each other in a linear and horizontal manner, in the process of history; on the other hand, as indicated by the metaphor 'layers of time', they are found to be overlapping, vertically, in the 'thickness' – to use a term adapted from the anthropologist Clifford Geertz – of a single historical moment.

Together these two titles can be said to cover most of the important aspects of intertemporality that I am discussing here – and could be summed up in a tentative definition of this rather vague concept. 'Intertemporality' then, as a conceptual parallel to 'interdisciplinarity', indicates a temporal structure of past, present and future that manifests itself both *diachronically* as a linear historical process, and *synchronically* as 'layers of time'. The rest of this paper will consist of a further discussion of this concept, and will attempt to make explicit some of the obvious intertemporal perspectives at work in the *Begriffsgeschichte*.

## The temporalities of *Begriffsgeschichte*

Essentially, the entire project of *Begriffsgeschichte* is founded on a theory of time, of temporality. There is not a single article or book by Koselleck which does not consider this issue in one sense or another. As concepts in the singular, however, 'time' and 'temporality' are misleading with regard to the project as a whole. Koselleck is not – or at least not primarily – concerned with the abstract, logical, philosophical problem of 'time', as we know it from Augustin, Heidegger, and Ricoeur. On the contrary, his focus is on 'temporalities', in the plural, meaning different ways of experiencing, imagining and conceptualizing time. "*Begriffsgeschichte*, the way we try to practice it," he writes, "cannot do without a theory of historical temporalities [*eine Theorie der historischen Zeiten*]" (Koselleck 2000b, 302).

At first glance, the temporality of *Begriffsgeschichte*, as represented in the *Geschichtliche Grundbegriffe*, seems relatively straightforward. All articles, on 'state', 'politics', 'democracy', 'farmer' and 'work', to mention only a few, are structured in more or less the same way, starting in Antiquity – if the history of the concept in question actually goes this far back – and then tracing the concept through history, more or less up to our own time. Nonetheless, the main emphasis is on the period from 1750 onwards, the *Sattelzeit*, as Koselleck has famously called it (Koselleck 1972, XV), when the modern world, often referred to by the notoriously vague term of 'modernity', is coming into being. So far then, *Begriffsgeschichte* seems to have very little in common with the notions of interdisciplinarity and intertemporality discussed in this article: *Geschichtliche Grundbegriffe*, in fact, gives the impression of being a fairly traditional work of social or intellectual history, concerned exclusively with the past as a linear, diachronic development.

However, a closer look at any one of the articles in the encyclopaedia is enough to convince us that this can hardly be the case. Let us choose the concept of 'democracy' and look up the period around 1780, at the very beginning of the *Sattelzeit*, a time in which we know a lot of things are happening to the notion of democratic government (cf. Conze/Koselleck/Maier/Meier/Reimann: 1972, 821-899, esp. 847-853). On the one hand, 'democracy' is still a concept within constitutional law, in the same way as 'aristocracy' and 'oligarchy, going back to Aristotle's treaty on the different forms of government, and used primarily in scholarly debates on matters of law and government; on the other hand, 'democracy' is emerging at the same time as a much more general political concept, used by different members of the public sphere to express their hopes or fears for the future, independent of any theoretical or philosophical debates on the advantages or disadvantages of various constitutional principles. According to diachronic temporality, this would indicate that one meaning and use of the concept of 'democracy' *precedes* or *succeeds* another; but in the relevant article in the *Geschictliche Grundbegriffe* this is clearly not the only possibility. In fact, these two meanings continue to exist alongside each other, simultaneously and in a sense as alternatives, for a certain period of time. To be able to explore this historical simultaneity of different conceptual meanings, we need a more sophisticated notion of the temporality of language than the one we have considered so far: 'diachronic succession'. Essentially, what we need is a notion of temporality which also takes into account the synchronic aspects of a concept within a specific debate or – to use Foucault's term – a specific discourse. Conceptual meanings, then, do not only succeed each other diachronically, but also enter into a synchronic structure of simultaneity, at a specific historical moment. This means that if we want to understand the meanings and uses of a concept, we must be able to place it within this synchronic structure, to explore its structural relations to other concepts as well as to other texts, writers, institutions and movements[9].

**Towards a theory of intertemporality: synchrony and diachrony revisited**
If our aim is to describe the conceptual changes going on around 1780, which have enormous consequences for the understanding of democracy in our own time, there is no use returning to the Saussurian dichotomy of *langue* and *parole*. On the contrary, our ambition must be, as Koselleck puts it, to overcome "the absolute alternative of diachrony and synchrony" (1992c, 125). At work in the *Begriffsgeschichte* are two different analytical strategies, which both aim at replacing this absolute alternative by a much more flexible structure, the structure of intertemporality. The last part of my article will be a presentation and discussion of these two strategies, which correspond to two different levels of theoretical reflection in Koselleck's work.

On the first level, and as a first strategy, synchronic and diachronic perspectives are related to each other in a rather traditional and basic manner, as described by Koselleck in the introduction to the first volume of *Geschichtliche Grundbegriffe*. Trying to establish the history of a concept, one must always start by considering the concept at a specific time and in a specific context. To describe this first step Koselleck actually uses the term "synchronic analysis" (ibid. 115), which he sees as a version of traditional historical criticism, *Quellenkritik*. To reveal the contents of a concept it is necessary to analyze the situation of the speaker and the addressee, as well as the possible intentions and interests at play, the immediate context and so on – a familiar practice in the work of every historian.

---

[9] For a further discussion of the structural or discursive aspects of Koselleck's works, from *Kritik und Krise* and onwards, see Jordheim 2001, 169-175.

It is, however, interesting to note that Koselleck is somewhat reluctant to develop this synchronic aspect of *Begriffsgeschichte* further. I can think of two reasons for this: firstly, because he, according to his own words, is wary that "linguistic semantics shall simply dissolve into a synchronic analysis of texts" (Koselleck 1992e, VI); and secondly because, in fact, one important ambition in all of his theoretical works is to attempt to redefine the entire notion of the structural, the systematic and the synchronic, in the light of a theory of temporalities. To a certain degree it is possible to understand this wariness, the synchronic for a long time having been the subject of choice of structuralist and post-structuralist theories of history. As in the case of the so-called New Historicism, one aim has been to replace the various concepts of historical time with concepts of space, such as 'discourse' and 'textuality of history', making it much more difficult to conceptualize and describe historical change (Montrose 1989, 15-37).

Anyway, at this first level of theoretical reflection the defining feature of *Begriffsgeschichte* is not the synchronic analysis but what Koselleck refers to as the "diachronic principle" (Koselleck 1972, XXI). Structurally speaking, the defining move of *Begriffsgeschichte* is when, in Koselleck's own words, "the synchronic analysis is expanded diachronically" (Koselleck 1992c, 115). The concept, he writes, is "detached from its historical context and its different meanings are traced through the succession of times" (Koselleck 1972, XXI). Finally, Koselleck continues, the "different descriptions of concepts in their contexts are added together in a history for the concept" (ibid.). This is in itself an important step, introducing a consistent theory as well as a method for showing how language – as represented in the 'key concepts' – actually changes through historical time. Explicitly integrating synchronic and diachronic perspectives on language and texts, Koselleck can be said to follow the same line of thought as we observed in Coseriu, Bakhtin and the Prague school, thus moving towards a theory of intertemporality.

**The next step: the diachronic within the synchronic**
There is, however, another way in which Koselleck integrates diachronic and synchronic elements, constituting what I claim to be the most important potential of both interdisciplinary and intertemporal analysis. If for a moment we return to the concept of 'democracy', there is at least one important aspect that has not been covered by what I have said so far. In fact neither the synchronic nor the diachronic analysis seems to be able to account for the fact that this concept, 'democracy', when being used around 1780, does not refer to its contemporary context alone, but also, and more importantly, to the past as well as to the future – more specifically, to the traditional, originally Aristotelian discussion of the forms of government on the one hand, and to the progressive political ideal of a future democratic society on the other. As a consequence, the relationship

between synchrony and diachrony is becoming much more complex: Firstly, the synchronic meanings or contents were added up – as Koselleck says – to a diachronic history of the concept; secondly, however, the diachronic element seems to reappear within the concept itself as a structural relationship between past, present and future.

At this point we have to consider Koselleck's redefinition of words like 'structure' and 'system'. For Saussure, these and similar terms constituted a way of freeing language from the predominance of time and diachrony in 19th century linguistics. In the case of Koselleck and the *Begriffsgeschichte*, however, it is the other way round. When Koselleck speaks of the "structural possibility" (1992c, 126) of historical concepts, or of their "systematic claim" (1972, XXI), it is precisely their temporal aspects he is talking about. According to Koselleck, every concept has "its own internal temporal structure" (1992e, VI), comprising all three dimensions of time: past, present and future. More precisely, his claim is that the semantics of every political or social concept includes both a *polemic* element directed at the present, a *prognostic* element directed at the future, and a *nostalgic* element directed at the past (1992c, 111)[10]. Hence, even though all concepts belong in a synchronically structured context, in a text, debate, or discourse, they still retain what Koselleck refers to as their "Janus-faces" (1972, XV), one facing backwards towards a nostalgically reconstructed past, the other facing forwards towards a prognostically envisaged future. The diachronic movement from the past through the present and into the future is reflected at a given historical moment, in the synchronic structure of a text, context or discourse, by the threefold reference of the key concepts – the *nostalgic* reference, the *polemic* reference, and the *prognostic* reference. Then again, the term 'reference' seems rather misleading, as Koselleck, at least to a certain extent, subscribes to a constructivist paradigm where meanings are constructed, not referred to. Thus it would probably be more correct to say that as they move through history the concepts are continually producing or constructing new pasts and new futures, as a way of making sense of the present.

### The simultaneity of the non-simultaneous
One last example of how this temporal or intertemporal structure affects the meaning of a concept is definitely called for, and so I will move from 'democracy' to 'revolution'. For an analysis of the concept of 'revolution' in the context of the fateful days of October 1917 when the Bolsheviks were rebelling against the Czarist empire, we might suggest the following temporal organization: firstly, the concept would be pointing *backwards* towards a past overshadowed by the French Revolution and the revolutions of 1830 and 1848, or maybe even further back, towards a pre-mo-

---

[10] "Nostalgic", "prognostic" and "polemic" are in fact my terms, not Koselleck's.

dern concept of 'revolution'; secondly, it would be pointing *forwards* towards the coming of a new era, the utopia of the communist society; thirdly, it would have an *interventionist* and *activist* element, summoning the workers to the barricades. And these three elements would coexist, would exist simultaneously as 'layers of time' that – to remain with Koselleck's own archaeological metaphor – must be excavated to enable a real understanding of the concept. This means, of course, that within the simultaneity of the Russian revolution, even within the very concept of 'revolution', there are conceptual and semantic elements that are obviously non-simultaneous, in the sense that they refer to or rather construct contents that lie either in the past or in the future, thus creating what can be regarded as *a diachronic movement through the synchronic moment* – a movement of experience and memory on the one hand or of expectation and hope on the other[11].

To sum up, intertemporality in the sense of Koselleck and the *Begriffsgeschichte* implies a twofold structure of time, or to be more precise, one temporal structure moving through another. On the one hand, as illustrated by the project of the *Geschichtliche Grundbegriffe*, there are all the synchronic contexts, moments and discourses, added up to a diachronic history of the concept; on the other hand, the concepts themselves, as they move through diachronic time, through all these synchronic contexts and moments, are simultaneously unfolding their own diachronic temporal structure, constructing their own pasts, their own presents and their own futures by means of the nostalgic, prognostic and polemic elements of their conceptual semantics. This means that every historical moment will exist in what Koselleck refers to as 'the simultaneity of the non-simultaneous' – 'die Gleichzeitigkeit des Ungleichzeitigen'[12] – where the past meets the future, both reconstructed in an instance of conceptual semantics, in an attempt to intervene in, reform or revolutionize the present.

Hence 'intertemporality', as a means of theorizing the study of philology, is in fact a way of understanding or at least trying to understand 'the simultaneity of the non-simultaneous', which in my opinion is one of the really great challenges of the global society. Take a word like 'terrorism',

---

[11] A broad discussion of this movement is found in one of Koselleck's most influential articles, originally published in 1975, see Koselleck 1992d, 349-375.

[12] As I read Koselleck, 'die Gleichzeitigkeit des Ungleichzeitigen' is one of the key notions in his entire work, appearing in several different contexts and at several different levels of analysis (historical, linguistic and anthropological). See for instance Koselleck 2000b, 9ff; 2000c, 306f; and 2000d, 164ff. A further discussion of this topic can be found in my forthcoming article "Die 'Gleichzeitigkeit des Ungleichzeitigen' als Konvergenzpunkt von Zeitlichkeit und Sprachlichkeit".

which we now encounter every day in the newspapers. To analyze this concept, with all its linguistic realizations in different languages, is to a large extent a battle with 'the simultaneity of the non-simultaneous'. What are the nostalgic elements, what kind of histories are being constructed, by Americans, by Europeans, by Arabs? What are the prognostic elements, which are the futures imagined and prophesized by fundamentalists and liberals on both sides? And last but not least: how does the concept of 'terrorism' intervene in the different political contexts of the present? As I see it, this line of thought represents at least one important aspect of the future of philology.

**References**

Arrowsmith, William: 1963. "Nietzsche on Classics and Classicists (Part II)". In: *Arion. A Quarterly Journal of Classical Culture* 2/1963, pp. 5-15.

Conze, Werner, Reinhart Koselleck, Hans Maier, Christian Meier & Hans Leo Reimann: 1972. "Demokratie". In: *Geschichtliche Grundbegriffe. Historisches Lexikon zur politisch-sozialen Sprache in Deutschland*. Edited by Otto Brunner, Werner Conze & Reinhart Koselleck. Volume 1, Stuttgart, Klett-Cotta, pp. 821-899.

Coseriu, Eugenio: 1974. *Synchronie, Diachronie und Geschichte. Das Problem des Sprachwandels* (translated by Helga Sohre). Munich, Wilhelm Fink Verlag.

Bakhtin, Mikhail M. & Valentin Volosjinov: 1986. *Marxism and the Philosophy of Language* (translated by Ladislav Matejka and I. R. Titunik). Cambridge, Mass., Harvard University Press.

Bakhtin, Mikhail M.: 1998. "Discourse in the Novel". In: *The Dialogic Imagination. Four essays by M. M. Bakhtin*. Edited by Michael Holquist (translated by Caryl Emerson & Michael Holquist). Austin, University of Texas Press, pp. 259-422.

Boeckh, August: 1966. *Enzyklopädie und Methodenlehre der philologischen Wissenschaften. Erster Hauptteil. Formale Theorie der philologischen Wissenschaft.* Edited by Ernst Bratuscheck, Darmstadt: Wissenschaftliche Buchgesellschaft.

De Man, Paul: 1993. "The Return to Philology", in *The Resistance to Theory*. Third edition, Minneapolis /London: University of Minnesota Press, pp. 21-26.

Gammelgaard, Karen: 2003. *Tekstens mening – en introduktion til Pragerskolen*. Roskilde, Roskilde Universitetsforlag.

Holquist, Michael: 1998. "Introduction". In: M. M. Bakhtin, *The Dialogic Imagination. Four essays by M. M. Bakhtin*. Edited by Michael Holquist (translated by Caryl Emerson & Michael Holquist). Austin, University of Texas Press., pp. XV-XXXIII.

Jordheim, Helge: 2001. *Lesningens vitenskap – utkast til en ny filologi*. Oslo, Universitetsforlaget.

Koselleck, Reinhart: 1972. "Einleitung". In: *Geschichtliche Grundbegriffe. Historisches Lexikon zur politisch-sozialen Sprache in Deutschland*. Edited by Otto Brunner,Werner Conze & Reinhart Koselleck. Volume 1, Stuttgart, Klett-Cotta, pp. XII-XXVII.

Koselleck, Reinhart: 1985. *Futures past. On the Semantics of Historical Time* (translated by Keith Tribe). Cambridge, Mass., MIT Press.
Koselleck, Reinhart: 1992a. *Kritik und Krise. Eine Studie zur Pathogenese der bürgerlichen Welt*. Seventh Edition, Frankfurt am Main, Suhrkamp Verlag.
Koselleck, Reinhart: 1992b. *Vergangene Zukunft. Zur Semantik geschichtlicher Zeiten*. Second Edition, Frankfurt am Main, Suhrkamp Verlag.
Koselleck, Reinhart: 1992c. "Begriffsgeschichte und Sozialgeschichte". In: *Vergangene Zukunft. Zur Semantik geschichtlicher Zeiten*. Second Edition, Frankfurt am Main, Suhrkamp Verlag, pp. 107-129.
Koselleck, Reinhart: 1992d. "'Erfahrungsraum' und 'Erwartungshorizont' – zwei historische Kategorien". In: *Vergangene Zukunft. Zur Semantik geschichtlicher Zeiten*. Second Edition, Frankfurt am Main, Suhrkamp Verlag, pp. 349-375.
Koselleck, Reinhart: 1992e. "Vorwort". In: *Geschichtliche Grundbegriffe. Historisches Lexikon zur politisch-sozialen Sprache in Deutschland*. Edited by Otto Brunner, Werner Conze & Reinhart Koselleck. Volume 7, Stuttgart, pp. V-VIII.
Koselleck, Reinhart: 2000a. *Zeitschichten. Studien zur Historik*. Frankfurt am Main, Suhrkamp Verlag.
Koselleck, Reinhart: 2000b. "Einleitung". In: *Zeitschichten. Studien zur Historik*, Frankfurt am Main, Suhrkamp Verlag, pp. 9-16.
Koselleck, Reinhart: 2000c. "Über die Theoriebedürftigkeit der Geschichtswissenschaft". In: *Zeitschichten. Studien zur Historik*. Frankfurt am Main, Suhrkamp Verlag, pp. 298-316.
Koselleck, Reinhart: 2000d. "Gibt es eine Beschleunigung der Geschichte?". In: *Zeitschichten. Studien zur Historik*. Frankfurt am Main, Suhrkamp Verlag, pp. 150-176.
Montrose, Louis A.: 1989. "Professing the Renaissance: The Poetics and Politics of Culture". In: H. A. Veeser (ed.): *The New Historicism*. New York/London, Routledge, pp. 15–37.
Nietzsche, Friedrich: 1977. "Wir Philologen". In: *Werke in drei Bänden*. Edited by Karl Schlechta. Volume 3, Munich/Vienna, Carl Hanser Verlag 1977, pp. 323-332.
Porter, James I.: 2000. *Nietzsche and the Philology of the Future*. Stanford, California, Stanford University Press.
Ross, Werner: 1994. *Der ängstliche Adler. Friedrich Nietzsches Leben*. Second Edition, Munich, Deutscher Taschenbuch Verlag.
Saussure, Ferdinand de: 1967. *Cours de linguistique générale*. Edited by Charles Bally & Albert Sechehaye in cooperation with Albert Riedlinger. Critical edition by Tullio de Mauro. Postface by Louis-Jean Calvert. Paris, Éditions Payot & Rivages.
Scheerer, Thomas M.: 1980. *Ferdinand de Saussure. Rezeption und Kritik*. Darmstadt, Wissenschaftliche Buchgesellschaft.
Thibault, Paul J.: 1997. *Re-reading Saussure. The Dynamics of Signs in Social Life*. London/ New York, Routledge.

# Cognitive Models

## Language and Thought in Cultural Studies

by

Mette Steenberg

Introduction
My intention in this article is to introduce a cognitive approach to the study of foreign languages. This approach allows us to study all phenomena pertaining to the 'cultural world' through the analysis of cognitive models situated at the level of conceptualisation and mediating the ground between language and culture. The scope of my argumentation will not be modest: my claim is that instead of allowing themselves to be reduced to utility disciplines, language studies must fight their way back to a central position within the Humanities. There is excellent reason for this: our language-based approach allows us to study cultural conceptualisation on a far more solid ground than non-language-based cultural studies, simply because linguistic categorization provides the most obvious access to semantic, content-dense categories of thought. To shed light on the relationship between language and thought I will discuss the Sapir-Whorf hypothesis and its relevance for current studies in cognitive linguistic.

Traditional philological studies grew out of the Renaissance project of reconstructing the ancient classical languages and literatures in which the Humanists found a model for all humanity. As such, the Philologies are born out of the hypothesis that the study of language is indispensable to the study of culture and history, which in the Humboldt-oriented university tradition was consolidated through a philological-historical methodological approach to insight into the classical world. The hermeneutic-historical ideal of *Geisteswissenschaften* remained strong until synchronic studies came to be foregrounded at the expense of diachrony, a process which took place in the second half of the 20$^{th}$ century.

In many respects, Modern Language Studies use the same philological-historical methodological approach, even though their ideological perspectives may be different. Where both the Renaissance Humanists and the New Humanists shared the ideal of mankind's full potential liberation through true disinterested knowledge, Modern Language Studies are constructed in the service of modern nations seeking consolidation through a national discourse. In many modern language departments, the literary canon creates a common point of reference and reflects a nation's self-conception.

Global citizenship and multicultural societies in which local discourses create a hybridity of voices have forced Modern Language Studies to switch from a unitary to a pluralistic approach to the study of cultures. The hypothesis of a tight relationship between language and culture remains a fruitful working paradigm, but the agenda is somewhat altered: since there can be no study of *the* culture of a nation, we are faced with the need to study the conflicting and intervening conceptions of identity. This necessity is witnessed to by the boom in Cultural Studies conducted with the help of critical discourse analysis, postcolonial studies and gender studies, together with an emerging host of social constructivist theories.[1] 'The cultural turn' has been on the agenda of Modern Language Studies for quite some time, with American language departments marking the furthest outpost of response to the necessity of a multi-cultural society.

The pros and cons of a switch from Philology to Cultural Studies in our own national debate are entangled with the fear of extension: what will remain of Philology if we give in to the demands of non-language-based cultural studies and start conducting our research and teaching on the basis of texts in translation? Probably not much. In this article, therefore, I would like to propose a viable approach to Cultural Studies, starting from the hypothesis that language studies hold a privileged position when it comes to analysing the conceptualisations of cultures[2].

## The Cognitive Linguistics approach to culture

Within the paradigm of Cognitive Linguistics, linguistic conceptualisations are conceptualisations of culture. The understanding and analysis of conceptual cultural systems have therefore been crucial for the cognitive linguistic paradigm[3]. Lakoff & Johnson's by now classic *Metaphors We Live By* (1980) demonstrates how our concepts are constructed on the basis of

---

[1] In the following I hope it will be clear that I do not see the cognitive approach as in any way contrary to these approaches, but rather as a substantial support, both theoretically and methodologically, in analysis of the conceptual structures that discourses utilise.

[2] This doesn't mean, however, that language is the only means of expression: aesthetics represents another, and so do social and legal systems.

[3] There is little space here to give a detailed account of the various definitions of culture within the cognitive paradigm, nor can I provide insight into the paradigm as such. I hope the reader will bear with me in this scratching of the surface, and can only suggest that those who are interested should follow up my references.

conceptual projections from concrete (bodily grounded) to abstract (discourse based) domains of knowledge. This cognitive theory of meaning leads to the formulation of a new epistemological position, Experientialism[4], which rejects both *objectivism* and *subjectivism*: *objectivism* in the form of metaphysical objectivism based on the idea of an external view which guarantees a truth-conditional logical correspondence between mind and world, since "being objective is always relative to a conceptual system and a set of cultural values" (Lakoff & Johnson 1980, 227); and the Romantic version of *subjectivism*, which postulates "that imaginative understanding is completely unconstrained" (ibid. 228). What they retain from the two positions is the insistence that objective knowledge is possible even when the idea of an external perspective is rejected in favour of the view that meaning is always meaning for someone from a specific internal perspective, because there are ways in which these processes of meaning are constrained. These conceptual processes – i.e. how meaning is shaped and constrained – are the core issues for cognitive linguistics.

This theoretical position grew out of epistemological questions raised by the Linguistic Relativity Hypothesis (LRH) formulated by Sapir and Whorf. Within this picture, we should not forget that at the time Lakoff was arguing against Chomsky and the modularity conception of language. The great challenge was to formulate a cognitive theory which avoided both pure Cartesian mentalism and cultural solipsism. Here Experientialism enters as an important theoretical contribution, which was to be developed later in separately authored books by Lakoff and Johnson (1987) into *The Embodiment Hypothesis*.

But what happens to objective knowledge if, as most practitioners of the Cognitive Linguistic paradigm seem to suggest, the only access we have to reality is through the conceptualisations formed by people and cultures of their interaction with their physical environment? This position would normally be associated with an intolerable relativism – intolerable because the notion carries with it the denial of unbiased knowledge. Lakoff (1987, Chap.8) turns the question around and asks whether relativism really is a problem for the scientific study of meaning. Given that the object of our study is the understanding of conceptual systems in their own terms, why would we need an external parameter by which to understand them? This does not deny, however, the need for a level of formalization, or a metalanguage, with which to analyse different parameters.

### The Principle of Linguistic Relevance
In his famous article on "The relation of habitual thought and behaviour to language" (Whorf 1956, 134-159), Benjamin Lee Whorf makes the claim that members of different cultures experience reality differently. This

---

[4] For the most recent version of experientialism se (Lakoff & Johnson, 1999).

argument is supported by contrasting the Hopi and the SAE concepts of time and space: "concepts of 'time' and 'matter' are not given in substantially the same form by experience to all men but depend upon the nature of the language or languages through the use of which they have been developed" (ibid. 158). However horrifying it may seem that even the substance of the world depends upon language, it is, however, another often cited passage from a later article on *Science and Linguistics* (ibid. 207-219) that has led to the liveliest disputes on the principle of linguistic relativity:

> We dissect nature along lines laid down by our native languages. The categories and types we isolate from the world of phenomena we do not find there because they stare every observer in the face; on the contrary, the world is presented in a kaleidoscopic flux of impressions which has to be organized by our minds – and this means largely by the linguistic systems in our minds. We cut nature up, organize it into concepts, and ascribe significances as we do, largely because we are parties to an agreement to organize it in this way – an agreement that holds throughout our speech community and is coded in the patterns of our language. The agreement is, of course, an implicit and unstated one, BUT ITS TERMS ARE ABSOLUTELY OBLIGATORY; we cannot talk at all except by subscribing to the organization and classification of data which the agreement decrees. (Whorf 1956, 213-214, author's emphasis)

In particular there has been wide discussion of his notion of reality as a flux of impressions which are only formed into stable structures by a process of linguistically 'carving up nature'.

There is however another version of the principle of linguistic relativity, which simply states that language somehow and to some extent shapes the manner in which human beings perceive reality, as is widely claimed in cognitive linguistics. This hypothesis can be broken down into two basic principles:

1) Determinism refers to the idea that the language we speak to some extent determines the way in which we conceptualise the world. This principle can be stated in a strong and a weak version, the strong implying complete identity between language and cognition.
2) Linguistic relativity refers to the idea that patterns of thought encoded in one language are unique to that language alone[5].

On the basis of untenable epistemological implications of the relativity principle, the argument most commonly put forward against relativism is the *translatability* criterion: if cultures and languages differ so radically translation should not be possible; therefore there must be points of

---

[5] It will be clear in the following that whereas the principle of linguistic determinism concentrates on the language-cognition aspect, the principle of linguistic relativism concentrates on the language-reality aspect.

commensurability. Commensurability refers to the idea of a shared platform of common standards, allowing a comparison on external grounds between two systems or worldviews: a *Tertium Organum*[6]; which is what Whorf seemed to expect from what he called the new sciences (1956, 248). Incommensurability also plays an important role in recent epistemological positions such as that of Kuhn, who claims that scientific theories are incommensurable because it is impossible to gain a perspective which is not intrinsic to a certain paradigm. This does not mean, however, that we cannot be taught to master alternative conceptual systems; as a matter of fact, that is what happens when we learn other languages. Commensurability is therefore a possibility, but only through experience; that is, not from a position external to the conceptual system but from an internal position like learning foreign languages. Our general conceptualising mechanism might in this sense count as a sort of common ground since it is our shared cognitive abilities that make it possible to acquire alternative conceptual systems. And so translation, in the broadest sense of cross-cultural communication, is possible.

While there has been a general reluctance to accept the strong version of the Sapir-Worf hypothesis, there is likewise a general agreement that language to some extent shapes our cognition. The question is, to what extent does it do so? Furthermore, which way should the arrow point, from language to cognition or from cognition to language? And how about the third component, reality? Not to mention culture, which seems to be left out of account[7]. One problem with the hypothesis is that even if it is falsifiable in principle, it is almost impossible to prove wrong, since that would require that groups within the same linguistic community should show testable differences in cognition which could be disentangled from effects induced by gender, social class, education etc: an almost impossible task[8].

---

[6] The need for a tertium comparationes is, as Enrique Bernárdez, in a paper read at ICLC, Spain, 2003, points out, a general concern in linguistics. He quotes Hansjakob Seiler (2000):..."Language universals research and language topology involve cross-linguistic comparison. For any type of comparison there must be two *comparanda* and one *tertium comparationes*, and for a scientifically based comparison both *comparanda* and *tertium comparationes* must be made explicit..."

[7] Enrique Bernárdez, in a paper read at the Language, Culture and Cognition conference, Portugal, 2003, surveys recent attempts to deal with the notion of relativity, one of which (Goddard, 2003) points out that whereas LRH "deals with the relations between language and cognition, culture is essentially left out"

[8] Not only impossible but also highly controversial. Could it be that as David Hull (2002) asks, it is the charge of racism, which was also levelled at Whorf, that makes leading cognitive scholars such as Steven Pinker insist on "monomorphic minds?" (cited in Bernárdez, forthcoming).

It has been easier to test the principle of linguistic relativity (the language-reality aspect). Here the claim can be stated thus: if language determines the world view of an individual, then cognitions in certain domains, such as colour, should also vary in those cases in which the languages terms referring to colours differ. However, the research on colour perception and colour terms conducted by Brent Berlin and Paul Kay (1969) shows no evidence that this is the case. On the contrary, people from cultures whose colour terms are widely disparate are not limited by linguistic labelling in their experience of colours. There is in fact much evidence that our perception of colour is both language- and culture-neutral. This evidence has been used to dismiss the relativity principle; however, even if it could be proved that reality is constant independent of our reference to it, the question would still remain why some cultures linguistically code for certain aspects of an experience while others code for other aspects[9].

The question of the degree of linguistic determinism is thus still pertinent to research conducted within CL[10], whereas the relativity issue has been challenged in the search for shared pre-linguistic mechanisms underlying the cognition of all human beings. Psychologist Eleanor Rosch, while, incidentally, setting out to prove the Whorfian hypothesis, came across such a 'universal' mechanism in the process of categorization[11]. On the basis of the Berlin and Kay focal colour test, she conducted experiments on the Danis, a non-westernized culture in Papua New Guinea speaking a language which possesses only two colour terms, and contrasted her results with those obtained from experiments on native English speakers with eleven basic colour terms at their disposal. Her research demonstrated convincingly that the process of categorization is language-independent; hence language does not determine cognition, since Dani- and English-speaking natives performed equally in naming and memory tasks. The categorization process is thus not carried out in relation to a linguistic category but to a semantic category, the focal colour being the most

---

[9] These questions are raised in CL under what could be called "The Frame and Attention Approach", including work by Fillmore, Langacker and Talmy (se chapter 5 in Ungerer & Schmid, 1996, for a very useful introduction and valuable suggestions for further readings to this approach)

[10] Dan Slobin's "Thinking-for-Speaking" Hypothesis (1996) proves an excellent working hypothesis for the coding processes that occur between conceptualisation and verbalisation in foreign language acquisition. See for instance Cadierno and Pedersen, this volume.

[11] For Elanor Rosch's research on categorization Ungerer and Schmid provides a first good step with a lot of useful references. Lakoff (1987 ch. 2) is also a valuable source, the most comprehensive however being Kleiber (1990). Rocsh (1977) and (1978) provides good non-technical insights and Rochs (1988) a most valuable overview on the whole issue.

salient, though it doesn't have to be in a focal position in order to function as the structuring principle. Rosch, going on to expand these findings to other categories, therefore termed the phenomenon *prototype* or *prototype effect*, on the basis of the quality or typicality effect displayed by category member ratings. Meanwhile, in cognitive anthropology, Berlin (Berlin *et. al.* 1974) conducted experiments on categorization which demonstrated that cognitive taxonomies function in a similar fashion around a basic level, showing prototype structure to be the most salient level of categorization, the one first learned and most easily retrievable in memory and naming. Another interesting thing about the basic level is that "generic level categories represent the preferred cognitive perspective. They seem to meet 'basic' cognitive needs because they pinpoint where the focus of human interest lies" (Ungerer & Schmid, 1996, 66)[12]. This result is important because it demonstrates that the cognitive organization of prototypes and basic levels overcomes the epistemological obstacles of relativism: communication across cultures can succeed because our conceptual systems are not entirely language-dependent; rather there is psychological evidence that we share conceptual mechanisms, and most importantly, this can be accounted for without having to deny cultural diversity. Basic level research thus makes it possible to defend a relativistic position without falling into the abyss of incommensurability.

This implies that whereas the mechanisms of categorisation are culture-independent, the content of categories is of course highly dependent on culture, a dependency that linguistic categories will code for. This "shows that cultural models do not only influence the selection of prototypes, but are equally important for the choice of the basic level perspective" (Ungerer & Schmid 1996, 70) This however is not evidence for a different carving up of reality, but simply demonstrates that our interaction with our environmental situation, or immediate context, influences the way we select objects and situations for attention[13]. To this extent language can be said to be relative to the world, without leading to the absurd claim that people are trapped within their language without any chance of cross-cultural understanding.

---

[12] Berlin's (1974) study of the classification and naming of plants in Tzeltal, a Mayan-speaking community, demonstrates how conceptual taxonomies will single out different objects for basic level categorization according to the specific relevance of that object to a certain culture: in this sense linguistic relativity does exist but the principles for the singling out is dependent on the specific environmental reality, which varies, and the specific cognitive principles which seem to operate across these differences, assuring the commensurability of meaning.

[13] Langacker's notion of *construal* seems to be the most promising in this respect.

## Domains of experience

But how are interaction and experience defined in cognitive linguistics? In *The Body in the Mind* (Johnson 1987) the answer to this question is formulated as *The Embodiment Hypothesis*. According to Johnson, our experiences are organized in schemas which are the ordering activity of our bodily interaction with our environment (ibid. 29). Schemas are dynamic in the sense that they both structure our past experiences and also allow for them to apply to any number of future situations. In *Women, Fire, and Dangerous Things* (1987), Lakoff distinguishes between conceptual and functional embodiment, where conceptual embodiment is the idea that "categories are a consequence of the nature of the human biological capacities and of the experience of functioning in a physical and social environment", and functional embodiment is "the idea that certain concepts are not merely understood intellectually; rather they are used automatically, unconsciously, and without noticeable effort as part of normal functioning" (Lakoff 1987, 12). But if our bodily interaction with the physical world is the basis for our conceptual system, how do different cultures develop? Don't we all share the same biological make up? Yet we create radically different conceptualisations and belief systems. The answer to this critique lies in the definition of the nature of 'experience':

> ...what we call "direct physical experience" is never merely a matter of having a body of a certain sort; rather, *every* experience takes place within a vast background of cultural presuppositions. It can be misleading, therefore, to speak of direct physical experience as though there were some core of immediate experience which we then "interpret" in terms of our conceptual system. Cultural assumptions, values, and attitudes are not a conceptual overlay which we may or may not place upon experience as we choose. It would be more correct to say that all experience is cultural through and through, that we experience our "world" in such a way that our culture is always present in the very experience itself. (Lakoff & Johnson 1980, 57)

It is important here to distinguish between on the one hand the cognitive mechanisms involved in the process of conceptualisation, which is thought to be more or less 'culture free' since at the neurobiological level cultural bias is hardly a relevant issue, and on the other hand the phenomenological level of experience which is cultural through and through, a distinction that I will dwell on in greater detail later.

It is also important to distinguish between the types of environment, or better, domain, in which our experiences take place. Lakoff & Johnson (1980) distinguish between three different kinds of experiential domains: the physical, the social and the emotional. While these domains might be structured and filled differently across cultures, the physical environment of the ethnic and linguistic groups of Navajo and the Chachi differs widely (see Enrique Bernárdez, *lengua y cultura de los Chachi*, in preparation). This situation will exert a significant influence on the individual's conceptualisation of space and the values attributed to a general schema of distance. The existence of such domains, however, can be regarded as possible examples of cross-cultural constancy, providing an argument against the whorfian arbitrary carving up of reality[14]. It is further argued that meaning is created through a process of metaphoric projection across domains, the most common projection occurring from the physical (including human biology) to the social or emotional domain. The detailed study of the embodiment of emotions by Zoltán Kövecses (in Lakoff 1987) offers such an account of how we structure our conceptualisation of anger, drawing on the structure of the physical sensation of getting 'hot' when emotionally agitated. This structure appears in examples like "he boiled with anger" (see Case Study 1 on Anger, Lakoff and Köecses 1987, for dozens of examples). Since these projections seem to occur in a highly structured manner across cultures, it is hypothesised that some domains, or at least some experiences, are correlated; that is, at a phenomenological level there seem to be systematic correlations between certain experiences. This claim has lead to the Primary Metaphor Hypothesis (Joseph Grady 1997), according to which basic experiences such as emotional intimacy and physical closeness are tightly correlated in what is called "a primary scene", supposedly existing cross-culturally. As much as it is true that we evaluate emotional intimacy in terms of physical closeness, the values attached to a general schema of distance might differ widely cross-culturally[15]. Let us return to the example above. Distance will probably be evaluated quite differently by the Chachi, surrounded by thick forest, and the Navajo, living in open country[16]. However, this does not indicate that some

---

[14] Per Aage Brandt (2000) proposes an architecture of semantic domains built upon the three above-mentioned basic ones. As much as I am hesitant to accept the idea of such a general design, I am very much in favour of the effort to provide a realistic grounding hypothesis in the study of cognitive linguistics. I am also sympathetic to the basic idea that the processes of meaning are regulated by its situatedness in a specific experiential domain.

[15] I have argued extensively elsewhere (paper read at the Cognitive Poetic Session at ICLC, Spain, 2003) for the existence of such a schema and how it can take on different evaluations depending on the cultural context.

[16] As Enrique Bernárdez' (forthcoming) study on cha'palaachi shows, the matter is complicated since a linguistic system can integrate spatial markers at many levels, even non-linguistic, which makes the endeavour of understanding the influence of cultures upon language phenomena a less than straight forward process: "Apart from relations at the level of pragmatics – or the socially and culturally conditioned use of language in general – and the vocabulary, where language-culture relations are fairly obvious, the many attempts to relate linguistic structures and cultural phenomena have failed. There is no such thing as the "cultural correlate" of say, the verbal tenses in a particular language, much less of verbal tense in general".

cultures might entirely lack a notion of space and that different cultures carve up reality differently. Whorf was clearly wrong on this point: reality, or rather the physical environment as we interact with it at the level of phenomenological experience, is so persistent and solid that it puts heavy constraints on how we are able to conceptualise our experiences. As the following citation shows, Whorf seems to turn the matter around and draw the wrong conclusions from the right insights:

> Whether such a civilization as ours would be possible with widely different linguistic handling of time is a large question – in our civilization, our linguistic patterns and the fitting of our behaviour to the temporal order are what they are, and they are in accord. (Whorf 1956, 154)

Contrary to this, I argue that we do not carve up reality differently because of the constraints that language puts on our conceptualisations, but that the nature of reality, in fact, puts constraints on our conceptualisations, and that language codes these conceptualisations in ways that inform us, upon analysis, about the experiences of reality that shaped them. As much as we are defined by our experiences, we are not therefore 'locked up' in our language, as Whorf seemed to believe. Adopting this perspective, however, is not to deny that language exercises an important role in cognition: here it is necessary to distinguish between several layers of cognition and different aspects of language. While there might be aspects of language and cognition that are "closed"[17] against readily changing re-conceptualisation, there will be other aspects such as our cultural models which upon scrutinizing analysis can be revised by discourse: for example, telling a story that activates less prototypical frames will necessarily create different focal points, and these will have effects upon the conceptualisations that make up our cognitive models.

Language should therefore never be reduced to a means of communication, neither within the academic world nor outside it: language is thought and, as such, it is highly ideological. If the academic world wishes to face up to its responsibility in this respect, the importance of the study of language and culture should not be underestimated.

### Idealized Cognitive Models

One way of studying language as thought is through cognitive models. Work in cognitive psychology and anthropology on prototypes and basic levels provided the ground for the development in cognitive linguistics of

---

[17] I am thinking here, of course, of Talmy's (2000) important distinction between open class and close classed forms in language.

the theory of Idealized Cognitive Models[18]. The elaboration of ICMs draws on Fillmore's research on frame semantics, and on schema theory (scripts: Schank and Abelson, 1977)[19].

Cognitive models can be defined as "stored cognitive representations that belong to a certain field" (Ungerer & Schmid 1996, 47) or domain of experience, e.g. restaurants, in Schank's and Abelson's famous example (Schank & Abelson 1977). They will often be organized as "cluster models", that is, constituted by several prototypically organized nuclei, as Lakoff's study of "motherhood" demonstrates (see Chap. 4, 1987). Since such domains will be filled differently by different cultures, as discussed earlier on, there might be good reason to consider them Cultural Models. The difference is that whereas cognitive models are thought to be context-underspecified, for instance applicable to any situation where people dine at a restaurant, cultural models are context-specified, e.g. filled by culturally specific rituals in which different cultures perform the restaurant script. Simplifying the issue, we might say that the cognitive model is closer to the schematic structure of an event[20]. It should be remembered that cultural models should never be equated with *the* model of a culture, since, as I said at the beginning of this article, there is no such thing as *Culture*, only individual cultures and thus individual models. However, since cognition is essentially *collective, cognition-for-action*, (Enrique Bernárdez, forthcoming) rather than individual internal and passive processing, cultural models are highly dynamic, like the schemas on which they function, and are stabilised principally through collective social practices.

Cognitive Models thus seem to constitute a felicitous combination of research in diverse fields, providing a solid platform for cultural studies which take seriously the effect language has on cognition while overcoming the barriers of linguistic relativism, since cognitive models are as much process-dependent as content-dependent[21]. With this interdisciplinary approach the notion of Cognitive Models becomes more relevant for

---

[18] Lakoff coined this term in his 1987 book: "The main thesis of this book is that we organize our knowledge by means of structures called idealized cognitive models, or ICM, and that categorization structures and prototype effects are by-products of that organization" (Lakoff 1987, 68). In the following I will simply use the term cognitive or cultural model as it is used in cognitive anthropology (Holland & Quinn 1987).

[19] See in particular Naomi Quinn (In Holland & Quinn 1987)

[20] Schemas are therefore of crucial importance to cognitive linguistics because their reality is hitherto the most viably functional *tertium comparationis*.

[21] It is important to remember that the term cognition covers both the physiological processes of cognition, as in neuro-biology, the psychological process, as in cognitive psychology, and the content of systems of conceptualisation, i.e. cognitive models.

foreign language studies since it is relevant both to linguistics, poetics[22] and, as already mentioned, cultural studies.

While it should be obvious that cognitive models e.g. of motherhood can take on a host of different instantiations, I do not claim that variation in cognitive models corresponds to differences in cognitive processing. Interestingly, cognitive models might provide yet another argument against the strong deterministic version, since it is possible to engage in practices that require shared cultural models but not a shared language (e.g. the cultural model of democracy), or to share a language but not cultural models (this is the situation people refer to when saying "we simply do not speak the same language" or "we have a communication problem"). This raises the interesting question of whether the consistency of cultures is actually more dependent on shared cultural models than on shared language. The USA is a case in point; for example, Americans firmly believe that any person of no matter which race, sex, religion, or language can become part of American society as long as she/he shares and strives to realise The American Dream. The American legal system is constituted upon defending and implementing this cognitive model, even though it can be argued that this very legal system is actually at odds with the cultural model of equality before the law. American foreign policy demonstrates the same eagerness to implement this cultural model outside the national boundaries. Contrary to expectation, this cultural imperialism still leaves room for a tolerant language diversity policy, maybe based on the assumption that cultural models have more weight than language.

The Danish language policy on the other hand seems almost to justify the Linguistic Relativity Hypothesis: language is culture through and through. It is on this background that the reluctance to accept anything but native-language qualifications and the fear of mother-tongue education should be considered. The argument seems to be that if non-Danish ethnic groups are prevented from thinking in their own language they will not be able to hold on to their own cultural models, and their integration into Danish society will be successful. But since cultural models are not solely grounded on language but principally on social practices among collectives of individuals, and since successful integration essentially means acquiring the cultural models that make for optimal interaction with different societal practices, language cannot really be held responsible. Besides, as any practitioner in the field of education can witness, learning is only possible when an individual has already established functional cultural models. Integration therefore does not depend on a process

---

[22] Recently a whole new field of Cognitive Poetics has emerged: literature, of course, as also Anne Marie E. Jeppesesn notices (In *Changing Philologies*, Hans Lauge Hansen (ed.) 2002, 39), being a valuable source of understanding and learning.

of substitution of cultural models, but on the adaptation of those already acquired, developing optimally functional models that will allow for successful interaction in the social practices that constitute the present state of Danish society. The maintenance and growth of society is generally dependent on the constant re-elaboration and re-conceptualisation of cultural models through practices, so that they can meet the needs of an ever-changing society. To this end a plurality of competing cognitive models is needed.

The pluralistic, dynamic view of cultures that I put forward here should not be taken as indicating the acceptance of any practices in any domain of society. In the domain of jurisdiction only one cultural model can be right at any one time; this does not mean, however, that the ethical models upon which the Danish nation grounds its laws should not constantly be revised through democratic debate.

I believe that the study of other languages provides us with ideal conditions for gaining insight into other people's cultural models and coming to understand alternative ways of conceptualising the world. The process by which we validate our own cultural models through confrontation with others' does not only give us insight into both our own and the foreign culture, but also enables us to confront these models with each other by means of translation, here understood in its broadest sense of any cross-cultural mediation[23]. I will therefore conclude by suggesting that not only do foreign language studies promote the understanding of other cultures, but they also develop a general competence which is needed at every level of our multicultural society, for bringing alternative cultural models into dialogue. This has been termed intercultural competence, or the competence of cross-cultural communication. On the basis of the views I have put forward here, I would like to emphasise that if our students acquire proficiency at cross-cultural communication and intercultural competence through their foreign language studies it is not because they are good at communication, but because they are good at understanding. Cross-cultural communication can only be successful in line with successful understanding of the cultural models each individual brings to bear in the process of communicative practices: an interaction which implies mutual (re-)examination of cultural models.

## References
Abelson, Roger P. & Roger C. Schank: 1977. *Scripts, Plans, Goals and Understanding*. Hillsdale/N.J., N.Y., Lawrance Erlbaum.
Berlin, Brent and Paul Kay: 1969. *Basic Color Terms. Their Universality and Evolution*. Berkeley, University of California Press.

---

[23] See for instance Susan Bassnett, and also the section on Translation in Hans Lauge Hansen (ed.): *Changing Philologies*, 2002.

Berlin, Brent et al: 1974. *Principles of Tzeltal Plant Classification.* New York, Academic.

Bernárdez Enrique: Forthcoming: *Intimate Enemies? On the relations between language and culture,* paper read at the Language, Culture and Cognition conference, An International Conference on Cognitive Linguistics. Catholic University of Braga, Portugal, 2003.

Bernárdez Enrique: Forthcoming: Social Cognition: Variation, language and culture, paper read at the 8th International Cognitive Linguistics Conference (ICLC-8). University of La Rioja, Spain

Brandt, Per Aage: 2000. "The Architecture of Semantic Domains. A Grounding Hypothesis in Cognitive Semiotics". *Revista Portuguesa de Humanidades,* Faculdade de Filosofia da U.C.P., Braga, Portugal.

Hansen, Hans Lauge (ed.): 2002. *Changing Philologies.* Copenhagen, Museum Tusculanum Press.

Holland, Dorothy and Naomi Quinn (eds.).: 1987. *Cultural Models in Language and Thought.* Cambridge, Cambridge University Press.

Johnson, Mark: 1987. *The Body in the Mind: The Bodily Basis of Meaning, Imagination and Reason.* Chicago, Chicago University Press.

Lakoff George. & Mark Johnson: 1999. *Philosophy in the Flesh.* New York, Basic Books.

Lakoff George. & Mark Johnson: 1980. *Metaphors We Live By.* Chicago and London, The University of Chicago Press.

Lakoff, George: 1987. *Women, Fire and Dangerous Things. What Categories Reveal about the Mind.* Chicago and London. The University of Chicago Press.

Rosch, Eleanor: 1977. "Human Categorization". In: N. Warren (ed.), *Studies in Cross-Cultural Psychology.* London, Academic.

Rosch, Eleanor: 1978. "Principles of Categorization". In: Rocsh and Lloyd (eds.), *Cognition and Categorization.* Hillsdale, N.J., Lawrence Erlbaum Associates.

Rosch, Eleanor: 1988. "Coherence and Categorization: A historical View". In: *Festschrift for Roger Brown.* Hillsdale, N.J., Lawrence Erlbaum Associates.

Schmid, Hans-Jörg & Frederich Ungerer: 1996. *An Introduction to Cognitive Linguistics.* London and New York, Longman.

Whorf, Benjamin Lee: 1956. *Language, Thought and Reality,* selected writings of Benjamin Lee Whorf, ed. John B. Carroll, Cambridge, The M.I.T. Press.

# Traditional and New Approaches to Theoretical Grammar Teaching

by

Hanne Leth Andersen, Merete Birkelund
and Thora Vinther

This article presents some considerations on the teaching of grammar in Foreign Language Studies at the Universities. After some reflections on grammar as an object of study and its placement within Foreign Language Studies, the focus will be on a number of French and Spanish examples of problems generated by the current approach to grammar in Denmark, and some grammar handbooks which might be relevant as alternatives to the traditional ones will be discussed.

As the Danish Language and Culture Network has undertaken to reflect upon the relationship between the three pillars which traditionally support Foreign Language Studies, we have found it natural to discuss the view of language underlying our teaching of grammar, language proficiency and linguistics. Our main topic of discussion[1] has been the change of focus in linguistic description from a mainly structuralist view with morphology and syntax as its dominant parameters to a more global description integrating on the one hand semantics and pragmatics and on the other linguistic variation. Variation in itself, and the plurality of themes and topics, can be considered one of the main characteristics of the research object of Foreign Language Studies at the Universities: hence the necessity of questioning the traditional boundaries and discussing the possibilities of collaboration.

Even with the focus narrowed to language per se, the object of study is still manifold, extensive and difficult to manage. Following the tradition of linguistic description, sentences and constructions can be presented as

---

[1] This text derives from discussions between the three authors and Karen Risager (University of Roskilde) and Nina Nørgaard (University of Southern Denmark).

fitting into a clear, well-defined structure, graphically represented by the figure of the triangle:

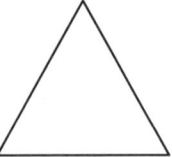

However, a glance at the unlimited language-using world around us will straightaway reveal examples that go against the system. We will be tempted to reject these as archaic, dialectal, vulgar, wrong or idiosyncratic if we do not remind ourselves that this clear-cut system is not the same thing as language itself, which spreads over a much broader area where the boundaries between language and other areas of knowledge are indistinct: such other areas are history, geography, sociology, language acquisition and psychology, to name but a few. This variation can be represented graphically as a series of fuzzy-bordered shapes:

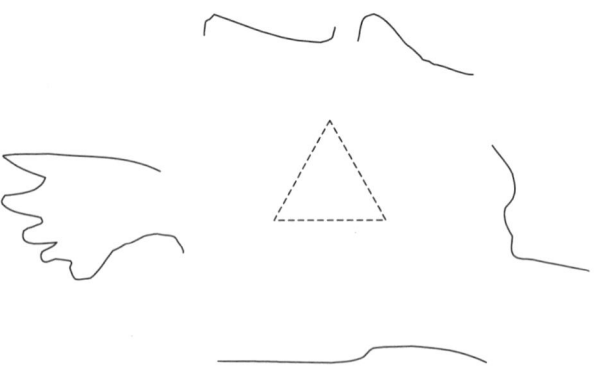

The challenge is to handle this understanding pedagogically, not only in the language-teaching disciplines, but also in all other classes where the foreign language plays a predominant role. If it is not within our reach to encompass and teach the language in all its diversity of usage, we must at least aim at getting students to recognize that language is a dynamic, ever-changing and multivariate organism, and not merely a set of rules which must be followed.

With respect to the teaching of grammar, we concur in the view that as a subject *per se* grammar is important and necessary at University level.

We are convinced that without a systematical introduction to grammar, with a related discussion of the subject, students will not acquire sufficient understanding and theoretical knowledge of the medium they use for communication in both professional and casual situations to be able to take a critical, scientific view of the linguistic expressions they deal with.

At very early stages of foreign language learning it is useful to have an all-round approach that integrates vocabulary and cultural information with the teaching of grammar. In this article, however, we shall consider the different elements of grammar at a more advanced level, where grammatical structure is a subject in itself. Here the teaching is usually separated from both literary and cultural issues and from productive oral and written practice.

As one of the oldest subjects within Foreign Language Studies at Danish Universities[2], grammar was the first discipline to subscribe to structuralist theories, and its roots are still deeply planted in structuralist thinking.

The clear distinction between linguistic material and linguistic function, and an awareness of the relationship between the two, led to brilliant results in Scandinavia in the 20th century. However, a closer approach to a more exhaustive language description will become possible if other aspects of the knowledge of grammar are incorporated than exclusively the form-based approach to constructing correct sentences.

Foreign Language Studies in Denmark have long since introduced the study of pragmatics, text linguistics, sociolinguistics and language acquisition theory in such disciplines as oral proficiency, textual analysis and in monographic courses, and grammatical research has long been engaged in applying other theoretical approaches. Still, grammar as a University subject remains a formal discipline engaged in discussing criteria for classification, defining terms and describing the advantages or disadvantages of various types of terminology, mostly from a language-inherent point of view.

There is no doubt that students profit from learning to think systematically about given data, but this skill should surely not be emphasised within the discipline of grammar at the expense of the students' proficiency in language usage and recognition of linguistic conceptualization. Henning Andersen (2001, 25) formulates this point very clearly when he explains that he does not see linguistic description as "a way for the linguist to organize his data", but as "a hypothesis about the competence of the speakers of the language". Claire Kramsch, on the other hand (1998, 31), defines language teaching in these ostensibly simple terms: "to confront students with the meanings associated with the specific uses of words". In this definition, 'meanings' is interesting because it gives priority to content against form, and 'specific uses' because it highlights the fact that this

---

[2] Literature was introduced later and still later the aspects of culture and society.

content is found not in an abstract system, but in concrete speech or writing situations governed by the need to communicate.

The Danish school of Functional Grammar especially, with its description of language rooted in the Saussurean sign concept, has inspired the inclusion of meaning in grammatical description in order to achieve a better comprehension of the language system being used. In this view of language, just as content and expression are inherent and equivalent aspects of the sign, so are semantics and pragmatics integrated parts which have to be taken into consideration in language description at all levels, and cannot simply be included or shut out from grammar at discretion.

**Problematic issues in the teaching of grammar**
In this context, however, it must be acknowledged that the relationship between form and meaning is far from simple, even though they are interdependent. A naive expectation would be that they coincide. But though they may do at some higher level, a quick glance at details will remind us, for instance, that the future tense in Spanish is also used to express suppositions and approximations about present facts, and that in Spanish (as in Danish and English) future actions can coherently be described with forms of the present tense.

Instead of describing this state of things as one general rule modified by a series of exceptions and instances of special cases, the challenge is, for instance, to describe the future tense in a way that makes it clear that in Spanish it is logical and coherent to use it to account for both future events and approximations about the present.

The relationship between form and meaning can also appear as a problem with respect to the category of *aspect*, which is grammaticalised in French and Spanish but not in Danish. The Nordic tradition, as exemplified by the widely used *Fransk Grammatik* by Pedersen, Spang-Hanssen and Vikner, first gives an account of the general semantic difference between the perfective and imperfective forms, then the role of adverbs, more or less as a relation of government, and finally their interplay with subordinate clauses as syntactic rules. In this concept of aspect, it is possible to describe it as a system of syntactic regularities. *Quand,* for instance, can be used with *imparfait* or *passé simple*: with *imparfait* for describing background or repetition, and with *passé simple* for describing a punctual action. But this strongly formal syntactic approach does not satisfy our present urge to provide a more global linguistic description. Moreover, the metaphoric description of the two forms as carriers of 'linearity' or 'punctuality', 'completion' or 'non-completion' is often confusing to students.

A more pedagogically and cognitively convincing approach would find its point of departure in meaning, as Comrie (1976) points out in his definition of aspect: "Aspects are different ways of viewing the internal temporal constituency of a situation". For Comrie the crucial distinction is whether there is transition from one state to another, and whether the action or event is seen from outside (globally) or from inside (still in progress). It is also important to integrate into the understanding of aspect the idea that it is not a question of *government* but of different linguistic elements, such as verbs, objects, tenses, adverbs, etc. functioning in interrelation as semantic choices.

For a complex concept like aspect, an adequate way into its use in the target language seems to us to go via an understanding of the notion and its manifestation in the mother tongue, whether morphological or lexical. Comrie's very general description of aspect as meaning opens up the possibility of investigating how this meaning is coded into different languages. Having grasped the semantic concept in Danish, where it is mostly lexically coded, it may prove to be much easier for students to grasp the morphological distinction between, for instance, *passé simple*, *passé composé* and *imparfait* in French, or preterite and imperfect in Spanish.

Another example of a problematic approach is the much discussed grammatical issue of Spanish constructions with *se*, the reflexive pronoun which can have the sense of 'oneself', though it is also used in a series of constructions that are not reflexive but have a passive or impersonal sense. During the last 50 years the trend in Denmark has been to describe the inventory of constructions with *se* as syntactic construction types. A diagram has been elaborated in which the constructions are paired according to whether they appear in all persons or only in the third person, and a set of arguments for matching the constructions with each other considers their potential to combine with the indirect object, the syntactic function of *se*, and whether the construction results in the active, passive or middle voice. In this country almost all Spanish grammarians make small variations on this scheme when describing these constructions.

This is very effective in class as widespread discussion of grammatical principles and syntactic tests is prompted by the diagram, and the students feel great satisfaction when they have mastered the details and can verify that 'it works'. Often one of the questions in the final examination relates to these constructions, and the students generally show that they are able both to present the diagram and to fit examples from the text into it, with the relevant arguments.

But if we aspire beyond placing the different constructions convincingly in relation to each other, the diagram will be found deficient in many respects because it fails to give information about semantic and pragmatic content, stylistic and social variation, and other related syntactical constructions which do not appear in the diagram, even though they are found in the speech of many native speakers. Some important questions are left unanswered: what is the meaning of each construction? Which registers do they appear in and what social signals do they transmit? How else can this meaning be expressed? Such discussions are missing in the traditional teaching of grammar, and we have to struggle to include them in the contents of the discipline. Currently it is left to the students themselves, with their linguistic intuition and hard-won experience, to acquire this knowledge.

**The importance of linguistic variation**
With respect to linguistic variation, the inclusion of spoken language would be of great value in grammar teaching: the difference between written and spoken language can be systematic, and a grammar based primarily on writing risks the omission of important features of the language. Variation is also often evidence of language change in progress, as language users tend more and more systematically to pick one option rather than another. This might be exemplified by the temporal system in spoken French. Here *passé simple* is almost always replaced by the perfect tense, *passé composé*. *Passé composé* thus has two different meanings or functions in spoken French:

1) the perfect tense, describing the past that is still relevant in the present
2) the past tense, describing the past that is detached from the present; narrative past

This creates a problem in the system. How can it be indicated that a situation or an event is not seen in its relation to the present and is thus not relevant at the moment of utterance? There seem to be two possible solutions. One is to use *passé surcomposé*, as in the two following examples:

a) il *a eu téléphoné* (he has had called)
b) il *a eu pris* le train vs il a pris le train (he has had taken the train)

Blanche-Benveniste (1997) states this quite clearly, describing the usage of "le passé surcomposé quand il s'agit de faits qu'on ne peut pas dater, parce qu'ils appartiennent à un passé indéterminé coupé du présent du locuteur", whereas the *passé composé* is used about "un passé qu'on peut dater". However, in the example given by Blanche-Benveniste: *J'ai couru le cent mètres le 14 juillet* (I ran [have run] the 100 meter on the 14th of July), *passé composé* can be used about an action seen as unconnected with the present exactly because of the presence of the date. It is thus not possible to think that the speaker has just run a hundred meters and might wish to express a consequence of this. Blanche-Benveniste's other example in this context does not include a date and it needs to be specified whether or not it is connected with the present moment. This is clarified by the use of the *passé surcomposé*: *J'ai eu couru le cent mètres* (I ran [have had run] 100 metres (at some point in the past)).

The other solution, for which Hanne Leth Andersen has found evidence in the 'Corpus d'Orléans'[3], is the use of *plus-que-parfait* with the same sense of making explicit the absence of direct connection with the present moment of the utterance. In the following sequence from the Orleans Corpus, in which a client is seeking information about different travel options, his purpose in line 3 is not to start discussing the article, as might have been understood had *passé composé* been used, but simply to make reference to his knowledge about Barbados:

- les Bahamas
- hein
- les Bahamas et la Barbade vous n' avez rien ? j' *avais lu* un article une fois sur cette île la Barbade
- mais si là euh laissez tomber
- ah ouais c' est ça
- c' est le prix de pour une personne
- ah ouais d' accord OK

The use of *passé composé* would be the expected solution according to the currently accepted system of spoken French, where *passé simple* is normally replaced by *passé composé*. But it is unsatisfying to the speaker because it leaves the point of the specific utterance unclear. We can thus explain an 'anomalous' use of a temporal form as a possible result of linguistic change caused by the need to express a meaning for which the language no longer offered an option. This gives yet another reason for including not only diaphasic, but also diachronic variation in the teaching of grammar.

It may not be easy to change the curriculum and traditional approaches to different grammatical issues, but until this is accomplished it is crucial at least to make students aware that there is more to grammar than just organizing the data.

## "Alternative" grammars

Acknowledging the difficulty of changing a deeply rooted educational tradition, we explored different types of grammatical description suggested in various alternative grammar handbooks. We shall discuss some of these, dealing with Spanish and French, and point out positive and negative aspects of these innovating works. Since 1976, when The European Council introduced the concept of 'niveau seuil' based on the notional functional principles of the communicative method, a number of grammatical handbooks that challenge traditional structuralist principles have appeared in different languages.

---

[3] Part of the Orléans Corpus is published on the net as a part of the Lancom Corpus, established by the ELICOP-group, 1997-2002, Département de Linguistique, Université de Louvain (K.U. Leuven).

With reference firstly to grammars of Spanish, we can mention Francisco Matte Bon's *Gramática comunicativa del español* (1992), which consists of two sections: 1. *De la lengua a la idea* and 2. *De la idea a la lengua*, where the second section deals with giving linguistic form to what a speaker wants to say; and Kattan-Ibarra & Pountain's *Modern Spanish Grammar, A Practical Guide* (1997), which also consists of two parts: "Structures" and "Functions". But these Spanish examples are somewhat problematic, because the so-called 'functions' are presented as a mixture of lexical notions, semantic areas, communicative formulae and less clearly defined speech-acts that are not always grammaticalised in the target language and are therefore very difficult to handle and systematize as productive tools for a language learner. Although they show great creativity in their semantic descriptions, and their attempts to systematize a content-based approach to linguistic material are interesting, these books are still very reminiscent of sophisticated language guides for tourists. Their bipartite structure can also be regarded as a problematic feature of these two books; an approach which integrated the semantic and formal aspects of the language would more satisfactorily demonstrate how a language establishes the relationship between form, content and communicative intention.

With respect to French, our search for the ideal grammar led us to an interesting recent work: Riegel et al's *Grammaire méthodique du français* from the mid 1990s. What makes this grammar different from others is that it introduces the multiplicity of linguistic aspects that are important to a comprehensive study of French language, from the morpho-syntactic level, i.e. forms and structures, to the level of utterance. The focus of the work is on the semantics and interpretation of linguistic forms, but in contrast to many – perhaps most – other traditional representations of grammar, much space is devoted to communicative aspects of language, for instance issues related to reference, speaker-hearer relations, textual structures and coherence, as well as to the importance of context. Thus Riegel's grammar goes far beyond the sentence level by emphasising language in context and communication.

Riegel's grammar does not present one overall theory or approach. The authors' attitude is that no single theoretical approach is capable of dealing with language and linguistics in a satisfactory way, and their grammar might consequently be criticised for being eclectic in its way of presenting the topics. Nevertheless, the authors are well aware of this problem and explicitly emphasise and justify their position in the foreword, where they say that it has been their aim to apply and propagate knowledge of recent theoretical discussions and linguistic descriptions. The authors have of course been selective in the works they have used, but their principle has been to introduce only the approaches which they regard as having attained the most convincing results.

The strength of Riegel's grammar is that it is more than merely a handbook and a tool for grammar courses and language acquisition. In fact it provides deep theoretical insight into the diversity of linguistics and the formation of linguistic concepts. It seems indeed that such an approach acts as a real catalyst to the awareness of language and the importance of critical scholarly positions/attitudes, so the book should be of use to the advanced reader.

On the other hand, the fact that it does not adhere to a single linguistic and theoretical approach might be considered its weakness, at least by students and language learners, who will be confronted with different linguistic viewpoints and not always be able to find definitive answers. Such a criticism is not relevant in so far as Riegel's objective is to present a holistic global understanding and comprehensive insight into the French language, and it satisfies the requirements of language teachers for an introduction to proper and adequate language usage with respect to different genres, registers, etc.

A comprehensive picture of the variety of theoretical discussions is presented by the approaches to mode and tense. These linguistic phenomena are described in the chapters dealing with morpho-syntactic forms and structures of the verb; however, they are also discussed in several other chapters, for instance those on propositions, text-structures and textual coherence, and the relations between speaker and hearer, utterances and context. This is a significant point for teachers who wish to go beyond the traditional bounds of simply teaching the language system: the verbal system is regarded not merely as forms and structures, but the focus has been directed beyond the sentence level and enlarged to embrace whole texts. Considering these linguistic phenomena from so many different angles makes it possible to regard them not only as elements in the language system, but also as important to the understanding of meaning and function.

In their discussion of mode, the authors make their starting point an account of the notion of modality which is more comprehensive than that found in any other grammar of the same extent as Riegel's. Their discussion of *mode* and *modality* is related to the utterance and to the importance of context and situation, with emphasis on the importance of spoken language and intonation for the interpretation of the modal value and semantic meaning of verbal expressions. In contrast to many traditional structuralist grammars, mode and modality are here considered as specific semantic phenomena which can be expressed by different verbal expressions.

With regard to verbal tenses, the grammar stresses the idea that grammatical tense does not necessarily coincide with the time denoted. This often presents French language learners with difficulties, since French has only one term, *temps*, in contrast to the two English terms *time* and *tense* and the German *Zeit* and *Tempus*. For that reason alone, it is sometimes difficult to explain such terminological and meta-linguistic problems to our students.

Riegel's concept of the chronology of the verbal tenses is similarly different from that found in most traditional grammars, as the authors insist on the importance of utterance and speech act theory, and this enables a greater understanding of the diversity of the French verbal tenses and their meaning.

To this extent, Riegel's *Grammaire méthodique du français* seems very close to being an ideal grammar, as far as linguistic description and comprehension are concerned. It applies a variety of theoretical linguistic approaches, thus giving a manifold input within most linguistic fields. The focus is on spoken language and its relation to written language, and on the importance of utterances and context, but the language system – i.e. the morpho-syntactic forms and structures and the grammatical rules – is still seen as the basis for communicative abilities.

The intention of Riegel's grammar is to be as innovative and far-reaching as possible, and it does indeed go further than traditional grammars, putting focus on the language system, meaning and function at equal levels. This global viewpoint or modular conception of language is very close to our concept of an ideal grammar. However, the lack of one specific theoretical approach and the multitude of suggested solutions do lead to a confused image of the language both theoretically and pedagogically.

An openly pedagogical approach to grammar which includes the pragmatic level is found in Henning Nølke (1997): *Fransk grammatik og sprogproduktion*. The main chapters deal with sentence grammar with a clear point of departure in morphology and syntax, arguing that most of the rules and principles of grammar apply to the sentence, whereas rules for texts depend on language use in specific situations.

As with the Spanish grammars mentioned above, this handbook is in two parts, the second, more 'alternative' one being the chapter "Fra tanke til tekst" (From thought to text). This interesting section goes beyond traditional sentence-based grammar, providing rules and principles for formulations in concrete situations. Here the overall approach is to "turn the grammar upside down", as Nølke puts it (p. 253), proceeding from semantic content to specific formulation, i.e. the production of language. The chapter presents the organisation of information in a sentence or a text and deals especially with discourse markers and speech-acts, with focus on the contrast between the mother tongue (Danish) and the target language (French) in questions, requests, etc.

When dealing with language in texts, Nølke highlights the importance of coherence and cohesion, using the metaphor of 'threads in the texture'. Thus, the grammatical means of making 'threads of subject' are personal pronouns and word order, and 'threads of point of view' enable the speaker to present his point of view with the aid of verbs of opinion, sentence adverbials, modal verbs, and the modal use of tenses, as well as the use of argumentative connectors. Finally, the 'logical threads' in a text are established by co-ordinate and subordinate conjunctions, certain verbs, and connectors. Specific attention is paid to connectors; of particular interest is the metaphor of the 'argumentative highway', with arguments as vehicles and connectors as traffic regulators (pp. 292-294).

Even though Nølke's grammar does not present an overall functional or pragmatic approach to all grammatical issues, in this particular chapter it does make a viable proposal for a concept of grammatical description which starts with meaning but does not allow the systematic organisation of forms to disappear from sight.

**Conclusion**
It should be clear by now that we have not yet found our "ideal" grammar, although the works we have studied have many positive features.

In general, we find it impossible to study and discuss the meaning of a sentence without knowledge of its contextual function. When our aim is to study language for comprehensive and conceptual purposes it will therefore be necessary to examine the use and function of language in concrete situations. That is why we can argue for a concept of language as the basic issue of Foreign Language Studies at the Universities. This basic issue has of course many different though interdependent aspects, which are combined in the search for a global description and understanding of the language. In such a global or modular conception of language no aspect can be excluded or considered more or less important than others. This seems to us to be the only reasonable way of doing grammar and linguistics, at least at University level, especially as we wish not only to understand language and to communicate efficiently, but also to understand ourselves in our context of life and verbal interaction.

Acknowledging our enormous debt to Sausssure's scientific stringency, with its clear-cut distinction between synchrony and diachrony, form and content, and between language system and language use, we can now advocate a more global view of language that will integrate diachrony, content and social variation into linguistic description, always on the basis of a clear understanding of what each of these concepts implies.

As compared to the strictly structural approach that culminated in the 70s but is still applied in most University teaching in Scandinavia, our view of language, with a grammar that integrates semantics and pragmatics, can be regarded as more open to the literary and cultural disciplines of Foreign Language Studies. But we do not neglect the conception of a linguistic system underlying each language. For instance, cognitive linguistics shows quite clearly how languages interact with our vision of the world, establishing lexical categories and placing information in different locations as they focus on different parts of reality. A specific language has a set of categories and constructions at its disposal, and the speakers of the language can use them more or less creatively and more or less dependently on their group membership, but always within the limits set by the system of the language in its very slowly development. As our example of the innovative use of *plus-que-parfait* showed, language change seems to be connected with language system and language use, but not directly with cultural change. Rather it seems to be the internal systematic coincidence of forms that provokes the change.

Consequently we conclude that language does not consist simply of windows towards other cultures or literatures, but is an organic system in itself, and a thorough knowledge of its structure at all levels is essential for the understanding of its nature as an instrument of communication among its users.

**References**

Andersen, Henning: 2001. "Markedness and the theory of linguistic change". In: H. Andersen (ed.), *Actualization: Linguistic Change in Progress: Papers from a workshop held at the 14th International Conference on Historical Linguistics, Vancouver, B.C., 14 August 1999*, pp. 21-57. Amsterdam, John Benjamins B.V.

Blanche-Benveniste, Claire: 1997. *Approches de la langue parlée en français*. Paris, Gap, Ophrys.

Comrie, Bernard: 1976. *Aspect: An introduction to the study of verbal aspect and related problems*. Cambridge, Cambridge University Press.

Hansen, Maj-Britt Mosegaard: 1999. "Aspekt". In: *Suppleringshæfte til Pedersen, Spang-Hanssen & Vikner: Fransk Grammatik*, pp. 57-72. Copenhagen, Romansk Institut, Københavns Universitet.

Nølke, Henning: 1997. *Fransk grammatik og sprogproduktion*. Copenhagen, Kaleidoscope.

Kattan-Ibarra, Juan & Christopher J. Pountain: 1997. *Modern Spanish Grammar, A practical guide*. London, Routledge.

Kramsch, Claire: 1998. "The privilege of the intercultural speaker". In: M. Byram & M. Fleming (eds), *Language Learning in Intercultural Perspective: Approaches through Drama and Ethnography*, pp. 16-31. Cambridge University Press.

Matte Bon, Francisco: 1992. *Gramática comunicativa del español 1-2*. Barcelona, Difusión.

Pedersen, John, Ebbe Spang-Hanssen & Carl Vikner: $2000^9$. *Fransk Grammatik*. Copenhagen, Akademisk Forlag.

Riegel, Martin, Jean-Christophe Pellat & René Rioul: $1994/1999^5$. *Grammaire méthodique du français*. Paris, Presses Universitaires de France.

# The study of literature
# – Does it matter, and if so, why?

by

Jørn Boisen & Pia Schwarz Lausten[1]

To some degree at least, the study of the humanities always seems to have been at odds with society, in a relation of fascination, repulsion and interdependence. Nevertheless, democratic societies have always acknowledged the use and even the necessity of independent centers of knowledge functioning by means of different rules than society as a whole and with other standards and values than financial and political power. This situation is apparently changing. The developments of recent years have posed new challenges for the humanities, new subjects to be explored and new disciplines to be organized, and this is basically fine; but a number of fundamental questions have also emerged concerning the role and use of the humanities now and in the future. The objective of this paper is to address these questions. It will take the form of a dialogue between two voices representing different perspectives on the issue. In the first part a pessimistic voice explores the negative consequences for the study of language and literature of globalization, of the ideology of neo-liberalism and of the more general condition of postmodernity. In the second part a more optimistic voice tries to give more definite form to the positive side of the argument by suggesting new relations between literature and society.

### The terminal paradoxes of literature

We live in an era of paradoxes, two of which are particularly relevant to the study of literature and foreign languages. Firstly, it is now simpler than

---

[1] The ideas and observations presented in this article are very much the result of a series of fruitful meetings within the network's literary group, comprising, among others, Lene Waage Petersen, Hans Lauge Hansen, Julio Hans Casado Jensen, Sofie Nielsen and Birthe Hoffmann in Copenhagen and Stig Ramløv Frandsen and Leonardo Cecchini in Aarhus.

ever before to have contact with other countries and cultures, and it is done more frequently. It is no longer necessary to transport our frail bodies right across Europe in bumpy stagecoaches in order to see Andalusia (as did H.C. Andersen). On the other hand, the study of language, that previously unavoidable labor for those wishing to maintain correspondences leading to knowledge and culture, has become strangely irrelevant as a personal or national enlightenment project. Secondly, we live in a society without significant material poverty. We have plenty of time and unrestricted access to all the culture the world can offer. On the other hand, interest in what used to be the essence of cultural and personal development, namely literature, has decreased in step with this development.

Marcel Proust's father was a doctor who wrote an important thesis on cerebral diseases and devoted his life to the struggle against cholera. He prospered, was awarded *La légion d'honneur* and became honorary citizen of the city of Toulon. His son never got a decent job. Nevertheless he once confessed to his maid: "Ah Celeste, if only I could be sure that I could do as much good with my books as my father does with his" (Albaret, 1973). Can a novel be as useful to humanity as effective measures against cholera? In fact, for a long period it was generally accepted that Marcel Proust's novel was just as useful as the writings of Doctor Proust, his successful father. Now, a hundred years later, we're not so sure. The notion of the usefulness of literature has gently faded from our horizon, like other notions once thought indispensable: God, Sin, Honor, Enlightenment, Culture. Why and how did this happen? Why does the general evolution of society seem systematically to undermine the old and honorable *humanitas*?

*Language and literature in the age of globalization.*
Characterizing our own time, we typically use terms like "globalization", "neo-liberalism" and "postmodernity" to designate the evolution that is imposing itself upon us. The study of literature in the modern philologies was to a very large extent the product of national Romanticism and its inherent wish to create a stable national identity. The history of literature was the story of the unbroken line of national geniuses, regarded as the spirit of the people incarnate. It was a kind of win-win situation: literature was granted honor and dignity as the finest expression of the nation, whilst the nation had the gratification of seeing its reflection in the flattering mirror of literary masterpieces. The national project had a tremendous appeal. It spoke to the masses, it spoke to the elite, and it spoke to all political ideologies; and it had a clear and definite goal. Literature and culture had an important place in this project, but they found themselves in the same paradox as history: the moment of their greatest popular appeal was also the moment when they were most misused.

In the present era of globalization this conception of literature, confined as a hostage within strict national boundaries, has long been abandoned and almost forgotten. However, an unfortunate side effect of this turn is that now that it is no longer used as a booster to the national ego, literature has lost the respect with which it was formerly regarded by the general public, and as we all know, the common opinion is what really counts in our old Protestant societies. (Anything else would be elitist, hence bad.) It may well be that national Romanticism insisted too heavily on the national aspect of culture, language and history, but it also gave the study of literature a legitimacy, a *raison-d'être* and a function.

Globalization has also had consequences for the study of foreign languages, but not necessarily those that might be expected. English now functions as a supra-national lingo, which has the enormous advantage that it facilitates contact between people all over the world. There are however also certain drawbacks to this. Firstly, internationalism is identified with the North Atlantic pop culture imposed on us by media. The rest of the world is like a dull province town: you know that it exists, but you're not really interested in it. Secondly, the English language has a monopoly on communication, which is therefore presented to us in an Anglo-American perspective.

The relation of small nation states like Denmark to the outside world outside can therefore be envisaged as a five-act drama:

1) The media only understand English;
2) So the sources they use to describe the world are exclusively British and American;
3) Which gives the public the impression that nothing ever happens outside Great Britain and the United States (otherwise somebody would write about it, right?);
4) Which reinforces the need for English;
5) And that's why the media only understand English.

Since the first and the fifth acts are almost identical, we have a nice circular composition. It is debatable whether the play is a comedy or a tragedy, but it is certain that it makes real first-hand knowledge of the world outside our own strangely irrelevant. If you want to know anything about Islam, Italian food or Provence, you watch a BBC documentary. The paradox of globalization is that contact with the world is in inverse proportion to knowledge of the world.

*Literature and the market.*
With globalization the market has come to be conceived of as a force of nature. The logic is that whatever emerges from the market is good, be-

cause otherwise it wouldn't have been able to emerge: all will be well if we put the market first. Thus the market is superior to any political control and guidance. There is no moral position superior to the fight for freedom; and so the idea of enlightenment, which operates with the ideal of educating people to certain civilized ways of thinking and behaving, should be abandoned. In the neo-liberalist vision only the wishes of the average man can be fulfilled. (Again, anything else would be elitist.)[2]

Even though the old ideals and hierarchies are no longer functional, humanity is not really liberated. On the contrary, we have been submitted to an authority far more frightening: the tyranny of the majority. Denmark there is a 'choice' of TV and radio stations, all telling us more or less the same thing at the same moment, and this is a pervasive paradigm. Neo-liberalism is a happy marriage of uniformity and freedom.

In the neo-liberal perspective only useful knowledge is of any relevance. And useful knowledge means knowledge that directly contributes to the material wealth of society. In the Danish welfare state the universities have been subordinated to the rules of the market for quite a while. Funding is granted to a department on the basis of its 'productivity', understood as the number of graduates who pass out of it each year, and the Ministry of Education fixes the price of graduates as a function of their estimated economic usefulness to society: in this perspective an engineer is worth 3.5 linguists.

*The decentered subject.*
Globalization and neo-liberalism are integrated parts of the overall postmodernist condition. It is generally agreed to envisage historical development in three phases: the pre-industrial phase, the industrial phase and the post-industrial phase; or, in a more philosophical perspective, the theocentric, the anthropocentric and the polycentric society.

In the theocentric society there is only one principle, namely God, who is the center of the universe and the supreme judge. When God gradually withdrew from ruling the world and separating wrong from right, Man took over and placed himself in the center. The individual, the thinking ego of Descartes, stands alone, opposing the universe and proposing himself as the measure of everything. This anthropocentric society is the modern world. The notion of the transcendent subject pervades modern art, literature and society. In order to understand the world one must first understand one's own mind, and in this process literature is a very helpful tool. The finest objective of literature is the exploration of that enigmatic universal standard situated at the center the universe: the infinite human being.

---

[2] In this account of neo-liberalism, we are borrowing the conclusions from Herbert Schui & Stephanie Blankenburg 2003.

In postmodern society the individual is no longer in the center; in fact Postmodernity has given up the whole idea of a center: it is polycentric or hyper-complex. It's a globalized world where we have the option of contact with a vast array of very different cultures, so it is no longer possible to limit ourselves to one single perspective; and since it is assumed that only complexity can reduce complexity, a whole range of rival perspectives come into play. Furthermore, society has multiple centers and thus multiple ways of describing itself. The subject is no longer transcendent, but social. Consciousness and the individual are defined by an ever floating system of relations, but neither consciousness nor the system of relations is any longer an absolute.

Polycentrism implies that the hierarchies that guided our understanding of culture and society in the past are no longer valid. A natural consequence of this is the moral, ethical and esthetic relativism, which has triumphed completely in the cultural domain. But it is a very strange kind of relativism. Classical high culture has been toppled from its pedestal and no longer demands more respect than anything else. There is no longer an absolute distinction between Shakespeare, cartoons and Playstation games. A glance at the cultural section of any newspaper will show that films, TV programs, pop music, classical music and books are treated in the same way, each from its proper perspective but all at the same level. The awareness of a work of art as something fundamentally different from a consumer product has been irremediably lost.

In the realm of the nation state, however, relativism is only apparent. A kind of tribal mentality still prevails. It is rarely stated directly, but there is a widespread feeling that the North Atlantic model – Scandinavia, Great Britain, the United States – is superior, and that the rest of the world would be far better off if it just followed our example.

This is the worst circumstance imaginable for the study of foreign languages, because it undermines two fundamental assumptions within the humanities: firstly, that it is possible and desirable to distinguish between different, hierarchically ordered levels of aesthetic expressions; secondly that we, the citizens of the North Atlantic societies, could learn something about the world and ourselves through the encounter with other cultures and other historical times. Our own times can be contrasted with the Renaissance, defined as a period of discovery of the past. The rediscovery of the magnificent civilizations of antiquity was the catalyst of a desire to learn other languages, because Renaissance man wanted to drink directly from these sources of wisdom and beauty. In the meeting with something strange and fascinating, reality was suddenly seen in another light, and the world was opened wide to the European spirit. But at our present moment of history we are entering a phase where the relevance of the past, of foreign languages and high culture, is vanishing.

*Culture as entertainment and consumption.*
And so what? Is it not possible to live a full and rich life without knowing about the Reformation and Proust, and without being able to speak German, French, Spanish and Italian? So it seems to many. The problem is, however, that we are *not* living full and rich lives. Danish society is going through an unprecedented identity crisis. The charges are familiar: the fragmentation of life, the atomization of civil society, the growing isolation of the individual, who claims recognition with more and more insistence and desperation. As Paul Virilio points out in *Cybermonde, la politique du pire*, previously evident and familiar concepts like "me", "here" and "now" have become problematic, because there is no longer any "them" "there" and "then" to define them by. On the one hand we are fascinated by what is distant, the strange world within our reach when we press the buttons on our keyboards and remote controls. But in the process we are losing touch with the near, concrete, political community of which we are part. On the other hand we are frightened by the discomforting contact with foreign and incomprehensible populations and try to shut out the world, seeking comfort in an imagined tribal identity.

In her essay "The Crisis of Culture" (1954) Hannah Arendt pointed out art's unique mode of existence within society, its ability to represent the everyday and at the same time create the conditions for moving out of the stream of practically oriented life.

> In common terms, culture means that part of the public sphere which is politically ensured by people's actions which offers a space for the presentation of those things, of which the fundamental fact is their beauty. In other words, culture shows how art and politics, regardless of their mutual bonds and tensions, are interlinked to the point of mutual interdependence. (p. 146)

But according to Hannah Arendt, culture had lost this function in public life. This problem within our civilization is not due to the fact that our society is a mass society, but rather that it is a global and completely liberal consumer society. Time that is not spent at work or resting is devoted to consumption for the sake of entertainment. Culture has entered this metabolism, not in the sense than art and high culture are spreading to the masses (which would in fact be nice), but rather that culture is modified and dissolved in order to create entertainment. The result is not mass culture, but mass entertainment that seeks its nourishment in the cultural product of the world. To think that over time and with the right attitude such a society would become more "cultured" is a fatal error, because it is inherent in the consumer mentality that it literally *consumes* everything it touches.

The fact that Hannah Arendt made this diagnosis as early as 1954 can be regarded as an indication that this state of affairs is not likely to pass with time, for the historical evolution, which might be hoped to change it, is actually its very cause. So who has the power to effect change? If God has disappeared and Man is no longer the master, then who is in control? The Earth merely moves through empty space with no hand at the wheel. In *The Art of the Novel* Milan Kundera says the following:

> When a phenomenon announces its imminent disappearance in advance, we are many that share this knowledge and maybe regret it. But when the struggle against death is coming to an end, we already look in another direction. Death becomes invisible. It has already been some time since the river, the nightingale, the small paths that cross the meadows, have disappeared from the consciousness of man. Nobody needs them anymore. When nature disappears from the globe tomorrow, who will pay any attention? Where are the heirs of Octavio Paz and René Char? And where are the great poets? Have they disappeared or have their voices become inaudible? In any circumstance it is an enormous change in our Europe: the past is unthinkable without poets. But if man has lost the need for poetry, will he notice its disappearance? The end is not an apocalyptic explosion. Maybe there's nothing more peaceful than the end. (pp. 60-61, My translation from the French original. JB)

One could seek comfort in the reflection that this state of affairs only makes more acute a relation that has always been problematic, namely the relation between society and culture. Artists have always seen themselves as being in some kind of opposition to society. Why is that? What's wrong with society? The Romantic poets were the first to become fully aware of their isolation in society. They saw it as populated by a petty bourgeoisie who lacked feeling for art and measured everything in terms of its immediate usefulness, and if they did become interested in literature, it was for the wrong reasons. Culture and literature were viewed as capital with which they could purchase higher social status.

In the globalized neo-liberal entertainment society the petty bourgeois cultural dream has come true. The petty bourgeois individual no longer despises culture for its uselessness, nor does he have complexes about it, for what is now considered culture mainly consists of events or entertainment served up all ready for consumption. Many great authors survived decades of rejection and poverty. The question now is whether their works can survive what the entertainment industry is doing to them. It can be seriously doubted whether the novels of Boris Pasternak have survived what Hollywood did to Doctor Zhivago.

The German Romantics used the term *philistines* to designate the petty bourgeoisie they despised. With its biblical connotation, this expression hints at an enemy of far superior numbers, into whose hands you might fall at any moment. Considering the problems of postmodern western society, and its way of discussing cultural matters, it is an open question whether the philistines have not already triumphed and planted their standard of TV programs with themed shopping bags in the headquarters of literature and high culture, by this victory making irrelevant the study of literature, history and foreign languages.

## The literary experience

*Decay or new challenges?*
The humanities have always had problems of self-legitimation, and even though we find ourselves in a particularly paradoxical historical moment, there is nothing new in politicians questioning the necessity of research and teaching that isn't directly socially useful. However, even the more 'hardcore' disciplines like chemistry and physics come under suspicion when their basic research cannot be transformed into practical uses. Furthermore, there is nothing new in the self-doubt of the humanities: the immediate necessity of philosophy and literature has been queried since the time of Plato and Aristotle. And neither is there anything new in premonitions of the death of literature: they were also issued when cinema and television were invented. Finally, the crisis in the national philologies is not so dramatic when it is recalled that they didn't even exist only 200 years ago, just as our present concept of literature did not exist before that time.

All this does not mean that we should avoid or evade the questions, which confront us. We should respond to them objectively and professionally, and regard them as offering new opportunities. To rethink the relevance of our discipline can pave the way for new insights and be part of a constructive process of evolution. Instead of thinking in terms of a threat against which we must defend our position with a return to tradition, we could envisage challenges that invite us to reformulate the relevance of literature even though it has lost its legitimacy. What can literature do, what does it actually do, and why do we consider it necessary to retain the study of literature within Foreign Language Studies today?

In the following section, the point of departure for answering these questions will be some fundamental reflections on the function of literature in general, i.e. on what literature can do and actually does, in addition to its more practical and visible functions such as providing knowledge about language and culture. Literature is of vital importance for the formation of our knowledge and conception of life.

*Literature as access to otherness.*
In the course of the 20th century many different theoretical approaches have influenced the studies of the national philologies with their different views of what happens when texts are read and interpreted. Marxist criticism, psychoanalysis, structuralism and others have introduced many useful tools for literary analysis, but they have also had the character of

more or less closed systems. In different ways they have represented the idea that you can talk objectively about literary texts and uncover their unconscious, underlying structures. Texts have often been viewed and used as documents or symptoms, with the interpreter as the authority. However, the object of the science of literature is not a definite objective field, but the result (at least in part) of subjective processes that call for different methods of elucidation, depending on such factors as genre. It seems important to maintain a plurality of literary theories and methods instead of seeking a single model. Consequently, the solution to the present crisis cannot be found in surrendering to the outside world's demands for objectivity and measurability. An alternative is suggested by the Danish professor Klaus P. Mortensen in his contribution to *Fortælling og fortolkning – videnskabsteoretisk set (Narration and interpretation – from the point of view of the theory of science)* (1998), in a position within humanistic scholarship that he calls dialectic or dialogic. It is a theory of text and interpretation that can provide the basis for an account of the epistemological function of literature, an account which is additionally extremely relevant to Foreign Language Studies since it underscores the privileged access of literature to the Other. Klaus P. Mortensen describes an exchange between text and reader that rests on the idea that

> a modern humanistic science doesn't allow itself to be fixed in the traditional subjective-objective dichotomy, because the so-called subjective and objective are relative and fluid positions in modern man's (self)reflexive project. The relation between reader and text isn't antithetical (Mortensen 1998, 106. My translation, PSL)

Klaus P. Mortensen claims that such a position presupposes the transcendence of the reader's self-perception, and that "exceeding a certain comprehension is a fundamental condition for all human cognitive evolution and social communication" (ibid.). This self-transcendence is possible because reading – understood as a dialogue that creates meaning – is not a purely individual pleasure. It takes place in a language that is not a subjective invention:

> When we think, and when we interpret what we perceive through our senses, we are ourselves already interpreted by virtue of our language, which is culturally created and formed (ibid. 107. My translation, P.S.L.)

Literature and interpretation are expressions of culturally instituted codes. But as Klaus P. Mortensen says, that does not mean that literature should be reduced to sociological documents:

> Although literature, like all other arts and sciences, is socially created, it does not only stand in a mimetic relationship to the existing signifying structures. It also relates in an interpretative way to the structures and expressive con-

> ventions that it uses and originates from, and therefore also influences them in a formative and converting way. (..) Literary texts are to a great extent a conscious game with and clarification of the codes that determine literature and the whole reality in which literature is made (ibid. My translation, P.S.L.)

Literature does not merely function as a means of achieving knowledge about beyond itself, it is also a valid epistemological form among others, e.g. sociology. And these forms do not necessarily exclude one another. During the reading process a historical consciousness comes into being in the form of

> a reflected attitude that does not only include the relation to literary texts and their context, but also the reader himself and the culture in which he has grown up or finds himself (idem 113. My translation, P.S.L.)

Literature, then, does not necessarily make changes or intervene directly in the social reality, but the reading of literature influences the reader's own way of experiencing, and, indirectly, his images and understanding of reality. The literary function can therefore be defined as the communication of a world of experience that challenges the reader's own way of experiencing.

Thus literature, and not least literature in foreign languages, gives a privileged access to the experience of otherness. As Iser put it in *The Act of Reading*, literature has a special capacity to open up one's horizon, leading to the recognition of one's own habits and the systems of meaning in which they are inserted. The fact that both text and reading come into being in a context of history and language that goes beyond subjectivity is very central to the understanding of the importance of literature, not only in the personal process of self-realization but also in the study of foreign cultures.

Literature has had an important role to play in the formation of individuals and of collective or national identities, and this function still remains. The self-understanding of nations rest upon the narrations and myths that are expressed in literary works, and it is still important to analyze the origin of these works in their national, historical and geographical context. The "archival" function of literature maintains knowledge of the past, a "then" against which we can measure our "now". However, the response of Foreign Language Studies to the new historical situation (testifying that the concept of the national is in crisis) must also promote a conscious openness between the different languages. This can be done by intensifying inter-linguistic projects and courses designed to strengthen students' awareness of the differences and similarities between cultures, and of the origin of cultures in interaction with other cultures and languages.

The national philologies must intensify this comparative dimension. One ways of doing this is to strengthen the focus on the encounter of cultures and the interchange of ideas from one area to another, from both a historical and a theoretical perspective. A comparative dimension presupposes the absorption of the student in one or two linguistic areas, since this specialization gives the profound knowledge of the culture, language and history of a single country necessary for the realization of an interdisciplinary comparative project.

*The function of language in the literary experience.*
Literature is rooted in and owes its existence to language, which thus plays a central role in the experience of reading a literary work. That is why a language is learnt best through its literature, just as one finds out most about colors by studying the art of painting. Literature explores the language's expressive range, testing and sometimes exceeding its boundaries. Language is fundamental to encountering and understanding another culture, with its specific symbolization derived from its geographical and historical experience. It is only through language, through the reading of literature in foreign languages, that we have the chance to really enter into the foreign culture.

The study of a foreign culture always contains a contrastive element. Looking at the other, we see ourselves reflected. We become conscious of our own culture and grow critical towards it, and such criticism and self-recognition are needed in the western world if our democracies are to persist and evolve. For this reason it is important that the teaching of foreign languages is strengthened.

The language of literature is replete with insights and unaccustomed ways of experiencing the self and the world. The work that goes on in texts of creating new significations, new experiences, and collective and individual identities – or, just as important, breaking down earlier significations and identities – takes place in the language and the form as much as in the content. So, as with other modes of aesthetic expressions, literary texts should not be approached only through their communicative function. Literature should not only be understood and analyzed rationally, but also experienced and perceived through the senses. Indeed, this is imperative for a full understanding of literature. Literature can be like a game, an open space which does not necessarily seek to communicate any rational message. Focusing narrowly on the communicative aspect, one risks the loss of the sensuous dimension of eye and ear, and the meaning that sound, rhythm, tone, and voice carry for one's experience of self and other.

The idea of literature we transmit to our students should be based on specifically literary categories like the use of language and sound effects, the conventions of genre and so on. At the same time, though, literature should be taught as a cultural product that is temporally and geographically anchored in a context, both as a result of this context and as one of its conditions.

*Literature and the mass media.*
Until now we have talked about literature in the classical sense of written texts, books. However, the book as cultural expression now faces competition from other media, and literature is no longer the central medium in the individual's process of cultural formation. Young people do not read so many books nowadays. They are more likely to experience narration in movies, computer-games, music, comics. This (r)evolution challenges the traditional concept of literary texts and gives reason to doubt the survival of literature as we know it. With the present flood of information and commercial messages from the mass media, the question is whether literature should be considered a 'counter-language', whether it should be preoccupied by its own 'death', or whether there is indeed a third possibility.

Instead of holding fast to a traditional, elitist concept of literature and resisting and refuting the new media because of their mass appeal, it may be more appropriate to engage the new reality in dialogue. In order to meet this challenge in the studies of the national philologies we must overcome the Romantic idealistic concept of literature as an autonomous phenomenon, replacing it with a more elastic idea of literary texts. This expansion of the concept of the text is already taking place in theory, but ought to be practiced more in the teaching of literature. In this respect it is fruitful to remember the historical determination of the concept of literature. Long before the 19$^{th}$ century, in some periods more than in others, literary discourse overlapped with and integrated other types of discourse, for instance scientific, technical and religious ones. From the time of Dante to (and including) the 16$^{th}$ century Italian Renaissance, the concept of literature included not only poetry, drama and prose fiction but also many other genres, such as letters, chronicles, treaties, diaries and so on. And it might be fruitful to rethink the Enlightenment's broader idea of genre too. This open and curious attitude became more closed in the 19$^{th}$ century, when literature became isolated as an exclusive concept. Today literature develops in dialogue with other expressions and forms of knowledge – images, movies, electronic texts – and this evolution should be taken seriously in university teaching. This intercultural meeting of different texts and media can be regarded as an instance of intertextuality, a concept from literary theory that goes beyond the narrow concept of literature, thus promoting dialogue between different interdisciplinary discourses. Intertextuality can function both as part of a meta-discourse on disciplinarity and inter-disciplinarity, and as a concrete theme in literature lectures.

It is also important to include in university syllabuses in foreign languages a consideration of the dialogue between literature and other forms of knowledge and discourse in order to draw attention to the fact that most texts, also non-literary texts, contain narratives or borrow literary narrative models. The forms of expression and experience of the new media can also be analyzed and interpreted using narratological methods, combined for instance with image analysis and other analytical methods normally applied to visual or technical aspects. Instead of considering this evolution as a dilution of the concept of literature, it should be emphasized that exportation or expansion of the concept to other areas is also going on. In recent decades *narrativity* has had a central significance in philosophy, psychology, history, sociology etc. (see Jan Gustafsson's contribution in this volume). This is associated with the trend in scholarship towards constructivism, and underscores the importance of literary theory, because of its experience with narratology and the tools it provides for describing and interpreting narratives, and not only written narratives but those found in texts of many kinds.

**References**

Albaret, Céleste: 1973. *Monsieur Proust*. Paris, Laffont.
Arendt, Hannah: 1993. "The Crisis of Culture: Its Social and Political Significance". In: *Between Past and Future*. New York, Penguin Books, (1954).
Iser, Wolfgang: 1987. *The Act of Reading: a theory of aesthetic response*. Baltimore, John Hopkins University Press.
Kundera, Milan: 1986. *L'art du roman*. Paris, Gallimard.
Mortensen, Klaus P.: 1998. "Komposition og konfiguration". In: B. Tufte & M. Hermansen (eds.): *Fortælling og fortolkning – videnskabsteoretisk set: forskningsantologi*. København, Danmarks Universitetsforlag, 105-137.
Schui, Herbert & Blankenburg, Stephanie: 2003. *Neoliberalismus: Theorie, Gegner, Praxis*. VSA-Verlag.
Virilio, Paul: 1996. *Cybermonde, la politique du pire*. Paris, Éditions Textuel.

# Cultural Orientation and Interdisciplinarity
## The German debate on
## *Literaturwissenschaft als Kulturwissenschaft*

by
**Sofie Nielsen**

Introduction
The debate in Denmark on disciplines and interdisciplinarity in Foreign Language Studies corresponds to similar discussions in other national contexts, for example in Germany, which will be the focus of this paper. I will begin with an account of the background to the German debate, including the introduction of the concept of 'cultural orientation' as a strategy for achieving interdisciplinarity. Next I will look at some of the problems of fulfilling these aims, particularly within literary studies. This will be followed by a consideration of the discussion of the object of literary studies as a way of defining the disciplinarity or identity of literary studies. In this connection I will try to show the importance of distinguishing between two aims of the discussion: (i) the legitimation of literature and literary studies; and (ii) a foundational discussion arriving at a cultural orientation of literary studies and projecting the possible basis for a significantly extended field of research which transcends the traditional canon of literary texts[1]. Finally I will summarize some of the characteristics of culturally orientated literary studies.

---

[1] In Foreign Language Studies there are additional questions to be considered owing to the different situation of the students (who are studying literature in a foreign language), the different objectives of the academic programmes (leading to employment) and the institutional frameworks (e.g. the size of the departments and their coexistence with other foreign languages). However, it will not be possible to go into these aspects in detail.

## Geisteswissenschaften Heute

In Germany the concept of culture has challenged the disciplinarity of the German university system since the early nineties. Virtually throughout the Humanities the concept of *Kulturwissenschaft* has been the keyword for attempts at renewal. Particularly concerning literary studies a vehement debate has taken place, which has become known as the debate on *Literaturwissenschaft als Kulturwissenschaft*[2]. From the beginning, the concept of *Kulturwissenschaft* was tied to the perspective of general structural changes within the system of sciences, particularly within the field of the humanities. This is mainly due to the tradition of *Geisteswissenschaften*, which has been regarded as yet another instance of the German *Sonderweg*. The ties between the conception of *Geisteswissenschaften* and German philosophic idealism made the concept seem outdated.

In 1991 the report *Geisteswissenschaften Heute* was published[3]. It recommended a cultural orientation or *kulturwissenschaftliche Orientierung* of the *Geisteswissenschaften* as a means of bringing the *Geisteswissenschaften* to the level of the Humanities in other Western countries[4]. This report has come to be seen as the starting signal for the discussion on the concept of *Kulturwissenschaft*, and as such it played an important role in the debate throughout the nineties. *Geisteswissenschaften Heute* only spoke of *Kulturwissenschaften* in the plural i.e. as a more neutral term for *Geisteswissenschaften* and not as a discipline on its own. The concept was used for the classification of a group of sciences comparable to the natural sciences: The existing disciplines within the humanities were to redefine themselves as *kulturwissenschaftlich* instead of *geisteswissenschaftlich*[5].

---

[2] The translation 'literary studies as cultural studies' does little justice to the semantics of both *Kulturwissenschaft* and cultural studies.

[3] The report was written by Wolfgang Frühwald, Hans Robert Jauß, Reinhart Koselleck, Jürgen Mittelstraß og Burkhart Steinwachs at request of the Science Council and the West German Rector's conference. (Frühwald et al. 1991)

[4] Similarly in *Die sog. Geisteswissenschaften. Innenansichten* by Wolfgang Prinz and Peter Weingart (1990) 'cultural orientation' was the keyword for renewal.

[5] Gerhart v. Graevenitz characterizes the difference between *Kulturwissenschaften* and *Geisteswissenschaften* with the question of whether *Geist* is to be regarded as the subject or object of culture: *Kulturwissenschaften* examine materiality, mediality, structures and history of cultures and cultural phenomena in order to find out how *Geistiges* is produced and constructed, whereas *Geisteswissenschaften* turn cultural products into objects that are understood as "Erscheinungsweisen des Geistes" (Graevenitz 1999, 98). Structurally, *Kulturwissenschaften* tend to cultural pluralism, and *Geisteswissenschaften* tend to unity and totality of the one human *Geist*.

## Cultural Orientation and Interdisciplinarity

An important aim of *Geisteswissenschaften Heute* was the introduction of a broad anthropological concept of culture:

> In dieser Perspektive befassen sich die Geisteswissenschaften mit Kultur als dem Inbegriff aller menschlichen Arbeit und Lebensformen, einschließlich naturwissenschaftlicher Entwicklungen. Ihr Gegenstand, der insofern auch die Naturwissenschaften einschließt, ist demnach *die kulturelle Form der Welt*. (Frühwald et al. 1991, 10; cf. 39-44)

The anthropological concept of culture did not only serve as a replacement of the traditional concept, which was synonymous with the *Bildungssphäre* and abstract values; the redefinition of *Geisteswissenschaften* as *Kulturwissenschaften* on the basis of a broad concept of culture served as a way of reversing the specialisation and compartmentalisation of disciplines. It must be seen in connection with the strategy of reviving the potential for interdisciplinarity within the existing German tradition, dating back to the Humboldt university reform in the early 19$^{th}$ century. Originally, the *Geisteswissenschaften* within the Faculty of Arts had been conceived as transcending, dialogical and integrative (Cf. Frühwald et al 1991, 45-72 and Böhme et al. 2000, 19-23).

### Cultural orientation

The focus on cultural orientation turned the attention to already existing traditions of *Kulturwissenschaft*. As demonstrated in *Orientierung Kulturwissenschaft. Was sie kann, was sie will* (Böhme et al. 2000), the traditions of *Kulturwissenschaft* are not always to be found along the lines of disciplines but rather in between and across disciplinary boundaries: The book describes the following approaches: *Völkerpsychologie, Kulturgeschichtsschreibung, Kulturphilosophie, Theorie symbolischer Formen, Psychoanalyse und Kritische Theorie*.

Along with the process of rediscovering *Kulturwissenschaft*, the reception of Anglo-American Cultural Studies accelerated. As Rolf Lindner says in *Die Stunde der Cultural Studies* (2000), from the 70s onwards there were several publications on the subject, but Cultural Studies did not really boom in Germany until 1999. The reception of Cultural Studies blended into the discussions on what constituted a German/continental tradition of *Kulturwissenschaft*, and this encounter made it clear that a more systematic comparison was needed. The formation of a continental variant of *Kulturwissenschaft*/Cultural Studies through a synthesis of different traditions can perhaps be observed in Germany more than anywhere else.

In Germany the reception of Cultural Studies is complicated by two main conditions: The disciplinarity of the German university system, and different notions of *Kulturwissenschaft*/Cultural Studies. Udo Göttlich and Carsten Winter suggest that the word 'studies' in itself shows the contrast between Cultural Studies and the tradition of strict disciplinarity in Germany:

> Bei 'studies' handelt es sich um den Versuch, unterschiedliche disziplinäre Perspektiven mit ihren theoretischen wie methodischen Zugängen zusammenzuführen und komplexe inhaltliche Fragestellungen zu nutzen – und gerade auch in ihrer Widersprüchlichkeit oder Kontextgebundenheit – zu erfahren. (Göttlich and Winter 1999, 31)

Göttlich and Winther emphasize the disciplinary independence of Cultural Studies and point out that much of the criticism aimed at Cultural Studies in Germany only makes sense from a disciplinary perspective. The talk of interdisciplinarity in Germany has little in common with Cultural Studies, because the calls for inter-, multi-, and transdisciplinarity all come from disciplines whose primary concern is, as Göttlich and Winter put it: "die Erhöhung der Leistungsfähigkeit der eignen Modelle und Theorien". (Göttlich and Winter 1999, 27)

As to the incompatible notions of *Kulturwissenchaft*/Cultural studies, Göttlich and Winter conclude:

> Die von Dirk Baecker geleistete Beschreibung der Kulturwissenschaft als 'garbage can' (Mülltonne), die er nicht wertend, sondern deskriptiv versteht, und mit der er auf das aufmerksam macht, was er als ein 'Fest loser Koppelung' beschreibt, darf deshalb weiter als die angemessenste Charakterisierung der Situation der bundesdeutschen Kulturwissenschaft(en) angesehen werden. Es handelt sich nach dieser Auffassung bislang um '[...] Konzepte, die nach ihren Problemen, und Probleme, die nach ihren Anlässen suchen'. (Göttlich and Winter 1999, 31)

What Göttlich and Winter are aiming at with this characterization of *Kulturwissenschaft* as opposed to Cultural Studies seems to be the absence of a certain kind of interdisciplinarity that is based on a problem-orientated approach to cultural phenomena. Interdisciplinarity should not be practiced as a way of enriching the methodological household of a single discipline but as a dialogue between disciplines about complex problems, where different forms of scientific argumentation have the chance to challenge each other. To understand why it is tempting to apply the garbage-can metaphor to the German situation, it is necessary to look at some of the prevailing variants of *Kulturwissenschaft*.

First of all there is of course the concept of *Kulturwissenschaften* as it was introduced in *Geisteswissenchaften Heute*. As Graevenitz points out, this can be understood as a way of defining the context of the disciplines (cf. Graevenitz 1999, 96).

Another similar definition is found in *Literaturwissenschaften und Kulturwissenschaften. Positionen, Theorien, Modelle* (Böhme and Scherpe

1996), where *Kulturwissenschaft* is not conceived of as a separate discipline but as a 'meta-level of reflection'. Whereas philology finds its objects of research in the ensemble of texts, *Kulturwissenschaft* does not have its own objects or problems, but is instead "eine Form der Moderation, ein Medium der Verständigung, eine Art Kunst der Multiperspektivität" (Böhme and Scherpe, 1996, 12)[6].

As to *Kulturwissenschaft* as a separate discipline, it is possible to define it along the same lines, as Hartmut Böhme does when he compares the object of *Kulturwissenschaft* to the function of a 'switchboard' or 'relay' – i.e. the ability to act interdisciplinarily and discover new objects of research (cf. Böhme 1998, 428).

These definitions show that cultural orientation is seen as a way of mediating between the disciplines: It is to serve, so to speak, as the theoretical basis for interdisciplinarity within the system of sciences. The substance is filled in by the disciplines, in this case literary studies.

An attempt to fill in the material of this cultural orientation is made in *Germanistik als Kulturwissenschaft. Eine Einführung in neue Theoriekonzepte* (Benthien and Velten 2002), in which the most important tendencies in current research are summarized. The selection of theories reflects the current hybridization of methods, and their common basis is that they all regard themselves as *Germanistik als Kulturwissenschaft* without giving up the philological basis of the discipline. The book contains introductions to: *Historische Anthropologie, Ordnungen des Wissens, Medien- und Kommunikationstheorie, New Philology/Textkritik, Performativität, Gender-Theorien, Alterität und Interkulturalität*. It presents a very precise picture of the 'state of the art', and shows how literary studies can redefine themselves within the context of *Kulturwissenschaften* along the lines of Graevenitz' description (cf. footnote 5).

Benthien and Velten raise the issue of whether *Kulturwissenschaft* should be regarded as a 'global paradigm' or as a supplementary methodical option. In the light of the hybridization of methods they argue that *Kulturwissenschaft* should be characterized as a paradigm, and one which is not new but the result of the (international) theoretical debates of the past 20 years (cf. Benthien and Velten 2002, 15-16). It would be absurd, they say,

---

[6] This comes quite close to the definition of *Kulturwissenschaft* as "Kennzeichnung einer prozeßorientierten wissenschaftlichen Praxis, 'die sich im semiotischen Sinne pragmatisch über Problemstellungen und nicht 'Forschungsgegenstände' legitimiert und definiert'" (Henningsen and Schröder in: Appelsmeyer and Billmann-Mahecha 2001, 9)

to question it fundamentally, since it has already been consolidated as a practice within literary studies[7].

There are many reasons why *Germanistik als Kulturwissenschaft* could serve as a model for culturally orientated literary studies, but – especially from the point of view of Foreign Language Studies – it is quite depressing that in their preface Benthien and Velten distance the scope of *Germanistik als Kulturwissenschaft* from the linguistic dimension of *Germanistik*:

> Im Titel des Bandes ist von 'Germanistik' und nicht von 'germanistischer Literaturwissenschaft' die Rede – was durchaus die korrektere Bezeichnung wäre, denn das dritte Teilgebiet des Fachs Germanistik, die germanistische Linguistik, spielt in dieser Einführung, wie bereits ein flüchtiger Blick ins Inhaltsverzeichnis zeigt, keine Rolle. Dies ist jedoch keine willkürliche Ausgrenzung, sondern trägt dem Umstand Rechnung, dass für die Linguistik, die sich mehr und mehr zu einer hoch spezialisierten Fachwissenschaft entwickelt, kulturwissenschaftliche Ansätze nicht entscheidend sind. Insofern haben wir anstelle des redundanten Titels Germanistische Literaturwissenschaft als Kulturwissenschaft die kürzere und eingängigere Version Germanistik als Kulturwissenschaft gewählt, im vollen Bewusstsein, damit nur jene 'zwei Drittel' der Germanistik zu meinen, für die das Paradigma der Kulturwissenschaft überhaupt in Anschlag zu bringen ist: Kulturwissenschaftliche Germanistik ist per se eine sich kulturwissenschaftlich orientierende Philologie. (Benthien and Velten 2002, 9)

The arguments justifying *Kulturwissenschaft* and linguistics excluding each other are not further developed here, but sadly this viewpoint is probably symptomatic of a widely shared attitude within literary studies. It is hard to disagree with the conception of linguistics as a highly specialized discipline, but this should perhaps rather be approached as a challenge to engage in interdisciplinary dialogue than as grounds for exclusion. This is especially the case when a culturally orientated philology is one of the topics of the discussion: Perhaps philology is the principle space where studies of language, literature and culture can be integrated. It seems indeed that it was exactly this kind of problem that *Geisteswissenschaften Heute* originally intended to resolve.

---

[7] With regard to literary studies in Germany today, this seems a fair claim. But nevertheless a critical voice should be allowed. Clemens Pornschlegel argues that the so-called methodical-conceptual paradigm of *Kulturwissenschaft* does not really exist. It is only constructed in the German reception of a number of individual heterogeneous French and English innovative approaches. He explains the German eagerness to see paradigms where there are none as an 'obsession with methods' that is inherent in the tradition of *Geisteswissenschaften* and its notion of absolute truth (cf. Pornschlegel 1999).

## Legitimating or rethinking literature and literary studies

Discussions of interdisciplinarity are inevitably followed by discussions of disciplinarity. Literary studies traditionally define themselves in relation to their object of research, i.e. literature, and the fact that the nature of this object is under debate is far from being a new situation produced by the protagonists of cultural orientation. The discussion exists in many versions: On the extended concept of text; on reconfiguration of the concept of World Literature; attempts at comparative openings, and issues concerning national literature, to name but a few. The discussion on *Kulturwissenschaft* can be seen as an extension of these, in that it sets the stage for a fundamental rethinking of the object of research. The question is not only which objects – things – are to be studied, but also how the object of research is to be understood in relation to a cultural orientation and a broad concept of culture. How are we to think literature in relation to other cultural products, for instance in relation to mass media or popular culture? It is not only a question of legitimating the reading of certain kinds of literature, but also of actually rethinking literature.

The question was raised in "Jahrbuch der deutschen Schillergesellschaft" in the provocative formulation *Are literary studies losing their object?* Never before had the editors received so many contributions to a discussion, and the tone was rather harsh (cf. Barner 1998, 457). The question of whether *Kulturwissenschaft* should be seen as a potential threat to the identity of the discipline was central in many of the contributions.

In these contributions Foreign Language Studies were represented in terms of many different lines of argument (some of which I will comment on in the following). But one point was expressed repeatedly and unanimously; it is exemplified here in the words of Hinrich C. Seeba:

> Anders als für deutsche Studenten der Germanistik ist für ihre amerikanischen Kommilitonen die Sprache deutscher Texte selber 'gegenständlich' geworden; sie ist nicht transparent, kein unverstelltes Fenster, durch das man auf eine dahinter liegende Wirklichkeit blickt, kein blanker Spiegel, in dem die Probleme 'abgebildet' werden, als wären sie immer und ausschließlich vorsprachlicher Natur. (Seeba 1998, 501f)

In Foreign Languages Studies especially, it is important to remember that literature as an object is composed of language, which for the student of a foreign language is itself an object. This should not only be regarded as problematic, since it is also an excellent justification for literary texts (*qua* the poetic use of language) to be seen as an indispensable object of study in Foreign Language Studies[8]. It can also motivate cooperation with the linguistic dimension of Foreign Language Studies.

---

[8] As is demonstrated in the argumentations of Martin Swales (1999), Hinrich C. Seeba (1998) and Erika Greber (2000).

Ansgar Nünning talks about a veritable explosion within the field of research in English studies, concurring with Doris Bachmann-Medick that this does not imply the loss of an object but rather the gain of other objects. He adds, however, that more reflection is needed on how to deal with this extended field of research from a perspective of *Kulturwissenschaft* (Nünning 2000, 354). Martin Swales is less confident about the extension of the field of research:

> Wir, die wir Literaturwissenschaftler sind, sollten wissen, daß bei dem Umgang mit dem wertvollen literarischen Text linguistische Intensität und ästhetische Qualität und historische Aussagekraft und erkenntnistheoretische Tragweite miteinander verwoben sind. Wenn wir das nicht wissen, wer soll denn sonst diese Art von Literatur verteidigen? [...] Sie [Werbung, Internet, Mode, Rockmusik, Baustelle und dergleichen mehr] sind überaus faszinierende Gegenstände der Analyse; und sie müssen berücksichtigt werden, denn sie liefern den Kontext unserer heutigen Literaturwissenschaft. Sie sind aber nicht deren Primärtext. Und, um auf das politische Argument zurückzukommen: sie brauchen keinerlei Subvention; die 'hohe' Literatur braucht sie aber – und erhält sie immer noch. (Swales 1999, 478)

For literary studies – *qua* a science of an art – literary texts are primary texts, and their poetic quality is essential. It is hard to disagree that it is necessary to know something about the context of these texts. As Hartmut Böhme points out: "Wenn man behauptet, der Kunstcharakter sei das Non-Aliud der Literatur, muß man, dies bereitet der Logik, hinreichend viel von dem verstehen, was das Aliud der Literatur ist." (Böhme 1998, 479).

But especially in the context of Foreign Language Studies, where it is the expectation that the dimensions of literature, culture and language will be connected, and not just for the sake of literature, literary texts, including their distinctive feature of poetry, should to a greater extent be seen as cultural products on the level of other cultural products appertaining to Foreign Language Studies.

The debate on the object of literary studies is a good example of how different strata in the discussion are interconnected. Political or normative lines of argument (such as Swales's) that serve as strategies for legitimating literary studies and literature are combined with conceptual theoretical and methodical discussions. This shows the need for reflection on concepts such as literature, literary studies, general education (*Bildung*) and subjectivity. Pornschlegel describes the problem as follows:

> Man befürchtet [...] das dunkle Ende der Literatur, die in lauter kulturellen Kontexten ihrer Spezifizität und Singularität beraubt zu werden droht, den Verlust von Geschichtsbewußtsein und (national-)sprachlicher Reflexionsfähigkeit, eine umfassende Nivellierung der kanonisch gewordenen Bildungsgüter, die im unterschiedslosen Einerlei kultureller Produktionen über-

haupt, irgendwo zwischen Waschmaschinen, Comic Strips und TV-Vorabendserien, verschwinden sollen, kurz, man befürchtet das Ende jener schönen Subjektivität, die zu bilden Germanistik einmal da war. Unreflektiert in diesen mehr oder weniger apokalyptisch vorgetragenen Befürchtungen bleibt, wie gesagt, lediglich der Literatur-, Literaturwissenschafts-, Bildungs- und Subjektbegriff selbst, der ihnen zugrunde liegt, gerade was seine identitätsstiftende Funktion angeht. Dieser spezifische Literatur- und Wissenschaftsbegriff steht mit einer 'kulturwissenschaftlichen Orientierung' der Germanistik in der Tat in Frage. (Pornschlegel 1999, 527)

At the core of the current discussions lies the question of the political and social function of literary studies and the critical examination of the inheritance of the *Geisteswissenschaften*. On the other hand, as Pornschlegel puts it, the reception of new impulses that are regarded as *kulturwissenschaftlich* may be of value in this process by virtue of their attention to historical contexts and the peripheries of text production, as well as to the construction of epistemic categories and to political processes. However, they do not solve the actual problem of the reconfiguration of traditions that have become dysfunctional (cf. Pornschlegel 1999, 531).

The discussion on *Kulturwissenschaft* is a reaction to a crisis of legitimation, and it will not come up with a resolution to this crisis if it is not combined with a discussion of the foundational questions that Pornschlegel raises. Only then will it be possible to find useful answers to what seems to be the fundamental question of *Kulturwissenschaft*: How to study literature and culture, or, to be precise, how to study literature as a cultural practice among other cultural practices.

**Literature as culture**
In the following I will summarize some features of a culturally orientated approach to literature. Such an approach would: a) be based on a non-emphatic concept of literature b) show a greater interest in the contexts of literary texts c) aim at a more empirical approach to literary texts (i.e. one that is based on everyday experience) d) be characterized by a constructivist understanding of science.

A special feature of the German discussion is that a modernized, extended concept of culture encounters a narrow, emphatic concept of literature, and this is what makes it so difficult to see literature as (merely) a cultural phenomenon among other cultural phenomena.

In his article "Was ist Literatur?" Peter J. Brenner answers this question, dismissing a regulative idea that has long determined all reflection on literature and is still prevalent: The idea that literature is one and indivisible, and that the theory of literature must accordingly be universally valid for all sorts of literature. In opposition to this essentialist concept of literature he argues that literature 'is not found' but 'is made'; that is, his approach is historical and pragmatic. Literature is made as a cultural practice when texts are produced, understood and used as 'literature' in the context of different argumentations (in delimitation of or approximation to other cultural practices).

With the motto "Literatur ist schön, fiktional und vieldeutig" (Brenner 1996, 14), Brenner surveys the history of theory in literary studies. He demonstrates a historical continuity in the assessment of what literature is, viz. variations of these three categories. In addition, he indicates three categories for the external relations of literature – originality, individuality and autonomy. Brenner regards it as crucial that none of these categories can serve as a criterion for distinguishing between literature and nonliterature. However, they share one feature: They all mark out literature as something special. Brenner concludes:

> Die Unterstellung, daß es so etwas wie eine einzige und unteilbare 'Literatur' gäbe, ist theoretisch nicht haltbar. Auch in ihrer reduzierten Form, daß nämlich zumindest 'die Literatur der westlichen Welt [...] eine Einheit, ein Ganzes' bilde, wirft diese These Probleme auf. Zwar kommt diese Formulierung ohne eine ontologische Bestimmung von 'Literatur' aus, da sie sich auf eine nachweisbare Kontinuität einer kohärenten abendländischen Literatur-, Theorie- und Rezeptionsgeschichte berufen kann; daß sich aber innerhalb dieser Kontinuität historisch, kulturell und regional höchst unterschiedliche Formen von 'Literatur' haben etablieren können, kommt auch ihr nicht in den Blick. (Brenner 1996, 33)

With the dethronement of the notion of the unity and indivisibility of literature it becomes possible to open out the concept of literature from an emphatic, essentialist and gnoseological definition to one that is historical, communicative and semiotic. What Brenner suggests is that literature should be regarded as 'nothing but' a cultural phenomenon, i.e. as a part of the symbolic system 'culture' and an aspect of cultural practice. Literature must be seen as something we 'do' or 'use', and writing must be seen as a form of social interaction, connected to a cultural practice. Brenner goes a step further in his diagnosis of the problem:

> Vielleicht ist es ja wirklich nur eine *affaire allemande*, um die es hier geht. Denn in der deutschen Theorietradition wird die Problematik verschärft durch die große Bedeutung, die die 'Dichtung' – im Unterschied zur Literatur, Poesie oder zur 'Dichtkunst' – seit dem ausgehenden 18. Jahrhundert für die wissenschaftliche Diskussion und das Selbstverständnis der Literaten gewonnen hat; ein Erbe, an dem die germanistische Literaturwissenschaft immer noch schwer trägt. (Brenner 1996, 34)

This localization of the problem is essential to an understanding of the German discussion on *Literaturwissenschaft als Kulturwissenschaft*. It shows the need for similar self-reflection on the history of theories within the

Foreign Language Studies in order to see differences and similarities in the national traditions upon which each is based.

Initially Clifford Geertz' (1973) interpretive cultural anthropology played a significant role in the discussion on *Kulturwissenschaft*. The concept of *Kultur als Text*, or rather the metaphor, was often used as a common basis for discussions on *Literaturwissenschaft als Kulturwissenschaft*.[9] But it seems to have had its day. Looking back at the discussions, what was important was not the concept in itself but the tendencies and aims that it reflected. It was seen as a productive way of extending the field of research, but the result was for the most part something different. One thing that *Kultur als Text* could be said to represent is an effort to pay greater attention to historical and social contexts. In a way it was a return to the endeavours (and problems) of *Sozialgeschichte*:

> Eine gegenüber den Kulturwissenschaften offene Literaturwissenschaft müßte ihren Platz genau in jener 'Lücke' finden, die zwischen poststrukturalistischen Texttheorien und deren Distanz zur Geschichte einerseits und der Sozial- und Funktionsgeschichte und ihren Schwierigkeiten, die Literarizität der Texte als geschichtliche Realität herauszuarbeiten andererseits liegt. (Vosskamp 1998, 506)

*Kultur als Text* represented a reaction to what Doris Bachmann-Medick called the "selbstreferentiellen Metakritizismus" (Bachmann-Medick 1996, 44) and to the increasing de-contextualization and de-politicization of literary studies. The focus on anthropology was not only a way of gaining an understanding of cultural pluralism that was so badly needed within the *Geisteswissenschaften*. The contribution of anthropology was the empirical (erfahrungsnahe) analysis of cultures and cultural symbolic systems and forms of life (cf. Bachmann-Medick 1996, 11). It may sound paradoxical, but the attempts at an 'empirical' approach originated from the concept of *Kultur als Text*. Perhaps for this reason the concept of *Kultur als Praxis* is gaining on that of *Kultur als Text*. Finally, *Kultur als Text* could be said to represent (as a tendency) an orientation towards a constructivist understanding of science. Following this line of thought, Geertz' theory may be described as a theory of cultural systems, where 'text' refers to the constructed nature of the object and of the activity of the ethnographer.

These are some of the tendencies that are represented by the metaphor *Kultur als Text*, and which are constitutive of a culturally orientated approach to literature. The most important aspect of the orientation toward anthropology is perhaps not the specific methods it makes available, but rather the concept of literature as a cultural practice and its potential for a dialogue with the study of other cultural practices. In other words, anthro-

---

[9] Two typical examples of this are *Kultur als Text* (Bachmann-Medick 1996) and *Lesbarkeit der Kultur* (Neumann and Weigel 2000).

pological categories can be applied to literature as they can to any other way of producing meaning (in this case a speech act). The orientation towards anthropology should thus not be regarded as in itself an interdisciplinary project, but rather as part of the basis that enables an interdisciplinary dialogue.

**References**

Appelsmeyer, Heide & Billmann-Mahecha (eds.): 2001. *Kulturwissenschaft. Felder einer prozeßorientierten Praxis*. Velbrück Wissenschaft, Weilerswist.

Bachmann-Medick, Doris (ed.): 1996. *Kultur als Text. Die Anthropologische Wende in der Literaturwissenschaft*. Fischer Taschenbuch Verlag, Frankfurt/M.

Barner, Wilfried: 1998. "Kommt der Literaturwissenschaft ihr Gegenstand abhanden? Zur ersten Diskussionsrunde". *Jahrbuch der Deutschen Schillergesellschaft*, 42. Jahrgang, pp. 457-462.

Benthien, Claudia & Hans Rudolf Velten (eds.): 2002. *Germanistik als Kulturwissenschaft. Eine Einführung in neue Theoriekonzepte*. Rowohlt Taschenbuch Verlag, Reinbek bei Hamburg.

Böhme, Hartmut: 1998. "Zur Gegenstandsfrage der Germanistik und Kulturwissenschaft". *Jahrbuch der Deutschen Schillergesellschaft*, 42. Jahrgang, pp. 476-485.

Böhme, Hartmut & Klaus R. Scherpe (eds.): 1996. *Literatur und Kulturwissenschaften. Positionen, Theorien, Modelle*. Rowohlt Taschenbuch Verlag GmbH, Reinbek bei Hamburg.

Böhme, Hartmut, Peter Matussek & Lothar Müller: 2000. *Orientierung Kulturwissenschaft. Was sie kann, was sie will*. Rowohlt Taschenbuch Verlag, Reinbek bei Hamburg.

Brenner, Peter J.: 1996. "Was ist Literatur?". In: R. Glaser & M. Luserke (eds.), *Literaturwissenschaft – Kulturwissenschaft. Positionen, Themen, Perspektiven*. Westdeutscher Verlag, Opladen, pp. 11-47.

Frühwald, Wolfgang, Hans Robert Jauß, Reinhart Koselleck, Jürgen Mittelstraß & Burkhart Steinwachs: 1991. *Geisteswissenschaften heute*. Suhrkamp Verlag, Frankfurt/M.

Geertz, Clifford: 1973. *The Interpretation of Cultures. Selected Essays by Clifford Geertz*. BasicBooks, A Division of HarperCollins Publishers, New York.

Göttlich, Udo & Carsten Winter: 1999. "Wessen Cultural Studies? Die Rezeption der Cultural Studies im deutschsprachigen Raum". In: R. Bromley, U. Göttlich, & C. Winter (eds.), *Cultural Studies. Grundlagentexte zur Einführung*. zu Klampen Verlag, Lüneburg, pp. 25-42.

Graevenitz, Gerhart v.: 1999. "Literaturwissenschaften und Kulturwissenschaften. Eine Erwiderung". *Deutsche Vierteljahrsschrift für Literaturwissenschaft und Geistesgeschichte*, 73. Jahrgang, LXXIII. Bd., pp. 94-115.

Greber, Erika: 2000. "Ein dritter Weg?" *Jahrbuch der Deutschen Schillergesellschaft*, 44. Jahrgang, pp. 336-342.

Lindner, Rolf: 2000. *Die Stunde der Cultural Studies*. WUV Universitätsverlag, Wien.

Neumann, Gerhard & Sigrid Weigel (eds.): 2000. *Lesbarkeit der Kultur. Literaturwissenschaften zwischen Kulturtechnik und Ethnographie.* Fink, München.

Nünning, Ansgar: 2000. "Anglistische Anmerkungen zu den Gegenstandsgewinnen einer kulturwissenschaftlich orientierten Literaturwissenschaft". *Jahrbuch der Deutschen Schillergesellschaft*, 44. Jahrgang, pp. 350-355.

Pornschlegel, Clemens. 1999. "Das Paradigma, das keines ist. Anmerkungen zu einer unglücklichen Debatte". *Mitteilungen des Deutschen Germanistenverbandes*, Heft 4 (Germanistik als Kulturwissenschaft), 46. Jahrgang, pp. 520-532.

Prinz, Wolfgang & Peter Weingart (eds.): 1990. *Die sog. Geisteswissenschaften. Innenansichten.* Suhrkamp Verlag, Frankfurt/M.

Seeba, Hinrich C.: 1998. "Kulturkritik: Objekt als 'subject'. Diskussionsbeitrag zum Gegenstand der Literaturwissenschaft". *Jahrbuch der Deutschen Schillergesellschaft*, 42. Jahrgang, pp. 495-502.

Swales, Martin: 1999. "Trahison des clercs? Gedanken zu dem abhandengekommenen – oder abgeschafften – Gegenstand der Literaturwissenschaft". *Jahrbuch der Deutschen Schillergesellschaft*, 43. Jahrgang, pp. 476-478.

Vosskamp, Wilhelm: 1998. "Die Gegenstände der Literaturwissenschaft und ihre Einbindung in die Kulturwissenschaften". *Jahrbuch der Deutschen Schillergesellschaft*, 42. Jahrgang, pp. 503-507.

# 'Advanced literacy'
## Bridging traditions in the study of language and culture

by

Francesco Caviglia

Introduction

That the criteria for being considered a member of the literate community have changed in the last few decades is clearly reflected in two recent surveys on literacy, the *IALS* survey on adult literacy (OECD, 2000) and *PISA 2000* on literacy at the age of 15 (OECD, 2000b and 2001). The traditional approach, which is still represented in the *IALS* survey, measures literacy on the assumption that the subject is at the receiving end of communication, and primarily verifies his or her ability to extract information from a text and to deliver it back. The level of difficulty of the reading exercises is graded according to such parameters as the presence of distracting information or the number of inferences necessary to answer a question: that is, according to the *computational* effort required for processing the sentences (OECD, 2000, 93-97). Implicit in the underlying conception of the reading and writing process is the idea that information is received and transmitted as if it were an object that migrates from one container to the other, from the page to the head or the other way round: the student has understood a text if the 'content' in his head corresponds to the contents of the text, as far as this can be tested. This view of reading and writing is relatively easy to evaluate and makes sense as long as language and text are regarded as means for *representing* reality, and learning – for which *reading* is one prerequisite-skill – is understood (maybe implicitly) as storing facts and rules in one's head.

In contrast to the *IALS* survey, the more recent *PISA 2000* survey entailed a more active role for the reader, who was required to recognize *genre*, *function* and *point of view* in a text and to collaborate with the text in the production of meaning by drawing inferences from her or his knowledge of the world. In other words, a certain degree of 'criticality' is an explicit requirement, in accordance with the spread of a view in which the function of communication is not only to transmit content but also to construct relationships and identities (Fairclough and Wodak, 1997); or, to use a formulation which I will prefer in this paper, 'to pattern expectations and values' (Raskin, 1982, 16; Raskin was actually referring to functions of art).

The claim of this paper is that much research on language and culture can be productively seen as a contribution to fostering *literacy*, which I would first define in general terms as understanding and mastery of the communication tools that permit us to orient ourselves and others in our complex world. However, like 'knowing' or 'learning', 'literacy' can be associated with a wide range of practices in our society. As an addition to this broad conception, I propose a distinction between two types of literacy: *basic literacy*, focused on the representational, face-value layer of language, and founded on a view of communication as the simple transmission of contents or as self-expression; and *advanced literacy*, which implies a view of reading and writing as a means for creating and transforming knowledge, for understanding and influencing others, and for constructing identities and relationships. The purpose of this paper is to discuss the concept of *advanced literacy* as a goal for the study of language and culture by providing examples of how this educational goal can become a source of research questions and a catalyst for dialogue between different paradigms in the study of language and culture[1].

## A literacy for the knowledge age

Electronic archives have already changed the way we locate information, and computer simulations may offer new approaches to the human scien-

---

[1] The definition of *advanced literacy* that I am proposing is heavily indebted to the research carried out by Carl Bereiter and Marlene Scardamalia over the last 15 years, into writing, learning and the mediational role of technology and social institutions. In the 1890s, supported by tools from experimental psychology and cognitive science, Bereiter and Scardamalia investigated the process of written composition and envisaged ways to assist it (Scardamalia & Bereiter, 1986; Bereiter & Scardamalia, 1987). Their subsequent work has focused on defining 'expertise' (Bereiter and Scardamalia, 1993) and on how to foster 'knowledge building', i.e. the ability to produce and manipulate new knowledge, which they consider a key skill for education that meets the needs of the *knowledge age* (Scardamalia & Bereiter,1999 and 2003; Bereiter, 2002a; Scardamalia, 2002). However, despite Bereiter's acknowledgement of the educational potential of the humanities (Bereiter, 2002a, 318-322), their work is mainly focused on elementary schools and on the natural and social sciences as content. An underlying ambition of my work in the last 10 years – most explicitly in Caviglia (2002) and Caviglia (2000a) – has been to help bridge their views of the learning process with some key conceptual tools developed within the humanities.

ces (Parisi 2000). The overwhelming presence of visual stimuli from TV and videogames, together with the 'hypertextual' reading practices promoted by computers, are probably jeopardizing the role of 'sequential' and 'reflective' reading and writing in favour of easier and shallower associative processes (Simone 2000). Yet reflective reading and writing remains a crucial empowering tool in our society. I do not believe that developments in Information and Communication Technology (ICT) require of us a radically different literacy from that already part of the more open traditions within the humanities, with roots in the written word but a keen eye for a variety of genres and media. Studies on the role of technology in shaping culture and cognition with focus on the past (e.g. Ong 1982; Gumbrecht 1985; Zumthor 1987) still offer key insights for understanding recent developments brought about by the technology of communication.

However, levels of literacy which were once the privilege of an elite have become a standard requirement for participation in the adult life of our culture, for at least two reasons. Firstly, a high level of literacy is a prerequisite for many attractive jobs, since "virtually every high-tech tool reduces the range of skills needed to accomplish tasks and puts more power into the hands of those with [...] general intellectual abilities" (Bereiter 2002a, 246). Besides, even if intellectual unemployment becomes an even worse problem in the future than it already is (Rifkin 1995), the access to a rich intellectual life remains a goal in itself, given the correlation between education and 'social capital' (Putnam 1996), i.e. the disposition to civic engagement and trust that is largely responsible for the well-being of a community. Some examples of once elitist and now increasingly standard educational requirements in European countries are that:

- mastery of one or more foreign languages, and understanding of the associated cultures, is a prerequisite for a range of work activities and for social life at large;
- writing has become almost as important as reading, since many workplaces and also leisure activities require writing skills (with optional multimedia extensions), partly as a consequence of the growing pervasiveness of technology-mediated communication;
- the ability to evaluate the trustworthiness and the non-explicit agenda of a source is vital in a society with a multiplicity of voices but little dialogue, with large concentrations of power in the media and at the same time the opportunity for many to publish or broadcast (almost) anything.

On a more general level, in a world where "the autonomous capacity of generating new knowledge" (e.g. Castells & Ince 2003, 133) is considered the key to development, adequate literacy ought to encompass an attitude to reading and writing (or their equivalent in visual media) with the purpose of furthering understanding.

*Advanced literacy as expertise in communication within a given domain.*[2]
The idea that 'knowledge' corresponds to a list of items in someone's head, or in a text, is a persistent one and still in good health, although nobody in the teaching profession would defend it explicitly today. According to this view, *knowing* something means having in one's head a 'copy' – or better, a representation – of a real-world object. The more accurate the representation, the fuller the knowledge[3]. This view makes sense for many aspects of cognition (including not-trivial ones: Einstein's theory of relativity can be seen in these terms). However, the idea of a mind as a container of facts and rules cannot account for other aspects of cognition, such as the role of implicit knowledge or 'having a sense for something', where 'something' often refers to things that really matter (e.g. language, interpersonal relations), or the way cognition is embedded in social praxis and tools.

But the container metaphor really does a poor job, according to Bereiter (2002a), when it is applied to learning and teaching. Here it stands more or less explicitly behind two possible unfortunate scenarios, rote learning (trying to stuff facts and rules into heads) or programs devised for 'learning to think'. The first scenario assumes that the social need is to master a stable body of knowledge without ever needing to revise it, which is by no means the case in the contemporary 'knowledge age'. The second scenario can be encountered in education when a subject or activity is considered to have a special potential for fostering 'thinking skills': Latin, for example, in the '60s in Italy, computer programming in the late '80s. Considering a single activity an all-round cognitive booster contradicts what we know of experts in the real world, who have typically developed their expertise through long and committed engagement with a given domain (Scardamalia and Bereiter 1993; see also below).

---

[2] For more details on and references to Bereiter's view of learning models, cf. Caviglia (2003, 18-25).

[3] The mind-as-container metaphor has even been re-instated as theory in cognitive science and artificial intelligence in the '70s and later, with knowledge represented as a set of facts and rules on which a 'computational unit' can operate. Prior to any other criticism, the weak point of that approach was its (often inexplicit) assumption that a computer with a single processor could simulate the processes going on in a human brain, if only the programmer could write in the appropriate rules. Traditional computer programs can indeed outperform most humans in highly formalised domains (from chess playing to medical diagnostics), but they fare less well in 'understanding' language; at any rate, the underlying 'architecture' of brains and traditional computers cannot be compared. More recent research on 'computer cognition' attempts to simulate the organisation of a network of neurons with a network of processors.

Bereiter discusses and accepts several contributions to the notion of 'knowledge', especially from traditions that highlight how cognition is embedded in social practice and tools, and goes on to suggest that educational goals should be expressed in terms of *understanding*. For example (from Bereiter 2002a, 01-104), understanding a person means:

- the ability to act intelligently in relation to the person (of course, there are many 'correct' ways of understanding a person, depending on your relationship to her/him);
- becoming interested in the person;
- envisioning the person in a broader context (family, occupations, personal history, etc.);
- the ability to talk about the person (her/his underlying motives, dispositions, strengths, weaknesses).

A deep understanding is demonstrated by an insightful resolution of problems involving the person and by telling stories that have depth of characterization; not least, deep understanding can only arise from deep involvement. Finally, there may be no single optimal understanding, but there are wrong (and possibly corrigible) forms of understanding.

If we now substitute 'a person' with 'a tool' (e.g., a computer) or 'a story', our definition of 'understanding' still holds: there are many appropriate ways of understanding. For example, understanding a joke may range from laughing at it to re-telling and adapting it to another audience, or to a deep analysis of the genre (e.g. Raskin, 1992).

*Deep understanding or expertise.*
What does it mean to possess a deep understanding, i.e. to be an 'expert' in an area? According to meta-research conducted by Bereiter and Scardamalia (1993) on the nature of expertise, there is no such thing as problem-solving or 'thinking' skills, and the transfer of skills across different domains is by no easy matter (see also below, *Lie-detecting as a step towards 'criticality'*). But experts in given domains do exist: these are people who:

- know a lot (have learnt a lot) in a given area;
- can exercise progressive problem-solving (that is, they are able to introduce new insights when they solve problems; they work on the edge of their knowledge and learn more while working).

Progressive problem-solving in a given area is also at the core of effective learning and expertise: experts succeed where long-time practitioners fail, because the latter stick to their routine. But how do people become experts in the first place? Bereiter (2002a, 254-266) further suggests that we distinguish between two components of the process:

- learning as the process that changes the individual's understanding of a given subject;
- knowledge building as work done to produce, refine and amend shared conceptual artefacts.

Both learning and knowledge building are worthwhile aims in education. 'Learning' can be regarded in its own right as activity focused on the single student and on his/her skills and knowledge in a given domain (what individual learners acquire is important; it is what they take with them when they finish school).

'Knowledge-building', on the other hand, means the production in a given working group of such objects as texts, projects or policies which represent an improvement over the current status of knowledge. These objects can be appropriated (*learned*) by others and then discussed, improved upon, and possibly discarded when a better alternative is available.

Knowledge building, then, means creating something new, rising above the previous 'state of the art'. If, for example, I learn to use a new word processor or to understand enough Swedish to be able to follow a lecture, the outcome of my efforts is that I can do something that I could not do before, but I have not (yet) made any contribution to the state of common knowledge. If participants in a seminar analyse the Readers' Letters section in an Italian Catholic magazine, and make what they have understood available to others, the group has built new knowledge (Caviglia, 2000). Of course, this activity of knowledge building has required individual appropriation (*learning*) of vocabulary, historical background, theories, and this is of no small importance. But it is the conjunction of the two dimensions of learning and knowledge-building that has produced both individual and collective progress.

The advanced literacy that I am proposing can be seen as expertise in communication and as both a prerequisite and a tool for knowledge building. For example, in the case of writing, *knowledge-telling* – i.e. writing according to a model of communication based on *transmission* of contents – is the strategy of the beginner writer ('basic literacy'), while expert writers use writing as a resource to transform and refine their understanding of a topic (Scardamalia & Bereiter, 1986).

Given the description of 'experts' proposed above, a view of advanced literacy as expertise gives rise to an awareness that it can hardly be context-independent: it takes, for example, a solid knowledge of an area of language, society and culture to recognize potential lies on a given topic, and this ability cannot readily be transferred across domains (Caviglia 2002a and below)[4].

From an educational viewpoint, advanced literacy should therefore be promoted in domains that are relevant and broad enough to be worth the effort, even when the transfer of abilities from one context to another may be problematic.

### Advanced literacy at work: three examples

The study of language and culture offers a wide range of possibilities for implementing the model of teaching and learning proposed by Bereiter. Much of the work done in secondary schools and universities is indeed knowledge building: this happens whenever a topic is analyzed and/or a project is developed that involves and challenges students and teacher alike, and where the aim is to rise above the previous level of understanding. This is at least what I aim at in my own 'research-based teaching': not the transmission of the results of research, but research (*knowledge building*), on an appropriate scale, integrated into the learning process. I cannot claim that our work group has discovered anything new. We were, perhaps, the only ones to investigate specific hoaxes or items of crime news, or to attempt a given problem of word choice. I am aware that most of the analyses we have carried out can hardly be considered an advance in overall knowledge on the topics. But 'originality' ought to be considered in relative terms:

> One major prejudice must be overcome if knowledge building, as real productive work similar to what goes on in industrial laboratories and university research centers, is to find a foothold in educational policy. This is the prejudice that bestows credit only on the first person to come forth with an idea. Although this may be a perfectly reasonable principle in patent law, when generalized it virtually denies the possibility of children's being real creators of knowledge; for rarely if ever will a child produce knowledge that is new to the world. But originality is always relative to context. If it should turn out that there are intelligent beings on another planet and that everything scientists on earth have discovered is already old hat to them, would that mean that Newton and Darwin were not scientists after all? (Bereiter, 2002b, 22)

Bereiter is thinking, of course, of children, and it is reasonable to expect that university students should eventually become capable of original work. But in education the process is often more important than the product, and I don't believe that reinventing the wheel should be despised,

---

[4] If we accept the idea of 'advanced literacy' as expertise in a given domain, then study programs keeping language and culture separate are likely to lessen students' chances of becoming 'experts' in anything. However, a discussion on this point would go beyond the scope of this paper.

as long as it means a better understanding of how the wheel works and why it matters.

## Lie detecting as a step towards *criticality*[5]

While a survey of approaches to *criticality* suggests that general skills for lie detecting may not exist, there are professions in which expertise in discerning lies is a requirement: judges, politicians, policemen, journalists, lawyers and criminals ought to have a good grasp of lying and lie-detecting. What does it take to recognize a printed or broadcasted lie, which is potentially the most dangerous kind? And does it make sense to analyse and produce lies as part of a secondary school curriculum in advanced literacy?[6]

First of all, it is worth questioning the need for instruction on this subject, given that small children usually learn how to lie and to mistrust others' statements simply by taking part in social life. However, a lie mediated by the printed word can be more difficult to spot than one told in a face-to-face situation, since literacy is far less natural than the spoken language and is acquired more slowly than either speech or body language. Besides, its asynchronous nature frees the liar from the risk of self-betrayal by unintentional body signals, while the differences in language proficiency among the population are much wider with regard to the written word. Furthermore, the institutions in charge of fostering literacy seldom incorporate a culture of questioning the reliability of written statements.

How can a didactic of the lie be implemented with students aged 14-16? The approach I suggest involves three different activities:

1. Students are asked to examine lies from fiction in order to make them aware that meaning is always constructed with the cooperation of the receiver (and not simply transmitted and received). They are instructed to consider the victim's expectations (fears and desires), the liar's aims, the form of the lie, the factual knowledge involved, and prompted to find similarities with real life situations;
2. Since a successful lie detector requires similar skills to a successful liar, students are asked to invent (innocuous) lies and discuss them,
3. Students are placed in controlled situations where they are lied to, and then discuss how they discovered (or failed to) discover the lie. The similarities with the other lies encountered in the course are highlighted.

---

[5] This section is based on Caviglia, 2002.
[6] See Caviglia (2003, 27) to explain why I am here using the term 'advanced literacy' instead of 'critical literacy' (as in Caviglia, 2002).

A reassessment of that experience confirms that working with lies can be a productive strategy for raising students' communication awareness, but also that lie detecting can hardly be learned on a general basis. I still believe that focusing on the motives and expectations of all the actors involved in communication, and on the identities and roles that they construct through discourse, would help lie detecting across different genres and topics. On the other hand, however, personal motives and factual knowledge about a given topic are decisive in triggering a critical attitude. Furthermore, though the categories of 'lie' vs. 'truth' used in the paper are appropriate for explaining the need for critical literacy, they may prove to be inadequate in many real-life cases.

Another limitation of a didactic of the lie as advanced literacy is that today's most dangerous lies are likely to be presented as scientific truth. While a sensitivity to potential lies might certainly help to develop antibodies against generic claims of scientificity, it would take a better and more widespread understanding of the areas involved to raise public awareness on issues that require a degree of sophisticated pre-knowledge, for example in biology or statistics or computer science.

In conclusion, language education and discourse analysis can cover an important portion of a curriculum in lie detecting, although a multidisciplinary approach will be necessary for dealing with real-life issues requiring 'critical information awareness'.

### Making sense of different discourses on crime and violence[7]

Though my work with lie-detecting ran into difficulties, the reactions of students and colleagues to the emancipatory goal of teaching how to read between the lines has been encouraging, and I have thus been induced to look for a more defined domain and genre. I have therefore progressed to various discourses on crime and violence, which I made an object of analysis in courses and seminars with Danish secondary school teachers and university students of Italian.

Examples taken from the coverage of crime in the Italian media offered a repository of source material for fostering 'advanced literacy' through better understanding of conflicting value systems (in this case, a shoot-the-perpetrator vs. a put-the-blame-on-society attitude to deviance) and of monological vs. dialogical approaches to discourse.

George Lakoff's analysis of liberal vs. conservative ideology in the USA, based on the hypothesis that both value systems are internally consistent (Lakoff, 1996), provided a model for describing the rationale behind different attitudes, while making it clear that taking a stand between value systems is not a matter that can be settled with the tools of discourse

---

[7] This section is based on Caviglia (2003, 88-111 and submitted).

analysis alone. But can the tools of discourse analysis substantiate the impression that a text or discourse is self-righteous or, on the other hand, open to dialogue?

Using examples from the press coverage of a murder committed in Northern Italy, Mikhail Bakhtin's dialogical principle[8] was applied as a benchmark for distinguishing dialogic texts from monologic (or self-righteous) ones. It could be easily recognized that whilst the dialogic texts grant an important role to the reader in meaning-making and a voice to the subject(s) written about, this is denied by the monologic texts. In addition, as in the previous experience with lie detecting, it was evident that creative storytelling, like the narratives constructed by such writers as James Ellroy or Georges Simenon out of the raw material of crime reporting, can be an expression of understanding and criticality at least as powerful as non-narrative criticism.

**Tools for language awareness: an experience using text corpora as L2 writing tools[9]**

Teaching Italian composition to Danish university students gave me the opportunity to look more closely at problems involving syntax and word-choice that the students were not able to solve with the tools at their disposal. In consulting the grammar or the dictionary (both mono- and bilingual) they often failed to recognize the most appropriate syntactic rule or the word which would have been the typical lexical choice for an Italian native speaker. When a low-cost, medium-sized Italian corpus became available, I proposed that it should be used as an alternative tool for dealing with syntax and word choice. Instead of consulting the rules to decide which preposition should go between word X and word Y, the student should search the corpus for occurrences of words X and Y connected with a preposition. This was likely to be the correct solution. In the case of word-choice problems, a search for patterns around keywords was likely to provide a list of co-occurring words, including, with luck, the one required (s. figure 1).

---

[8] E.g. Bakhtin 1986, 161; Bakhtin 1984, 318; Todorov 1984, x; also re-read in the light of the notion of 'involvement in dialogue' developed among others by Deborah Tannen 1989, 1997.

[9] This section is based on Caviglia, 2000b.

'Advanced literacy'

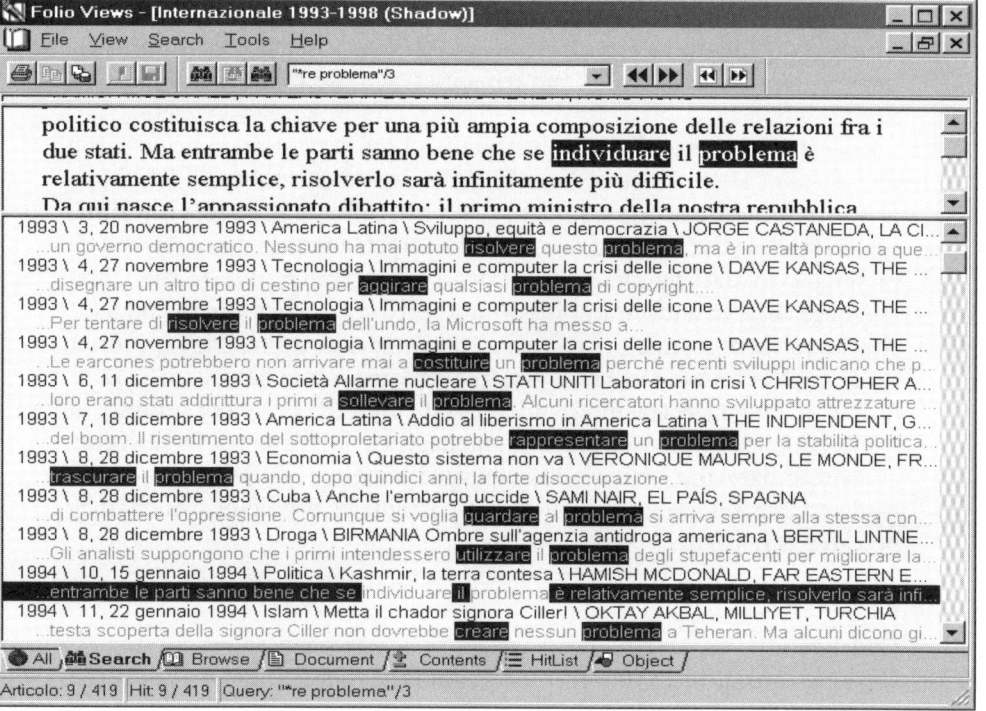

Figure 1
A few verbs associated with "problema" (= *problem*): see the collocations "risolvere", "aggirare", "costituire", "sollevare", "individuare" (the query "*re problema"/3 means "take all the occurrences of '*re' endings (= likely infinitives) followed by 'problema' at a maximum 3-word distance").

It soon became evident that this approach could be applied to less trivial problems: for example, whether or not to use the subjunctive, or deciding which of two words with apparently the same meaning is the more appropriate to a given context.

With four year's experience behind me, I can claim that at least eight of 10 syntax or word-choice problems acknowledged as such by my Danish students can be resolved by putting an appropriate query to the corpus. However, only half the students eventually become regular users of the text corpus, although they all receive instruction and support in learning the technicalities. Why?

Formulating a query on a text corpus, the activity I had devoted most emphasis to, is less difficult than I believed at first: I would now consider it a matter of *basic literacy*, a skill slightly more complex than locating a word in a dictionary on paper. The real difficulty with text corpora is making sense of the results of a query, i.e. how to recognize patterns of form and meaning within raw, unprepared data. This requires two skills which I consider to be aspects of *advanced literacy*: sensitivity to similarities and differences in syntax and semantics, and the ability to induce rules from examples.

Does it make sense, from an instructional point of view, to begin using text corpora at the stage of Second Language Acquisition (L2)? Using a text corpus in L2 confronts students with two difficulties at the same time: understanding the tool and decoding the target language. It might well be preferable to start familiarizing students with text corpora in their first language (L1). In a more ambitious perspective, a curriculum in language education from a joint L1/L2 perspective might be a challenging project for researchers and teachers trying to overcome a peculiar *Catch 22* condition of language teaching: students are indeed on shaky ground in respect of both language and meta-language when talking about L2 syntax and vocabulary, but when meta-language is taught as subject matter in L1 students are seldom confronted with language problems which they perceive as relevant.

## Conclusion

My long-term project is to further explore the requirements of advanced literacy and on this basis develop a *toolbox for advanced literacy* in the form of a list of *conceptual tools* with associated teaching material. Experience with the three projects outlined above suggests a few general goals as focus of educational intervention:

- an attitude to reading and writing (or their equivalent in visual media) with the purpose of furthering understanding;
- an awareness of the role of the subject's expectations in guiding the process of understanding (of a situation as well as of a text; see Tannen, 1993); this entails in turn that understanding the context of communication is crucial, and that advanced readers are conscious of their own expectations and the limits of their background knowledge; the same is true of advanced writers' understanding of their audiences;
- a disposition to consider texts (in the broad sense) as *solutions*, as tools to gain leverage over aspects of personal and social life, as problem-solving actions devised to satisfy a need; a *functional* approach as proposed by Raskin (1982) for the analysis of art can act as the unifying rationale for a set of concepts developed in language and cultural studies, from Bakhtin's *dialogical principle* to more recent 'cognitive' approaches (cf. a discussion in Caviglia, 2003,13-14, 26-33);

- an awareness of the connection between, on the one hand, the form and function of communication, and on the other, the ability to recognize, imitate and discuss structures of language and communication (e.g. words, sentences, images, narrative or argumentative patterns). Examples of recent research on the 'function of the structure' are Nølke's (2002) extension of Bakhtin's dialogical principle to linguistic analysis or Raskin's (2001, 2002) conceptual model for analysing the ways in which a short fiction film tells its story.

Hans Lauge Hansen (2002) and Hanne Leth Andersen (2002) have recently proposed teaching as one common ground for cooperation and dialogue across disciplines and traditions. This paper is an attempt to take up their suggestion and to demonstrate that teaching ought not to be considered a by-product of research activity, but rather a source of questions for research, and a field of cooperation and also competition among the sub-disciplines in the quest to answer those questions.

This is not to say that any research ought to be subordinate to teaching, but is rather an attempt to address the problem of the lack of impact of much research in the humanities. My point is that a body of research exists which has the capacity to enhance our understanding of culture and communication, but which remains disconnected from teaching practices due to poor mediation between the culture of research and the culture of teaching.

> I wish to thank Leonardo Cecchini and Hans Lauge Hansen for valuable comments on earlier versions of this article, Richard Raskin for his invaluable assistance as supervisor of the PhD-thesis on which this article is based, and Hanne Leth Andersen for her suggestions and support.

## References

Andersen, H. L. : 2002. The situation of the Foreign Language Studies. "Modern language studies in current educational planning". In: H. L. Hansen (ed.), *Changing philologies: contributions to the redefinition of foreign language studies in the age of globalisation.* Copenhagen, Museum Tusculanum Press; 41-50.

Bakhtin, Mikhhail: 1984. *Problems of Dostoevsky's poetics.* Minneapolis, University of Minnesota Press. Original essays written in 1923 and 1961.

Bakhtin, Mikhhail: [1974] 1986. "Toward a methodology for the human sciences." In: *Speech Genres & Other Late Essays*, C. Emerson & M. Holquist (eds), Austin, University of Texas Press; 159-172.

Bereiter, C.: 2002a. *Education and mind in the knowledge age.* Mahwah, New Jersey, Erlbaum.

Bereiter, C. : 2002b. "Liberal education in a knowledge society". In: B. Smith (ed.), *Liberal education in a knowledge society.* Chicago, Open Court. Retrieved from *http://www.ikit.org/fulltext/inpresseducation.pdf* on December 1st, 2002; 11-33.

Bereiter, C. & M. Scardamalia: 1987. *The Psychology of Written Composition*. Hillsdale, NJ, Erlbaum.

Bereiter, C. & M. Scardamalia: 1993. *Surpassing ourselves: An inquiry into the nature and implications of expertise*. Chicago, Open Court.

Castells, M. & M. Rice: 2003. *Conversations with Manuel Castells*. Cambridge, UK, Polity.

Caviglia, F. (ed): 2000. "Valori degli italiani : un percorso intorno alla famiglia". *(Prè)pub* of the Romansk Institut, Aarhus University, n. 177-178. Also online: <http://www.hum.au.dk/romansk/tidsskrift/>, seen 5.5.2002.

Caviglia, F.: 2000b. "A text corpus as a companion to the strategic second language writer". *(Prè)pub* no. 179 (November 2000). Also in Caviglia (2003; 178-189).

Caviglia, F.: 2002. "Lie Detecting as a Step Towards Critical Literacy". *L1-Educational Studies in Language and Literature*, 2, 179-220. Also retrieved 20.10.2003 from *http://ipsapp008.kluweronline.com/ips/frames/toc.asp?J=4686&I=6*

Caviglia, F.: 2003. *Tools for advanced literacy: functional approaches to reading, writing and storytelling*. Ph.D. dissertation submitted in July 2003 to the University of Aarhus, Department of Media and Information Science. Retrieved 10.11.2003 from http://www.hum.au.dk/romansk/romfrc/papers/elenco.htm [The defence is expected to take place in December 2003].

Caviglia, F. (submitted). "Understanding public discourse about violence and crime: a challenge for critical discourse analysis at school". In: Caviglia (2003; 88-111); a shorter version is currently submitted for publication.

Fairclough, N. & R. Wodak: 1997. "Critical discourse analysis". In: T.A. Van Dijk (ed.), *Discourse as social interaction*. London, Sage; 258–283.

Gumbrecht, H.U.: 1985. "The body versus the printing press: Media in the early modern period, mentalities in the reign of Castile, and another history of literary forms". *Poetics* 14, 209–227.

Hansen, H. L.: 2002. "A change of paradigm in language studies". In: H. L. Hansen (ed.), *Changing philologies: contributions to the redefinition of foreign language studies in the age of globalisation*. Copenhagen, Museum Tusculanum Press; 63-76.

Lakoff, G.: 1996. *Moral politics*. Chicago, University of Chicago Press.

Nølke, H.: 2002. "La polyphonie comme théorie linguistique". [Polyphony as language theory.] In: M. Carel (ed.), *Les facettes du dire. Hommage à Oswald Ducrot* [The aspects of the spoken word: Hommage to Oswald Ducrot]. Paris, Kimé; 215–224.

OECD (ed.): 2000. *Literacy in the information age. Final report on the International Adult Literacy Survey*. Paris, OECD.

OECD (ed.): 2000b. *Measuring student knowledge and skills. The Pisa 2000 assessment of reading, mathematical and scientific literacy*. Paris, OECD.

OECD (ed.): 2001. *Knowledge and skills for life. First results from Pisa 2000*. Paris, OECD.

Ong, W.: 1982. *Orality and literacy: The technologizing of the word*. London, Routledge.

Parisi, Domenico : 2001. *Simulazioni. La realtà rifatta nel computer* [Simulations. Reconstructing reality by computer]. Bologna, Il Mulino.

Putnam, R. D.: 1996. "The Strange Disappearance of Civic America". *The American Prospect* vol. 7 no. 24, December 1, 1996. Retrieved from *http://www.prospect.org/print/V7/24/putnam-r.html on 12/10/ 2003.*

Raskin, R.: 1982. *The functional analysis of art,* Aarhus, Arkona.

Raskin, R.: 2001. *Kortfilmen som fortælling.* Aarhus, Systime.

Raskin, R.: 2002. *The Art of the Short Fiction Film. A Shot by Shot Study of Nine Modern Classics.* Jefferson, NC and London, McFarland Publications.

Rifkin, J.: 1995. *The end of work. The decline of the global labor force and the dawn of the post-market era.* New York, G. B. Putnam.

Scardamalia, M. & C. Bereiter: 2003. "Knowledge building". In: James W. Guthrie (ed.), *Encyclopedia of education, Second Edition.* New York, Macmillan Reference USA.

Simone, R.: 2000. *La terza fase. Forme di sapere che stiamo perdendo* [The third phase. Forms of knowledge we are losing]. Bari, Laterza.

Tannen, D.: 1993. "What's in a frame? Surface evidence for underlying expectations". In: *Framing in discourse* 14–56). New York, Oxford University Press. First published in 1979.

Tannen, D.: 1989. *Talking voices: Repetition, dialogue and imagery in conversational discourse.* Cambridge, Cambridge University Press.

Tannen, D.: 1997. "Involvement as dialogue: Linguistic theory and the relation between conversational and literary discourse". In: M. Macovski (ed.), *Dialogue and critical discourse.* New York/Oxford, Oxford University Press; 137-157.

Thomas, W. P. & V. P. Collier: 1997. "School Effectiveness for Language Minority Students". NCBE Resource Collection Series, No. 9, December 1997. Retrieved from *http://www.ncela.gwu.edu/ncbepubs/resource/effectiveness/* on December 1st, 2002.

Todorov, T.: [1981] 1984. *Mikhail Bakhtin: The dialogical principle.* Translation by Wlad Godzich. Minneapolis: University of Minnesota Press (ed. orig. 1981, *Mikhail Bakhtine. Le principe dialogique.* Paris, Éditions du Seuil).

Woods, C.: 2001. "Bridging the creative and the critical". *L1 – Educational Studies in Language and Literature* 1; 55–72.

Zumthor, P.: 1994. "Body and performance". In: H.U. Gumbrecht & K.L. Pfeiffer (eds), *Materialities of communication.* Stanford, California, Stanford University Press; 217–226. [Originally published in German 1988 and 1991.]

# Towards a Sociocritical Theory of the Text

by
Edmond Cros

If we look back to the 1960s we observe a radical reconfiguration of the idea of the text, resulting from the rapid expansion of general linguistics and literary semiology. This idea was detached from the 'philosophy of truth'; it defined a 'new object' that was described as a 'translinguistic device' and considered as a signifying practice that never ceases to work and is irreducible to objective signification. While retaining the theoretical concepts implicit within this idea, sociocriticism is essentially concerned with what the text transcribes; that is to say, with the modalities of the incorporation of history, not at the level of content but at the level of forms. For sociocriticism, this plurality is the product of the dynamic and dialectical process of history. It is because it incorporates history in a way that is specific to it that the text presents itself as a translinguistic device. In the present article I seek to map out these paths of complex, heterogeneous and contradictory meaning and to identify both their nature and their effects.

Sociocriticism aims to bring out the relations existing between the structures of literary (or cultural) work and the structures of the society in which this work is deeply rooted. This theory claims that the encounter with ideological traces and with antagonistic tensions between social classes is central to any reading of texts. However, unlike most sociological approaches to literature, which leave the structures of text untouched, it assumes that the social nature of the literary work must be located and investigated *within* the text and not outside it. A patient and exact reconstruction of the semiotico-ideological elements must therefore be elaborated in order to show how the historical process is deeply involved in the writing process. Indeed, it is necessary to consider the different ways of incorporating history in the text. On this point, a series of questions must be emphasized:

- Which kind of historical material is required?
- How should the text incorporate this historical material?
- Which theoretical and methodological approach can enable the critic to bring into view the process of the history's incorporation?

Before attempting to answer these questions I shall recall that every theory is founded on two points:

1. a philosophical conception implying an view of history which questions the nature of the historical process;
2. a poetic conception referring to the function of the text.

So, what is the process of history? What is the text? How does the text work? To elucidate the first point I refer to Marxism, which links the discursive formation to the ideological and social formations. There is indeed a relation between the infrastructure and the superstructure but this relation is neither automatic nor direct. Between the two levels (and within them) a series of various instances must be distinguished, each belonging to a specific historical time. At any given moment of history, some instances seem advanced, ahead of their time, whilst others seem delayed, behind the times. Insofar as the delayed is always attracted by the advanced, the gap between the two instances and the series of gaps existing in the totality of the system produce the dynamism of the process. These historical gaps produce semiotico-ideological traces and various kinds of effects in the literary work, observable especially in the textual spaces of the contradictions. That is why in my critical reading I start from the intratextual microsemiotics organized by these contradictions, which enable us to reconstruct the social and ideological formations.

Now, how does the text function? At its start the text establishes its rules of repetition: it repeats a short series of messages, but not in a monotonous (or identical) way, through the different levels or categories of the texts (i.e. time, space, discursive material, myth, topics etc., depending on the nature of the text). These messages are generated in an abstract intratextual space that I name the 'Genotext'.

### Genotext and Phenotext

The genotext is a semiotic field that appears to be ordered but at the same time is torn and ruptured by 'ideological junctures'. It is made up of a combinatory system of genetic elements responsible for the global production of meaning and vectors of conflict. All these genetic elements function in a pluri-accentuated form, and I assume that these contradictions reproduce the contradictions of the social and ideological formations.

But the genotext does not exist in the text, where we deal only with the phenotexts. Materializing, or actualising, the genotext, the phenotexts appear in all categories of the text, with each category tearing and deconstructing the genotext according to the specific rules of its own functioning. The expression of time, for example, produces a result, an actualisation, very different from the actualisation operated by the expression of space. These terms do not refer to the notions of Julia Kristeva (Kristeva 1969, 280-283), but are borrowed from human geography. To understand what I mean, it is necessary to recall the notions of 'Phenotype' and 'Genotype'. The Mediterranean woman is a genotype, but she does not exist: all that exists are various women living on the different shores of the Mediterranean Sea, with similar characteristics. From (and by means of) these characteristics an abstract figure is elaborated.

The genotext is not exactly a structure, but it becomes a structure by constructing itself within the different phenotextual actualisations of the same text. In the phenotext, the ungrammaticalized enunciation of the genotext and the characteristics appropriate to a given level both operate in the framework of a signifying process to actualise in an apparently incoherent and fragmented way the semantic latencies of the same utterance: the genotext. This genotext exists only in this multiple and concrete actualisation – the Phenotext – and corresponds to an abstraction reconstituted by the analyst.

**Genotext and history**
In so far as the genotext is the way by which the text incorporates history, we can understand that the elements incorporated, in the form of strong contradictions, are the fundamental ones, which produce the future of a given society and constitute its more important stakes.

How does the Genotext operate? Where does it come from? Using a spatial metaphor, we may imagine the point of intersection of two axes, a vertical and a horizontal. On the first axis is the 'interdiscourse', which materializes both the mental structures and the ideological formations produced by a social formation. The discourse of time upon itself is read on this axis; in other words, interdiscourse translates into semiotic operations the socio-historical conditions in which a speaker is immersed.

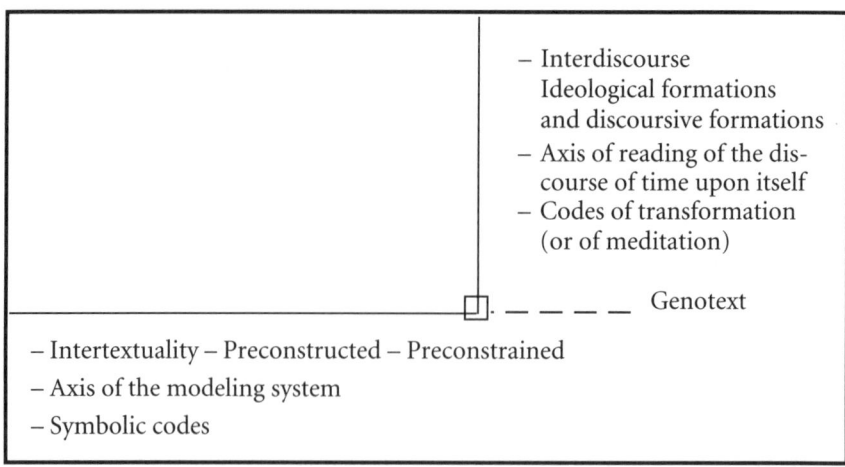

On the horizontal axis we find the intertext, (pre-asserted, pre-constructed, pre-constrained), i.e. all the linguistic material destined to give shape to meaning.

**What do I mean by interdiscourse?**
To explain what the term genotext means to me, I would like to recall two notions of Lucien Goldmann: the transindividual (collective) subject and the level of the no-conscious (Goldman 1966). At any moment of our lives each of us belongs to a series of collective subjects (generation, family, geographic origin, profession...). We pass through many of these various collective subjects in the course of our existence, and as we do so they bestow on us their social values and world vision by means of their specific discourses. Every transindividual subject inscribes in its discourse the indexes of its spatial, social and historical insertion, and consequently generates a specific microsemiotics.

The totality of the discursive material we use throughout our lives is made up of this mosaic of discourses. For this reason, the text selects its signs not within language but within the totality of semiotic expressions acquired/proposed by the collective subjects. This transindividual subject invests the individual consciousness of each individual participating in it by means of a specific microsemiotics, which transcribes in signs the totality of the aspirations, frustrations and vital problems of the group, providing a kind of "readout" of the ways each group is immersed. Reconstructing the microsemiotic level of the text enables us to reconstruct the social formation in which is the writer immersed.

Goldmann's notion of the transindividual subject calls for further precision insofar as it seems to operate for him only at the level of the implicit values of a literary work. That is why I sought to describe its effects in a more precise way, and tried to describe the levels where these indexes may be found. It seems to me that the most obvious traces are located on the paradigmatic axes, on the ready-made expressions and the 'lexies'. The way they become lexicalized transcribes social values systems. The changes that modify them transcribe modes of living and of socioeconomic insertions, the evolution of mental structures in the milieus producing them.

Now, how does the discourse of the transindividual subject function or operate? Goldmann distinguishes between three different levels of consciousness; to the first two (unconscious and alert consciousness) he adds the no-conscious. The no-conscious is a creation of the collective subject. It is different from the Freudian unconscious in that it is not repressed and therefore does not need to overcome resistance in order to become conscious, but it can only be brought to light through scientific analysis. Indeed, in reproducing the social and discursive practices of the collective subjects we are saying much more than we know or wish, and are thus usually reproducing the social values of different collective subjects. That is the space and the level of the genetic process that is of interest to sociocriticism. From this point of view we can better deal with the following basic issue: whilst the social and personal visibility of the writer is of very small extent, we assume that the visibility of the literary work is sometimes very large. How does the critic explain this difference? As far as I can see, the difference is the result of the functioning of the no-conscious.

As a matter of fact, beyond the field of social visibility proper, there extends another one, which is interiorized but not consciously responsible for the intratextual microsemiotics. These microsemiotic elements reproduce the social values of the different collective subjects to which the writer belongs. Relations with the world are neither perceived nor perceivable at the level of immediate experience. The different discourses and different types of behaviour appertaining to the subject always hold more meaning than the subject can know or wish to know. This supplement of meaning is stocked in the intratextual microsemiotics made up by and around the semiotic material of the no-conscious of the collective subject implied in the writing process. In making the semiotic system work in writing, the writer always says more than he or she understands and more than he or she apparently grasps.

In order to make this presentation more clear, I suggest a cursory glance at a text of the Spanish Golden Century, Mateo Alemán's picaresque novel *Guzmán de Alfarache*, edited between 1597 and 1604.

> *Conforme a lo cual*, siempre se tuvo por dificultoso hallarse un *fiel amigo y verdadero. Son contados, por escrito están* y lo más en fábulas, los que se dice haberlo sido. Uno solo hallé de nuestra misma naturaleza, el mejor, el más liberal, verdadero y cierto de todos, que nunca falta y permanence, siempre sin cansarse de darnos; y es la tierra.
> 
> Esta nos da las *piedras de precio*, el oro, la plata y más metales, de que tanta necesidad y sed tenemos. Produce la yerba, con que no sólo se sustentan los

ganados y animals de que nos valemos para cosas de nuestro servicio; mas juntamente aquellas medicinales, que nos conservan la salud y aligeran la enfermedad, preservándonos della. Cría nuestros frutos, *dándonos telas* con que *cubrirnos y adornarnos*. Rompe sus venas, brotando de sus pechos dulcísimas y misteriosas aguas que bebemos, arroyos y ríos que fertilizan los campos y facilitan los comercios, comunicándose por ellos las partes más extrañas y remotas. Todo nos lo consiente y sufre, bueno y mal tratamiento. A todo calla; es como la oveja, que nunca le oirán otra cosa que bien: si la llevan a comer, si a beber, si la encierran, si lo quitan el hijo, la lana y la vida, siempre a todo dice bien.

Y todo el bien que tenemos en la tierra, la tierra lo da. Ultimamente, ya después de fallecidos y hediondos, cuando no hay mujer, padre, hijo, pariente ni amigo que quiera sufrirnos y todos nos despiden, huyendo de nosotros, entonces nos ampara, regogiéndonos dentro de su proprio vientre, *donde nos guarda* en *fiel depósito*, para volvernos a dar en vida nueva y eterna. Y la mayor excelencia, la más digna de Gloria y alabanza, es que, hacienda por nosotros tanto, tan a la continua, siendo tan generosa y franca, que ni cesa ni se cansa, nunca repite lo que da ni lo zahiere dando con ello en los ojos, como lo hacen los hombres. (Alemán, c.f. Rico 1967, II. My italics.)

Insofar as my approach implies the necessity of taking into account the exact verbal materiality of the signs invested in the text, I will use the English translation of James Mabbe (1622-1623) to emphasise the linguistic differences.

And therefore (these things considered) it hath ever beene held one of the hardest and dificultest things in the world, to finde out a *true and faithfull friend*.

Of which sort, many are spoken of in ancient stories, and we finde a great number of them recorded of olde, and painted forth unto us in your feigned fables; but that there either now are, or have beene such heterofore as are there deciphered unto us, I doubt very much, at least I am fully perswaded, they were very *rare and few*. One only friend have I found to be true, and is of the same nature and condition, as we are. And this friend of ours, is the best, the bountifullest, the truest, and the faithfullest of all other; for this is never wanting to its friend, but continues firme and constant for ever, nor is at any time weary of giving: And this good friend of ours (that I may not hold you any longer in suspence) is the Earth.

This affords us *pretious stones*, gold, silver, and divers other metals, whereof we stand in need, and so earnestly thirst after. It bringeth forth grasse, and all sorts of herbes, wherewith are not only fed our flocks of sheepe, our cattell, and other beasts for the use and servise of man, but those medicinable simples, which conserve our health, free us from diseases, and if we fall into sicknesse, set us upright againe, preserving this life of ours, in a sound and perfect state of health. It yeeldeth us all sorts of fruits, that are either savourie to the taste, or nourishable to the bodie. *It gives us wooll, and flax, and by consequence, all kinde of woven stuffes, wherewith we cloath, and adorne*, this naked flesh of ours. It opens its owne veines of its owne accord, whilest from its full brests, sprout forth those sweet and delicate waters, which we drinke;

those brookes and rivers, which get the fields with childe, and make them friutfull, and not only that, but doth facilitate commerce, and make an easie way for trafficke, bringing the strangest and remotest parts of the world to shake hands, and to live in a league of love and friendship together. Nay more, it is so good, and so sweet a friend, that it suffereth, and willingly consenteth to all that we will our selves. Be shee well or ill used by us, all is one to her, so as we be pleased. Shee is like a sheepe, from whom you shall heare no other language, but *Omnia bene*: All is well. Leade her forth to feed, or bring her to the waters to drink; shut, and penne her up, or let her loose; take her lambkin from her, her milke, her wooll, nay her very life, to all shee always answers *bien*: all is well. And all that *bien*, or good that we have on earth, the Earth gives it us. And for an upshot of all, when we are now dead, and lye stinking above ground, when there is neither wife, father, sonne, kinsman, nor friend, that will abide and endure our companie any longer, but does all of them utterly forsake us, and flie from us; then, even then, doth not shee refuse us, but huggs us, and makes much of us, and opening her owne wombe, *takes us in unto her, where we quietly lye, as it were* **in deposito**, *till shee render afterwards a faithfull account of what shee hath received*, and delivers us up to a new and eternall life. And amongst many her other excellencies, one of the worthiest things in her, and deserving most commendation, is; That shee doing so much for us, as shee doth, and that so continually and without ceasing, being so generous, and so franke-hearted, that shee is never tyred out, never growes weary, yet doth shee not looke for any requital, shee neither askes, nor expects any returne of kindeness, nor doth shee talke and tell of it, not twit thee in the teeth with it; which some kinde of friends, more usually, then commendably, doe. (Mappe Part II, Book II, chapter 1. My italics).

First of all, let us briefly evoke the social formation in the Spanish Golden Century. If we wish to present a panorama of its various social interests, we will have to take note of the prosperous position of commerce and of the brotherhood of great cattle breeders, which regrouped in La Mesta. These came to the fore at the expense of the cloth-makers and the agricultural producers. The government of Charles V encouraged the exportation of the best wool to northern Europe and imported the cloth that Spain afterwards exported to *las Indias*. Thus, for example, it was permitted for cattle to pass through cultivated fields, thus ruining them. Aleman's text was written at the very moment when the flood of silver coming from America reached its maximum, generating a strong polemic opposing two systems of thought that have coexisted with and struggled against each other, the ideas concerning the role of gold and precious metals in a State's prosperity: is gold the "only sign of individual prosperity or of the greatness of a state? Or, on the contrary, is it the sign of the dissolution of true wealth, that consists only in the production of goods necessary for life?" (Vilar 1974, 192). From this point of view we can better understand the new contradiction opposing the production of agricultural and industrial goods to the accumulation of money (by means of commerce or the importation of precious metals) as the best way to create economic prosperity. As a matter of fact the interests of the cattle breeders are linked to trade and the bankers' activities.

The text examined is meant to praise the faithful and true friend who gives you all he possesses without asking for anything in return. It develops a commonplace, a *topos*: praise of the Earth's fecundity, the myth of the Golden Age, the life of early man when Nature gave its wealth spontaneously (Lucretius, *De natura rerum*). Man only has to reach out his hand to collect fruits. There is no need for work. This theme is loaded with the condemnation of exploration, by land or sea, for the sake of commercial gain and the acquisition of individual property. Effort, work, private wealth – such things are banished. Later, in Virgil's *Georgics*, another formulation of the myth appears, developing the idea that the Earth is fecund if it is well cultivated. This new formulation is linked to the notion of progress in agriculture being due to the beneficent intervention of the gods. The *Georgics* were written at the request of Maecenas, who thus gave support to Octavian's plan of reviving in the Roman people the ancient virtues of their race, especially the taste for agriculture. This theme creates at the heart of the former one a space of conflict, insofar as it translates the same notions (happiness and virtue) into contradictory figurative languages (effort vs. idleness – private property vs. collectivism). From the *De natura rerum* to the *Georgics*, the commonplace of the praise of the Earth changes from an atheistic discourse to an ethico-religious one in the service of a political project.

Aleman's text operates in the hollow of this commonplace. The honey and the wild fruits of the Latin descriptions have been omitted, and all that remains is the much more general form of 'fruit'. Four products are added: metals, grass, cloth, water. From *grass* to *cloth* and to *sheep*, a panegyric movement is constructed glorifying breeding. Let us observe what occurs with the concept of water, traditionally linked to that of life ("without water no man or any other animal can sustain life"). Here, however, its chief merit is to permit trade and communication between peoples most distant from each other. This perspective on overseas adventures, stressing the importance of international trade and animal breeding, reveals the point of view deconstructing the *topos*. The transgression of the interdiction of commerce observable in all the Latin texts occupies the entire textual space. *The commonplace is completely inverted.*

That is what makes the concision of "*dándonos telas*" (giving us clothes) remarkable: it erases all the process of material transformation. As a matter of fact neither the field of agriculture nor of industry is invested in the text. This absence, this gap, obviously reproduces the absences existing in the social formation between distinct historical times.

Let us now investigate the writing itself. On a first reading some phenomena of semantic and semiotic diffraction or deconstruction of set phrases can be observed:

1. The first concerns "*piedras de precio*" ('costly' stones in Mabbe's translation, and not the 'precious' stones corresponding to the ready-made expression, 'piedras preciosas'). On the original formulation has thus been superimposed the concept of the monetary exchange of valuable stones at the expense of the metaphorical virtuality of objects that would be estimable with respect to other criteria: emotional or aesthetic, for example.
2. In Mabbe's translation, the ready-made expression "*cubrir y abrigar*" (to clothe and to 'shelter') is altered to "*cubrir y adornar*" (to clothe and to 'adorn'). From being a product of the first necessity, 'cloth' becomes adornment, an index of social position, as much an object of covetousness as silver or gold.
3. A similar deconstruction appears in "*fiel amigo y verdadero*" (faithful and true friend). The usual formulation is: '*buen y verdadero amigo*' (good and true friend) The Spanish term *fiel* used in this text is very interesting, insofar it indicates for example a servant who 'does not rob' his master, and also designates the official who checks the weights and prices of goods in the markets.
4. "*Son contados*" (in English, literally, 'counted'). In the paradigmatic axis the more widely used adjectives are *raros, pocos, escasos* (rare, few...). In this paradigmatic axis the text selects a term obviously connoted in a similar way to the other examples mentioned.
5. But the most surprising deconstruction is offered with the expression: "*donde nos guarda en fiel depósito*" (in English, literally, 'where we are in a safe bank deposit'). The English translator understands the sentence very well and he develops it, explaining that the Spanish expression belongs to the vocabulary of banking.
6. We could add a series of set expressions from the vocabulary of commercial law (in dotted lines in the text published here) such as: "*conforme a lo cual*" ('according to'), "*por escrito estan*" ('set down in writing').

The semiotic material of the discourse is thus seen as a representation of the world of transaction with its activities, its values, its rules of behaviors and juridicial organization. Tracing in this manner the textual markers of a dominant discourse, it reveals the ideological system responsible for the deconstruction of the *topos*.

## Conclusion

The discourse invested in the text and operating as producer of the deconstruction is thus clearly brought into view: it is a discourse of a given collective subject, of the merchant and the merchant capitalism implying a definite historical time. This discourse generates the microsemiotic level that we have pointed out and constituted by the deconstructions of the ready-made expressions, which have been analysed. The discourse implies a fundamental value, the *exchange*, i.e. the contrary of the *gift*. While the writer claims that he is showing us the model of the perfect friend who gives all he owns without asking anything in return, the view of the world he reveals is obviously very contradictory. I can therefore define the major element of the genotext as the contradiction between *to give* and *to exchange*. This function is brought into view, at least in my analysis, in three levels or three phenotexts: the explicit theme (the total generosity of the faithful friend vs. the range of the verbal material used to describe it); the myth; and the discursive material in itself. A more detailed analysis brings into view more textual categories functioning in the same way: the religious problematic, for example, questioning the relations between human merit (an exchange between human acts and salvation) and the Holy Goodness of God, who grants us salvation without checking whether we merit it. Last but not least, I must mention the confessed social commitment of Mateo Aleman, who supports the reform of begging in Spain, pleading that we should give alms only to the poor who are not able to work. This new conception introduces the notion of merit, and consequently of exchange, in a contradictory way, because the traditional Catholic conception does not permit any limitation to charity. If we can credit a letter he wrote to a friend, Aleman composed his book in order to give his support to this social reform, which derived from the Protestant countries of Europe and gave rise to fierce polemic in Spain.

We can thus now better understand that the historical material invested in the genotext corresponds to the major stakes of a society at a given moment of its history, and can observe how the historical material is the vector of the textual production's dynamic process.

### References

Alemán, Mateo: 1987. *Guzmán de Alfarache*. Barcelona, Planeta.
Cros, Edmond: 1971. *Mateo Alemán: Introducción a su vida y obra*. Madrid, Anaya.
Cros, Edmond: 1988. *Theory and Practice of Sociocriticism*. Minneapolis, University of Minnesota Press.
Goldman, Lucien: 1966. *Sciences humaines et philosophie*. Paris, Gonthier.
Kristeva, Julia: 1969. *Semiotiké. Recherches pour une sémanalyse*. Paris Seuil.
Lucretius: 1937. *De natura rerum*. London, Heineman, Loeb Classical Library / Cambridge, Mass., Harvard University Press, 3rd edition (revised) pp. 406-407.
Rico, Francisco (ed.): 1967. *La novela picaresca*. Barcelona.
Vilar, Pierre: 1974. *Or et monnaie dans l'Histoire 1450-1920*. Paris, Flammarion.
Virgil: 1947. *Ecloges, Georgies, Aenid*. London, New York. Loeb Classical Library.

# The Construction and Deconstruction of Nation and Identity in Modern Belgium

by
Inge Degn, Lisbeth Verstraete Hansen,
Anne Magnussen, Jens Rahbek Rasmussen[1]

Introduction
Traditionally, the study of European languages and literatures has been organized in discrete departments, each of which studied one language, e.g. French, and the literature, culture and history of the nation chiefly associated with it, in this case France (rather than Belgium or Switzerland). However, recent decades have seen the field of study expand in several directions. Though the degree of hospitality shown to the new no doubt varies greatly from one university to the next, a language and literature department may now be expected to deal with colonial and postcolonial literature as well as with the multiculturalism of the metropolis; with mass literature and popular culture as well as with the traditional canon; and with cultural and social practices as well as with texts.

It is against this background that we offer a paper dealing critically with the national frame of reference in the study of foreign languages and literatures. We shall be examining concepts such as nation, state and identity from a range of disciplinary perspectives – linguistics, literature, history, and the social sciences – with a view to developing and testing a number of tools that can be used in various contexts. It is our hope that this may help us to identify, and with luck meet, some of the challenges to our fields of study which the current social, political, and cultural changes entail.

---

[1] The working group also had Gert Sørensen and Charlotte Werther as members and discussants.

In itself the case presented below may be said to exemplify the new openings that have characterized language and literature studies in recent decades. Belgium has attracted much attention, not all of it favourable, because of its bilingualism, and it is often seen as a 'problematic' nation. But we shall argue that Belgium is in fact rather typical of our times; it is one of an increasing number of countries comprising several competing languages, cultures, and identities, and both the creation of the Belgian state in 1830-31 and its reorganization as a federal state in 1970 reflect general European developments.

In the wave of nation states emerging in the 19th and early 20th centuries, the study of national history, literature, and culture was diligently pursued, contributing to what has later been termed "the construction of the national". The nation state as the focus of identity and political organization became the preferred, and rarely challenged, framework for both the internal organization and the international co-operation of the peoples. Towards the end of the 20th century, however, supra-national political co-operation on the one hand, and the resurgence of regional identities on the other, combined to challenge the monopoly of the nation state (already under pressure from economic globalization) as an organizational framework. One result of this was a massive theorization of concepts such as nation, identity, and culture (Anderson 1983, Gellner 1983, Hobsbawm and Ranger 1983, Hobsbawm 1990, Smith 1986).

In the context of this paper, the national historiography acquires importance in both cases. First it helps create and confirm the nation and (the changes in) the national identity; later it partakes in its deconstruction as new discourses and narratives are constructed or (re)invented. It is this rupture in the national narrative that will be discussed below on the basis of the Belgian example.

Following the Austrian linguist Ruth Wodak, a leading authority on critical discourse analysis, we assume that national identities, as special forms of social identities, are produced and reproduced, as well as transformed and dismantled, discursively (Wodak 1999, 3-4). If we are to speak of a nation, there must be a certain measure of common narrative identity[2] to be found across different communities and media. Belgium's existence as a nation is thus reflected in various discourses of history, politics, society, and literature, and not least the history of literature with its reflections on the contribution of the arts to the debate on problems of national identity. We analyze a few of these genres, partly because we regard them as especially useful in discussing issues of national identity, partly because they may open up for a debate on interdisciplinarity in the teaching of foreign languages and literatures.

---

[2] In this context the concepts and theories of narrative identity (Ricœur) and narration of the nation (Hall) seem of great interest, cf. below.

Analyzing the selected texts, we employ a concept inspired by the discourse-historical approach developed by Ruth Wodak and the Vienna School of Discourse Analysis; in the discussion of how the history of literature uses comics, obviously other methods and theories, not least from the field of visual analysis, must be added. Examining different kinds of texts should force us to consider which theories, methods or concepts may be used across the four strands of foreign language study (the linguistic, the literary-aesthetic, the cultural, and the historical-sociological), and to what degree it is possible or desirable to integrate these strands.

**Belgian identities**
Two factors in particular make Belgium seem 'unnatural' to foreign observers, and to many Belgians as well. Firstly, it became a sovereign state as a result of Great Power politics in 1831, apparently without the historical roots usually deemed necessary for a nation state. Secondly, the co-existence of two national languages, French and Dutch/Flemish (*nederlands*) makes it easy to label Belgium an artificial construction, which should be dissolved into its 'natural' nations, Flanders and Wallonia[3].

Before discussing these issues, it may be useful to look at the two main and apparently incompatible positions in the debate on nations and nationalism. The first position, 'primordialism', which prevailed among 19th century nationalists, assumes that nations go back at least to the early middle ages (Geary 2002), though for centuries most of them were suppressed by native or foreign kings and aristocracies. (An even more extreme version can be found in national histories, when e.g. the hunters who happened to leave the earliest traces somewhere in present-day Denmark are hailed as 'the first Danes'). For the second position, 'modernism', to which most post-1945 historians have subscribed, national identities are 'invented' or 'imagined' by 19th-century nationalist intellectuals who through education and the media managed to persuade the people to accept them.

Recently, however, several scholars have pointed out that the concept of peoples and nations predated 1789, if only because the European elites were steeped in the Bible and the classics, where both are met with frequently (Smith 1991, Hastings 1997, Ilsøe 1991). National identities predate mass nationalism, and the European nation states came into existence along different trajectories, deriving from:

---

[3] Strictly speaking German is also an official language, but its use is effectively limited to 75,000 speakers in the province of Eupen-Malmedy in eastern Belgium.

1. territorial, multinational states where one nation subsumed other ethnic or linguistic groups (France, Britain); here political continuity masks change and makes the nation state difficult to date;
2. 'cultural nations' which were unified politically c. 1870 (Italy, Germany);
3. dissolved multinational empires (e.g. Habsburg which divided into the core state of Austria and the peripheral states of Czechoslovakia, Yugoslavia etc. – usually comprising more than one nation, leading eventually to further splits).

Seen in this perspective, Belgium is an early example of a post-imperial peripheral nation state (cf. fig.1), which in 1831 split off from the Habsburg empire, just as the states in Central and Southern Europe would do after 1918, except that in the Belgian case the split was delayed by two rather coincidental and short-lived political unions with France 1794-1814 and the Netherlands 1815-1830.

The image of a particularly 'artificial' nation nevertheless haunted Belgians for many years. The state's survival was far from guaranteed, for in Belgium and abroad there were people both wanting and expecting it to reunite with either France ('Reunionists') or the Netherlands ('Orangists'). Maybe that was why Belgian nationalists were so eager to highlight Belgium's contributions to medieval Europe, not least in providing leaders for the crusades such as Godefroid de Bouillon, whose statue adorns Place Royale in Brussels (Morelli 1995b, 35-66; Koll 1998). But as pointed out above, Belgium is no more 'artificial' or 'constructed' than other nation states. If we take Anthony D. Smith's three key criteria for a nation – a historic territory, common myths and historical memories – Belgium easily fulfils them (Smith 1991, 14). All of the post-1713 Southern Netherlands is included in present-day Belgium, except for Dutch Limburg and the Grand Duchy of Luxemburg which in 1839 were detached (against the wishes of the inhabitants) from Belgium in exchange for the Dutch king's accept of the Belgian secession. Conversely, the important industrial area around Liège was an ecclesiastical state until the French occupation 1794-1814 united it with the Southern Netherlands (and administered the entire territory as a part of France).

Before 1713, parts of the Southern Netherlands had been ceded to the Dutch Republic (North Brabant) and France (Artois and southern Hainault, comprising the towns of Dunkerque, Arras and Lille.) The latter region had changed rulers regularly: ceded to the French king in 1312, it was restored to the Spanish Habsburgs in 1559 before reverting to France. It remained linguistically mixed for a long time: André Malraux's grandfather, a Dunkerque shipowner, spoke Flemish to his death in 1909 (Weber 1977, 81). Even the French-speaking inhabitants long retained a 'Southern Netherlands' identity; on the other hand, Louis XIV never ceased to regard the whole of Flanders as properly belonging to France (Collins 1999, 170-172, 186-189). But during the War of the Spanish Succession, the British and the Dutch managed to alienate the population, who had hailed them as liberators, "by behaving as though they were conquerors and exploiters". People accepted their new French identity and stuck to it, as the British and Austrians were to discover to their cost in 1792-94 (Lottin 1991; Parker 1977, 258).

Before the Dutch achieved their independence in the late 16$^{th}$ century, the Southern and the Northern Netherlands had been united under the Habsburgs – the 17 provinces of the Low Countries corresponding roughly to present-day Benelux – and before that, in the late 14$^{th}$ and 15$^{th}$ centuries, most of them had belonged to the Burgundian state, whose court basked in a last golden age of chivalry. It was in these centuries that the Flemish towns peaked, economically and culturally, and 'the Flemish school' of painters came to be regarded as proto-Belgians by the new state (Huizinga 1924).

The traditional interpretation of the 16$^{th}$-century split between the Northern and Southern Netherlands – that it was caused by the Calvinist reformation in the North, which the Catholic South refused to accept – was acceptable to both Dutch and Belgian historical writing: Holland saw themselves as the successors of the rebellious Protestants, Belgium of the loyal Catholics. But in fact it was not the religious differences that created the border, but vice versa (Geyl 1955, 211-233). The initial opposition to the Spanish Habsburgs in the 1560's spread all over the Netherlands, though the Calvinists were in a minority in the north as well as in the south. But the Spanish army, having successfully defeated the rebellion in the south, failed to do so in the north because of English intervention. A military frontier having been established, the Spanish counterreformation forced the Protestants to flee and take refuge in the north – an act of 'religious cleansing' which established the northern Netherlands, alias the Dutch Republic, as Protestant (albeit with a considerable Catholic minority in the areas that the Dutch regained after 1621), and the southern Netherlands as Catholic. Justus Lipsius was thus entirely justified in calling the Spanish general Alexander Farnese, Duke of Parma, 'the founder of Belgium' (*conditor Belgii*) (Parker 1977, 215; Lacrosse 1997, 16).

The Belgians did not regard the Spanish Habsburgs as foreign oppressors. Spanish seems to have been used as a polite language besides French at a time when most people, even in Brussels, spoke Flemish, something Voltaire later complained about. In 1713 they transferred their loyalty to the Austrian Habsburgs, at least as long as these respected the rights and privileges of the individual principalities, towns and estates; it was Joseph II's attempt to impose his reforms on Belgium that ignited the Brabant revolution in 1789-90 (Roegiers 1998, Vos 1998). The Belgian national anthem, *La Brabançonne*, which refers to centuries of slavery, ("Après des siècles d'esclavage / Le Belge sortant du tombeau..."), is thus an interesting example of identity construction through victimization (Stengers 1980, Morelli 1995a).[4]

On the other hand, the experience of the Southern Netherlands in the constant wars with Louis XIV and his successors had led to hostility towards France, exacerbated by the French occupation 1794-1814, and the fifteen years together with Holland created similar feelings towards that country. Whichever part of the country they came from, the Belgian elite were by 1830 francophone but anti-French. Attempts were made to create a literature which reflected *"l'âme belge"*. This meant a focus on Flemish history and culture, especially art, and this was true of both French and Flemish writers – Costers *Légende d'Ulenspiegel* (1867) and Henri Conscience's *De Leeuw van Vlaanderen* (1838) were seen as parallel efforts.

*Interpretations and Reinterpretations.*
The cultural/linguistic split between French and Flemish speakers from the late 19th century led to many reinterpretations of Belgian historical identity, most of them insensitive to the historical context. It was often overlooked that the Southern Netherlands had been divided into regions and principalities, with different linguistic regimes and national compositions. This political particularism prevailed into the 18th century: the Austrian rulers swore to respect the individual privileges of each region, though admittedly they also promised to keep the Southern Netherlands united.

Initially the Flemish movement only insisted on linguistic equality and the use of Flemish in education and the courts. The idea of political devolution came later, when Wallonia's economic dominance was broken; until c. 1960, industrialized Wallonia had been far more prosperous than rural Flanders (leading to a substantial labour migration from north to south). After the collapse of the iron, steel and coal industries, the situation was reversed, and there is today Flemish resentment at having to 'subsidize' Wallonia.

The linguistic development in Belgium is far from unique. In all nation states, the power elite created a standard national language. Those who did not speak it could choose between individual mobility and social action (Witte & Van Velthofen 1998, 15, 27). The speakers of Low German (and other German dialects) opted for mobility, accepting a common German identity and a standard language which relegated Low German to dialect

---

[4] The lines quoted do not appear in the two first versions of *La Brabançonne* from 1830-31, but only in the third revised version from 1860.

status; the Flemish-speaking Belgians chose social action and eventually mounted a successful challenge to the status of French.

As noted above, Belgium owed its existence as an independent state to Great Power politics, and arguably its origins – and its historical experience as the cockpit of European wars – gave Belgian nationalism a European touch. One of the major points of the seven-volume *Histoire de Belgique* by the great Belgian historian Henri Pirenne was that Belgium had always spanned the divide between Germanic and Romance Europe, building a bridge between the two cultural areas and (it was implied) combining the best elements of both. In that perspective the clash between *francophones* and *nederlandstalige* Belgians takes on added meaning. A national identity based on bilingual tolerance, and thus an example to Europe, is crumbling, and although little seems to indicate that Belgium will actually disintegrate in the foreseeable future, the constant Flemish demand for more autonomy is a real threat to the Belgian state, be it federal or con-federal[5]. Despite the seemingly clear-cut division between the two major communities, it is far from clear how a partition of the country could be realized. The Belgian federal institutions[6], which are the result of complicated and seemingly endless negotiations, are but one face of the coin, the other being the identities that are constructed, changed and deconstructed in this reconfiguration of the nation-state. So when the francophone Belgian historian Jean Stengers states that only Flanders is an authentic 'nation-in-waiting', whereas Wallonia merely qualifies as a linguistic community (Stengers 1990, 97), it must be understood in the context of this process of changing identities.

**Critical Discourse Analysis and the issue of nation and identity in Belgium**
National identities, as special forms of social identities, are produced, reproduced, as well as transformed and dismantled, *discursively* (Wodak, de Cillia, Reisigl and Liebhart 1999, 3-4).

The historians' writings provide us with information on the historical background of Belgium today, but they are themselves also part of the discursive construction of their object. The same is true for other academic disciplines; a particular area is the analysis of current issues in political science[7], which may become part of the political debate proper. In what follows we are firstly going to introduce a classification of Belgian histori-

---

[5] It should be stressed that many Flemish Belgians regret these developments. See Schaepdrijver 1993 and Reybeneau 1995.

[6] Devolution operates on two levels, into regions (Flanders/Brussels/Wallonia) and communities (Flemish/French/German-speaking).

[7] Two such texts were originally part of the corpus for the present discussion, but had to be left out for reasons of space.

cal writing reflecting the stages of the process that has led to the transformation of the Belgian state, secondly we will sketch out first an analysis of a historical article and then of a political manifesto.

The writing of history, at least in part, reflects developments and tensions in society. Henri Pirenne aimed in his writings to show that the Belgians belonged to a glorious nation with a proud past, and that national union preceded the political union; this can be seen as a response to the pressure put on the nation in the decades around 1900, not least by the development of the Flemish movement. The Belgian national identity reached its peak between 1900 and 1925, but in the thirties Flemish demands for cultural recognition were vigorously put forward. A distinct Flemish historiography emerged which rejected the idea of Belgium as a unitary state. From the seventies onwards, historians are less interested in what is shared than in differences, preferring to write the history of the component communities and regions; it is at this time that a specifically Walloon historiography emerges[8]. Belgium is again seen as an artificial construction, though this does not prevent a Belgian point of view from being still very much present.

The author of the statement quoted above, to the effect that Flanders is an authentic 'nation-in-waiting' whereas Wallonia only qualifies as a linguistic community, was the leading historian Jean Stengers, who died in 2002 at the age of eighty. On the cover of the last of his many books, the two-volume *magnum opus* on Belgian national feeling, *Histoire du sentiment national en Belgique des origines à 1918*, we read that "[1918] marks in fact the end of an epoch"[9], i.e. the epoch where the nation and the national sentiment went unchallenged (Stengers 2000, Stengers and Gubin 2002). On several occasions Stengers has addressed what he labels the reinterpretation of historical events, e.g. the different readings of what happened around the founding event of the Belgian state, the revolution in 1830. This is also the subject of his contribution to *Les Grands mythes de l'histoire de Belgique, de Flandre et de Wallonie* (Morelli 1995), which we shall subject to an analysis using the principles of Critical Discourse Analysis, more specifically the discourse-historical approach developed by Ruth Wodak and the Vienna School of Discourse Analysis (Wodak, de Cillia, Reisigl and Liebhart 1999; Wodak and Reisigl 2001a; Wodak and Reisigl 2001b; Wodak 2001).

---

[8] *La Wallonie, le pays et les hommes* (4 vol.), ed. By Rita Lejeune and Jacques Stiennon 1975-81, and *Histoire de la Wallonie*, ed. By L. Génicot, 1973 are early examples of this development.

[9] *Mais 1918 (…) marque réellement la fin d'une époque …*

*The discourse-historical approach.*
In Ruth Wodak et al., 1999, the historical-discursive approach is presented as an *interdisciplinary approach* [that] *combines historical, socio-political and linguistic perspectives in a methodologically pluralistic approach* [that uses] *various methods of data collection and the analysis of different sets of data – political speeches, newspaper articles, posters and brochures, interviews and focus groups (...)* [in order to get] *a detailed picture of an identity* [in various settings and] *to identify and contrast competing configurations of national identity as well as divergent narratives of identity.* It does so by taking into consideration as *context: linguistic co-text, extra-linguistic social and institutional* [*context*]*, and the intertextual og interdiscursive references in the text.* In their analyses Wodak et al. also draw on a number of theories and concepts, among them *narrative identity* (Ricœur 1990) and *the narration of the Nation* (Hall 1996). In other words, this framework presents an approach to issues of history and contemporary society based on pragmatic linguistic analysis, and which includes theories of narrative and narration (Ruth Wodak et al. 1999, 7-30).

A central element in the historical discursive approach is the analysis of strategies. Five strategies are specified, which can all be seen as part of 'positive self-representation' and 'negative other-representation', viz. 1) referential strategies or nomination strategies, 2) predicational strategies, 3) argumentation strategies and funds of topoi, 4) perspectivation, framing, or discourse representation by which speakers express their involvement in discourse and position their point of view in the report, description, narration, or quotation of events, 5) intensifying strategies/mitigation strategies (Wodak and Reisigl 2001a; Wodak and Reisigl 2001b; Wodak 2001). Below we shall subject two texts to an analysis using this model of strategies, Jean Stengers' article on the 1830 revolution and a contemporary political manifesto published on the Internet. The analysis further draws on a more comprehensive analysis of newspaper articles from the Belgian daily *Le Soir* (Degn in press).

*Jean Stengers' treatment of the 1830 revolution.*
An analysis of nomination (categorization) and predication (negative and positive traits) helps to identify how Stengers himself views the 1830 revolution and how he views alternative interpretations. Stengers characterizes the 1830 revolution as national and liberal; it was made against a foreign power, the Netherlands, and it was caused by the perceived lack of civic rights for Belgians. Stengers' account stresses the shared and unifying elements of the revolution, while at the same time blotting out or denying the differences between linguistic groups, regions and classes. Now this story of fundamental harmony has been challenged by a range of alterna-

tive narratives, emphasizing the very differences that Stengers played down. The Walloons emphasize their role in the event and stress their Frenchness, referring to the importance of 'reunionism' (the irredentist movement for reuniting with France) in 1830. The Flemings for their part disclaim any participation in the revolution, without however showing the slightest sympathy for the 'Orangist' position (that is, a continued union with the Netherlands). Marxist readings emphasize the economic and social aspects. Finally the artificial character of the nation is stressed by those who do not believe in its survival. Stengers points to a number of quotations from between 1983 and 1994, all of which construct differences and underline the artificiality of the state. In his view, 'authentic history' (Stengers' own term) has been undermined by the repeated use of discourses that he characterises as 'deviant'[10].

Stengers argues that although the divisions and differences stressed by these alternative narratives were undoubtedly present in 1830, they were of no importance; only after 1900 were they 'resurrected' and magnified out of all proportion[11]. Stengers strongly refutes the 'myth' that Flemings and Walloons were united against their will in 1830, and denies that there was anything remotely resembling two peoples at the time. In other words, he defends an interpretation stressing the national unity of Belgium and exposes what he regards as the 'mythical' claims of Walloons and Flemings.

In the final point of his discussion of the artificiality of the state, Stengers makes an interesting move. Until now, he says, he has been speaking as an historian, and therefore avoided taking sides on a political issue. He thus posits a contrast between the scholarly character of his analysis and an openly political judgement, regarding the issue whether a state that unites populations with different languages is necessarily artificial[12]. He does answer the question, however, albeit implicitly, for he refers first to Switzerland and then to Alsace being French. His implicit argument draws on the topos of the opposing concepts of *Kulturnation* and *Staatsnation*, with an intertextual reference to Ernest Renan's famous speech on the nation: "Qu'est-ce qu'une nation?" (1882), where these concepts are theorized. Renan's speech underlines the peoples' will (in this case the Alsatians') against the 'German' concept of a nation built on language, race, soil and blood, obviously implying that the *Kulturnation* is bad and the political

---

[10] *Ces dérives par rapport au 1830 de l'histoire ne sont certes pas générales – et même loin de là – , mais, en gros, on a le sentiment que la dérive se fait beaucoup plus fréquente que l'histoire authentique* (Morelli 1995, 146).

[11] For a more thorough treatment see Stengers and Gubin 2002.

[12] *(...) qu'un Etat ne peut être qu'artificiel lorsqu'il réunit des populations de langues différentes* (Morelli 1995, 146).

*Staatsnation* is good[13]. What one perceives here is an argumentation in favour of the Belgian nation state by means of a topos.

This may help to explain Stengers' views of Belgian, Flemish and Walloon national sentiment. Clearly Belgium is his frame of reference and identification, whereas he does not recognize Wallonia nor a Wallonian claim for a particular identity. As a predicational strategy his statement can be seen as a backgrounding of Wallonia, which gives priority to the nation proper, Belgium. His argument further implies that the nation state can accommodate Flanders, although obviously this also depends on the willingness of the Flemish to be part of that state.

*The Brussels Manifesto.*
The distinction between the *Kulturnation* and the *Staatsnation* is also central in the next text, *Le manifeste bruxellois*, published in the spring of 2003 (www.manifestobru.be). The text is a manifesto aimed at gathering the citizens of Brussels for a cause, securing greater liberty of action for Brussels through certain institutional changes, and inviting dialogue. These changes are meant to benefit the region of Brussels and the people living there. The sender presents itself as a cross-party, almost 'unpolitical' group. The present analysis concentrates on the introduction to the manifesto and its conclusion, with the heading: "The creation of a Brussels Community"[14].

By its extensive use of nominalisation and the passive, and similar forms of occultation of the agent, the text is made to appear as rather neutral. It advocates a specific view and a political agenda: the abolition of the division in linguistic communities and the adoption instead of multicultural future-oriented institutions[15]. It contrasts, by means of referential and predicational strategies, a negative division of the country based on communitarian (cultural and linguistic) arguments with a positive multilingual and multicultural vision for Brussels. It is not specified who is responsible for the partition, though some adversary is implied; the authors for their part, at the very end of the text, refer to themselves as a 'we' who intend to promote 'democratic debate'[16]. The argumentation is supported

---

[13] Cf. also Gubin in Stengers and Gubin 2002, 121. The authoritative use of Renan here is interesting in comparison with the judgement expressed by Wodak and al., 1999.

[14] *La création d'une "Communauté bruxelloise".*

[15] *l'abandon du clivage bi-communautaire et l'adoption d'une conception multiculturelle tournée vers l'avenir de ces institutions.*

[16] *Plusieurs solutions existent sans doute pour répondre aux besoins des Bruxellois et elles devront être précisées dans le cadre du **débat démocratique** sur l'avenir de Bruxelles **que nous entendons promouvoir*** (emphasis added).

by the use of flag words (besides 'democratic', words like 'multilingual', 'multicultural', 'future'), while their opposites are not made explicit except for the words 'bi-communitarian' and, later, 'communitarian'[17], which in this context must be seen as a stigma word that is implicitly coupled with the past. In a further perspective this must be seen as part of a positive self-representation and a negative other-representation. The neutral and objective style can be seen as a mitigation strategy, aiming at avoiding accusations of 'the other', accusations that are still present anyway in the predications of the state of affairs.

Of the culturally based bi-partition it is said that this is no longer appropriate[18]. The indication that it is time to pass on contains an intertextual reference, viz. to a political statement dating from 1970, when the process of federalisation and the dismantling of the Belgian State took off. Gaston Eyskens, Prime Minister 1968-1972, was reported to have said: "'The old Belgium' [*La Belgique de papa*] has passed away"[19]. He himself strongly denied ever having said this: "I never pronounced the old Belgium dead. What I said was that the unitary state and its structures and functions as defined by law, had been overtaken by reality"[20]. The intertextual reference seems to imply rather strongly the need for changing the institutions, and probably also contains a hint that it is pay-back time.

Quite surprisingly considering the rejection of the division in communities, the manifesto ends with a proposal to create a Brussels Community, but stresses that this should be essentially multilingual and multicultural[21]. The vision outlined in the conclusion would be a combination, a merging of the political-territorial region and the linguistic-cultural community. It can be seen as an attempt to transcend the logic under accusation with its loss of 'identity-distance', as "hybrid, multicultural identities represent a

---

[17] *le partage progressif du pays sur des bases communautaires.*

[18] *Ce clivage est maintenant dépassé par les faits.*

[19] *La Belgique de papa a vécu.*

[20] *Je n'ai jamais declaré que la Belgique de papa était morte. J'ai dit que l'Etat unitaire, tel que les lois le régissaient encore dans ses structures et dans son fonctionnement, était dépassé par les faits* (André Mean 1989, 11).

[21] *Dans cet esprit, en plus des suggestions émises dans les points qui précèdent, nous proposons la création d'une "Communauté bruxelloise". Une telle institution permettrait notamment de soutenir un enseignement multilingue, des activités interculturelles, des services publiques et des médias bruxellois multilingues. Elle permettrait de simplifier le paysage institutionnel bruxellois en reprenant l'ensemble des compétences communautaires à Bruxelles. Enfin, la création de cette institution entraînerait une révision des aspects de nos structures fédérales trop exclusivement centrés sur les deux grandes communautés.*

potential corrective element which can counteract the practices of exclusion and differentiation." (Wodak et al. 1999, 17).

Our analysis of these texts has identified several competing configurations of national identity in Belgium, as well as the ever ongoing effort to find new solutions to the problems of modern society, which also imply the construction of new narrative identities. Stengers and the authors of the Brussels Manifesto represent extreme positions on a scale going from unity to plurality, from a uniting of differences under a shared identity to a common organization allowing for a multiplicity of hybrid identities.

**The construction of identity in comics and histories of literature**
Thus (political) historians contributed first to the construction of national identity in the nineteenth century, and then to its deconstruction in the twentieth. We find a similar logic in the writing of Belgian histories of literature, and this similarity points to the significance of narrative as one of the key concepts capable of building bridges – within a constructivist framework – between the different components of language studies. The discussion here differs from the former examples by having as its point of departure other kinds of material, namely histories of literature and comic strips, which require additional concepts and analytical frameworks.

In general, the nineteenth-century paradigm of literary history involved an explicit contribution to the creation of national identity, complementary to the efforts of political history. The paradigm was based on the idea of the nation as a unity in terms of language, politics and culture, the nation being constituted by its territory and, most often, by a common language. It aimed at establishing a canon of those literary works that most fully expressed the specific characteristics of the nation. The history of national literature was the story of the literary development leading towards a perfected expression of the national spirit. Within these overall delimitations, authors and texts were divided into periods, often based on historical events. These periods were again subdivided into movements, trends or schools based on the predominant aesthetics, as well as into the main genres of poetry, drama, narrative prose and essay. The underlying premiss of this kind of history of literature is that there is a direct, unmediated reference between literature and society, fiction and reality, text and context (cf. Perkins 1992).

But the writing of a history of Belgian national literature was, and is, complicated because the linguistic differences seem to question the idea of national unity. It is therefore unsurprising that most of the histories of literature begin by reflecting on what their very object is and how it should be named – Belgian literature in French or French literature from Belgium.

The 1980's saw the beginning of a particularly thorough rewriting of histories of literature, inspired by the contemporary restructuring of the

Belgian state. Especially influential were those articles and histories of literature which took up Marc Quaghebeur's hypothesis that *déshistoire* was a national characteristic of the French-speaking Belgians (Quaghebeur 1982), the concept of *déshistoire* referring both to the Belgian reality and to the representation of this reality. Quaghebeur argues that the national historiography is a permanent falsification as it builds upon the assumption that the two language communities are willing to share the same idea of Belgian identity, something which political developments in the 20th century seem to belie[22]. This kind of historiography sees national identity as existing in reality, whereas according to Quaghebeur it is nothing but a construct, a fiction that should now be replaced by another, more appropriate construct.

A central plank in Marc Quaghebeur's argument is the special relationship between the francophone Belgians and French. The French language is supposed to express a particularly clear and logical vision of the world, which contrasts sharply with the complex Belgian reality. This has made it even more difficult for the French-speaking Belgians to understand and describe their own history. Further he argues that the uneasy relationship between language, history and reality has brought forward a kind of 'irregular' literature. This label, *les irréguliers,* encourages greater tolerance and flexibility within the literary field by admitting such genres (until recently regarded as illegitimate) as crime novels, *chansons* and comic strips, where French-speaking Belgium, with names like Georges Simenon, Jacques Brel and Hergé, has a lot to offer (Halen 1998). The concept of *les irreguliers* is furthermore characterised by a privileged relationship between word and image, which Quaghebeur sees exemplified in a direct line from the founding text of French-language literature, *La Légende d'Ulenspiegel* (1867), via the surrealists and the logogrammes of the *Cobra* poet Christian Dotremont to the comics[23].

Thus, with the introduction of the concept of *déshistoire,* several Belgian literary historians become part of a deconstruction, rather than a construction, of the historical context of the national literature. This new history of literature revolves around such concepts as rupture, negative identity and heterogeneity, and establishes itself by continuous opposition

---

[22] (...) *la perception de l'histoire, passée comme présente, paraît en Belgique plus particulièrement tronquée que dans nombre de pays occidentaux. La mythologie développée par l'histoire officielle n'est jamais devenue un véritable support de la conscience collective parce qu'elle oublia que tout mythe se fonde quelque part dans un réel – lequel suppose un usage précis du langage* (Quaghebeur 1982, 14).

[23] *Entre texte et image, les lettres belges ne cessent de développer un rapport original. C'est une de leurs réponses les plus profondes et les plus singulières au drame de la langue vécue comme norme et comme absence de corps matriciel* (Quaghebeur 1990, 26).

to the very pillars of the French identity model – continuity and homogeneity – and not least to the universalist discourse implied in the use of the French language.

It must be pointed out, though, that even if the *content* of this kind of history of literature differs radically from its predecessors, its narrative *form* and its identity-creating *function* do not. When the national identity is being dissolved and needs to be replaced by a post-national or regional identity, which for a great part may only be formulated negatively, this negativity is legitimized by historical references in precisely the same way as in the traditional histories of literature, except that in this case the references are to the alleged artificiality of the creation of the state. In the new histories, Belgian literature is seen as a mirror of the national/regional *désidentité*, partly because of its peculiarities of form and genre, partly because in its content a certain *de-belgification* – the authors avoid or evade a clear reference to Belgium – is claimed to be a direct and observable manifestation of *déshistoire*.

The discourse analysis approach of Ruth Wodak and her co-authors makes it possible to identify some of the strategies used by the Belgian researchers in their construction of a post-national identity for the French-speaking Belgians. This new narrative of national Belgian literature from the 1980s onwards may also, however, be approached differently, and one possibility is to look more closely at how the new narrative is documented. As mentioned above, a specific way of including images is now seen as a characteristic of national literature. Comic strips is one of the genres often used as documentation of the 'irregular' characteristics of Belgian literature in French, and in certain cases also more specifically of the *de-belgification* – or decontextualization – of this literature.

The comic strip *Tintin au Congo* could be used as an example of the latter, primarily due to the fact that in the revised 1946 edition of the strip, a series of specific references to Belgium present in the 1931 edition had been removed. Based on these modifications, one could take the strip to prove the argument of the Belgians' uneasy relationship to concepts such as history, language, reality and identity. Within this perspective, *Tintin au Congo* supposedly documents the negation or impossibility of a Belgian affiliation, and the protagonist (Tintin) appears as the de-nationalised hero incarnate, moving in a de-historicized and universal environment with no reference to any specific point in time or space[24].

---

[24] Tintin has often been described in this way: "(…) Tintin and Maigret seem to go through walls and move in time without leaving any trace. Instead of growing old they seem to remain unchangeable. Neither do they seem to have any sexual problems. I wonder whether we do not witness with this a negation of any kind of division? Tintin and Maigret are apolitical persons. The author hides – or neutralizes – his philosophy of life underneath a general morale that

We shall try to demonstrate why the use of *Tintin au Congo* as documentation for the *irregularité* and decontextualization of French Belgian literature implies both an oversimplified view of the genre of comic strips, with its original combination of writing and drawing, and a deliberate effort to ignore the context of the comic: its reception and circulation in society, its history including references to the genre and the aesthetics of comic strips in an international context. By using a broad framework of concepts and analytical tools, it is possible to offer a more convincing and subtle analysis of the ways in which comic strips such as *Tintin* can be seen as part of the construction and/or deconstruction of national identities.

*"Tintin au Congo", perspectives for an analysis.*
*Tintin au Congo* was first published in 1931 in the Belgian daily newspaper *Le vingtième siècle*, where the weekly supplement for children "Le petit Vingtième" carried two pages each week. However, the coloured version of the story published in 1946, and unchanged in later editions, is far better known, and it is of specific interest here due to the changes made concerning Tintin and his Belgian identity.

Several changes and deletions were made from the 1931 edition to the one of 1946 (Tintin.com 2003). A specific example is to be found on the last page of the story where Tintin's identity is changed from Belgian to European. However, the example that is quoted most often is the sequence where Tintin is teaching a group of Congolese pupils at a Catholic mission. In the 1931 edition he teaches history with a specific reference to Belgium as the fatherland of the pupils[25]. This is replaced by a maths class in the 1946 edition[26].

At first sight, these examples may seem to support the argument that *Tintin au Congo* documents a decontextualization of Belgian literature and thus exemplifies the phenomenon of *déshistoire*. Several objections may

---

in many ways refers back to interwar Belgium. The country that would have liked not to carry the scars of history, and that dreamt of escaping socially related political conflicts, developed a social system that should help avoid this kind of conflict. Had it not been the world's richest colony? Should it not be possible to become a welfare paradise? Tintin, who rights all wrongs, and Maigret, the ordinary man's police inspector, are products of a subtle denial that allows people to move openly through history. In this way, their creators avoid taking refuge in the countless mediations that their colleagues of the fine literary arts find obligatory." (Quaghebeur 1993, 53. Our translation)

[25] *Mes chers amis, je vais vous parler aujourd'hui de votre patrie: La Belgique!...* (Peeters 1990, 31).

[26] *Nous allons commencer, si vous le voulez bien, par quelques additions. Qui peut me dire combien font deux plus deux? ... Personne? ...Voyons, deux plus deux? ... Deux plus deux égalent?...* (Hergé 1962, 36).

legitimately be raised, however[27]. The first concerns the way in which this interpretation separates the visual and the verbal elements of the comic strip. The implication that the 'Belgiumness' of the story relies on the verbal references alone is a consequence of this separation, which ignores the complex ways in which words and images interact within the narrative form of the comic[28].

The field of semiotics has long had a prominent position within language studies. Semiotics, both in C.S. Peirce's version and in de Saussure's 'semiology', may serve as an interesting point of departure for the discussion of the comic strips form, and more specifically, in the case of *Tintin au Congo*, of the consequences of removing the verbal references to Belgium. Especially the concepts of icon, index and symbol, which are part of C.S. Peirce's definition of the sign relation, are useful for describing the way in which image and writing interact. In the case of the class given by Tintin, a more complete analysis would include the symbolic or conventional characteristics both of the relationship between teacher and pupil and of the narrative of which the specific scene is part. The indexical character of the scene in question would include both the narrative context of the scene and the context in which the comic strip album is produced and interpreted. The latter leads to a further objection to seeing *Tintin au Congo* as documentation of a decontextualization of Belgian literature. From a semiotic point of view (C.S. Peirce), the comic strip album is necessarily always interpreted within a specific context of both space and time. This means that the analysis of the album, as well as of the genre which it belongs to, will have to include the history of the comic strip or of the genre.

Comic strips have undergone a whole range of modifications, ruptures and ramifications in terms of both genre and aesthetics. From the seventies an adult audience was added to the traditional children's audience. Furthermore, comic strips have been included in the deconstruction, or at least the questioning, of oppositions such as high and low culture and of the postmodern in the broadest possible sense. The history of the comic strip, as well as that of the *Tintin* series, differs very much from that of fifty years ago. Banal though this may sound, it helps draw attention to the importance of stating the precise context within which a comic strip such as *Tintin au Congo* may serve as documentation for a specific trend or idea within literary history. For instance, Tintin and his universe frequently appear in intertextual references in other comic strips, and the graphic style that Hergé came to represent, *la ligne claire*, has been reproduced and

---

[27] One objection which we cannot pursue here is obviously that the change is related to the strongly anti-colonial mood in the early post-war years.

[28] For recent discussions of this issue see e.g. Varnum and Gibbons 2001.

modified over time. At least from the 1980s readers of comic strips were, in the words of Jim Collins, sophisticated semioticians capable of seeing through manipulation and stereotypes as well as of establishing and interpreting intertextual references in ways that were not characteristic for earlier comics audiences (Collins 1991).

In the specific case it should be argued that *Tintin au Congo* 2003 differs greatly from *Tintin au Congo* 1946 when context, reception and history are taken into account. There is a series of possible theoretical and methodological frameworks for the analysis of a comic strip such as *Tintin au Congo* as part of a specific context. Combining familiar concepts such as genre, context, aesthetics, style, fiction and non-fiction with one of the several versions of discourse analysis and/or sociological method enables us to analyze histories of literature and the ways in which they are documented. Thus there is a clear potential within the existing framework of language studies for the present type of interdisciplinary approach to the study of nation and identity.

The impossibility of using the figure of *Tintin* as documentation for the decontextualization of Belgian literature lends support to the argument that the new literary histories from the 1980s onwards are not substantially different from their predecessors in terms of constructing a narrative of Belgian literature. In this sense the analysis of comic strips also partakes in the overall discussion in the present article concerning the construction and deconstruction of Belgian national identities.

## Perspectives

Our paper has tried to utilize approaches, theories and methods from different disciplines in analyzing a specific area. The essentially constructivist perspective which we have adopted most certainly does not render a thorough knowledge of the area and its history redundant; on the contrary, such knowledge is indispensable for the very discussions made possible by the combination of different approaches. Our main aim has been to show how the perspectives that we have selected may enable students to apply their critical and analytical skills to a field where ready-made solutions or 'correct' opinions are not available, and we have tried to provide a particularly clear illustration of this by choosing a field where national and academic traditions clash, and where key concepts such as nation and identity are in a state of flux.

## References

Anderson, Benedict: 1983. *Imagined Communities. Reflections on the Origin and Spread of Nationalism*. London, Verso.

Collins, James B.: 1999. "State-building in Early Modern Europe: The Case of France". In: Victor Lieberman (ed.), *Beyond Binary Histories: Re-imagining Eurasia to c. 1830*. Ann Arbor, University of Michigan Press.

Collins, Jim: 1991. "Batman: The Movie, Narrative: The Hyperconscious". In: R. Pearson & W. Uricchio (eds.), 2001, *The Many Lives of the Batman*. BFI Publishing.

Degn, Inge: in press. "Identity Discourse and the Construction of Images". Conference paper at Images 2002, Aalborg University.

Deprez, K. & L. Vos (eds): 1998. *Nationalism in Belgium: Shifting Identities, 1780-1995*. London, Palgrave.

Geary, Patrick: 2002. *The Myth of Nations: The Medieval Origins of Europe*. Princeton, NJ, Princeton University Press.

Gellner, Ernest: 1983. *Nations and Nationalism*. Oxford, Blackwell.

Génicot, L. (éd.): 1973. *Histoire de la Wallonie*.

Geyl, Pieter: 1955. "The national state and the writers of Netherlands history". In: *Debates with Historians*. London, Fontana.

Halen, Pierre: 1998. "Primitifs en marche. Sur les échanges intercollectifs à partir d'espaces mineurs". In: *Identités en mutation. Socialités en germination*, B. Jewsiewicki et J. Létourneau (dir.), *Les Nouveaux Cahiers du CELAT*. Ed. Septentrion.

Hall, Stuart: 1996. "The Question of Cultural Identity." In: S. Hall, D. Held, D. Hubert & K. Thompson (eds.), *Modernity: An Introduction to Modern Societies*. Cambridge, Cambridge University Press; 595-634.

Hastings, Adrian: 1997. *The Construction of Nationhood: Ethnicity, Religion and Nationalism*. Cambridge, Cambridge University Press.

Hergé: 1962. *Tintin au Congo* (1946). Casterman.

Hobsbawm, Eric: 1990. *Nations and Nationalism since 1780. Programme, Myth, Reality*. Cambridge, Cambridge University Press.

Hobsbawm, Eric & Terence Ranger (eds): 1983. *The Invention of Tradition*. Cambridge, Cambridge University Press.

Huizinga, Johan: 1924. *The Waning of the Middle Ages*. (Reprinted. 1984, St. Martins Press)

Ilsøe, Harald: 1991. "Danskerne og deres fædreland. Holdninger og opfattelser ca. 1550-1700". In: O. Feldbæk (ed.), *Dansk identitetshistorie*, vol. 1. Copenhagen, C.A. Reitzel; 27-88.

Koll, Johannes: 1998. "Belgien : Geschichtskultur und nationale Identität". In : Monika Flacke (ed.), *Mythen der Nationen*. Berlin, Koehler & Amelang.

Lacrosse, J.M.: 1997. "La Belgique telle qu'elle s'ignore". *Le Débat*, no. 49; 12-41.

Lejeune, Rita & Jacques Stiennon (eds.): 1977-81. *La Wallonie. Le pays et les hommes*.

Lottin, Alain: 1991. "Louis XIV and Flanders". In: M. Greengrass (ed.), *Conquest and Coalescence: The Shaping of the State in Early Modern Europe*. London, Edward Arnold.

Mean, André: 1981. *La Belgique de papa*. Bruxelles, Politique & Histoire.

Morelli, Anne : 1995a. "La construction des symboles « patriotiques » de la Belgique, de ses régions et de ses communautés". In: A. Morelli: 1995b; 191-204.

Morelli, Anne (ed): 1995b. *Les grands mythes de l'histoire de Belgique, de Flandre et de Wallonie*. Brussels, Editions Vie Ouvrière.

Parker, Geoffrey: 1990. *The Dutch Revolt*. Harmondsworth, Penguin.
Peeters, Benoît : 1990. *Le monde d'Hergé*. Casterman.
Perkins, David: 1992. *Is Literary History Possible?* Baltimore & London, The Johns Hopkins University Press.
Quaghebeur, Marc: 1982. "Balises pour l'histoire de nos lettres". In: *Alphabet des lettres belges*. Brussels, La Promotion des lettres.
Quaghebeur, Marc: 1990. "Belgique: Une littérature qui n'ose pas dire son nom". *Écriture*, no. 36, Lausanne.
Quaghebeur, Marc: 1993. *National eller regional identitet. Om Belgiens franskprogede litteratur*. Oversat og bearbejdet af Ole Wehner Rasmussen. Copenhagen, Akademisk Forlag.
Reybeneau, Marc de: 1995. *Het klauwen van de leeuw: De Vlaamse identiteit van de 12de tot de 21ste eeuw*. Leuven, Van Halewyck.
Ricœur, Paul: 1990. *Soi-même comme un autre*. Paris.
Roegiers, Jan: 1998. "Belgian liberties and loyalty to the House of Austria". In: K. Deprez & L. Vos (eds): 1998; 23-32.
Schaepdrijver, Sophie de: 1993. "België als idee". In: G. van Istendael (ed), *Het nut van België*. Amsterdam/Antwerpen, Atlas; 83-106.
Smith, Anthony D.: 1986. *The Ethnic Origins of Nations*. Oxford, Blackwell.
Smith, Anthony D.: 1991. *National Identity*. Harmondsworth, Penguin.
Stengers, Jean : 1990. "Belgian national sentiment". In: R. Bryssinck (ed.), *Modern Belgium*. Brussels, Modern Belgium Association.
Stengers, Jean: 1980. "Belgian national sentiments". In : A. Lijphart (ed) : *Conflict and Coexistence in Belgium: The Dynamics of a Culturally Divided Society*. Berkeley, University of California Press; 46-60.
Stengers, Jean & Éliane Gubin: 2002. *Historie du sentiment national en Belgique des origines à 1918. Le grand siècle de la nationalité belge*. Brussels.
Tintin.com. http://www.tintin.be/ 22.07.03.
Varnum, Robin & Christina Gibbons (eds.): 2001. *The Language of Comics. Word and Image*. Jackson, University Press of Mississippi.
Vos, L.: 1998. "The two Belgian revolutions". In: K. Deprez & L. Vos (eds); 33-41.
Weber, Eugen: 1977. *Peasants into Frenchmen: The Modernization of Rural France, 1870-1914*. New York, Stanford University Press.
Witte, Els & Harry Van Velthofen: 1998. *Taal en politiek: De Belgische casus in een historisch perspectief*. Brussels, VUB Press.
Wodak, Ruth & Martin Reisigl: 2001a. "Discourse and racism". In: D. Schiffrin, D. Tannen & H. Hamilton, *The Handbook of Discourse Analysis*; 372-397.
Wodak, Ruth & Martin Reisigl: 2001b. *Discourse and Discrimination. Rhetorics of Racism and Antisemitism*. London, Routledge.
Wodak, Ruth: 2001. "The discourse-historical approach". In: R. Wodak & M. Meyer (eds): 2001. *Methods of Critical Discourse Analysis*. London.
Wodak, Ruth, Rudolf de Cillia, Martin Reisigl & Karin Liebhart: 1999. *The Discursive Construction of National Identity*. Edinburgh.
www.manifestobru.be/

# Construction Grammar and Second Language Acquisition:

## A Cognitive Understanding of Language in a Contrastive Perspective

by

Johan Pedersen & Teresa Cadierno

Introduction
Our previous research in the areas of Spanish grammar and second language acquisition (= SLA) respectively is theoretically positioned in various ways in relation to Cognitive Linguistics. With regard to SLA, the adoption of the Cognitive Linguistics framework (e.g. Langacker 1987/91; Goldberg 1995; Talmy 1985; Croft 2001; Tomasello 1998) is a relatively new approach. Similarly, SLA has only recently been an object of study in cognitive linguistic research. Cognitive linguistics thus represents an obvious potential for interdisciplinary work in Modern Language Studies: the application of basic cognitive linguistics principles may throw light on a number of issues within SLA. In particular, it offers a theoretical framework for contrastive studies that enables research into how the construction of semantic structures in the first language (L1) and the foreign language (e.g. L2) is related to general human cognitive capacity, and to the cultural behavior that characterizes the L1 and L2 user. On the other hand, the study of SLA may provide some very interesting data for testing hypotheses concerning the formation of grammar in a language formulated in the cognitive linguistic framework.

The aim of this paper is twofold: (a) to outline the overall role of Cognitive Linguistics in the study of language and culture and its implications for the study of Second Language Acquisition (SLA); and (b) to discuss the reciprocal contributions of Cognitive Linguistics and the study of adult SLA. Specifically, we will present some concrete cases of research to demonstrate how cognitively-based contrastive analyses of learners' first and second languages can be fruitful for foreign language studies.

The paper is divided as follows: First we will outline the role of culture in Cognitive Linguistics. In the next section we will discuss Cognitive Linguistics as a common ground for usage-based frameworks, and the implications for the study of SLA. Subsequently, we will look more closely at the reciprocal contributions of Cognitive Linguistics and SLA, and present some cases of recent research. Finally we will briefly discuss some pedagogical implications of the Cognitive Linguistics Framework.

**The role of culture in Cognitive Linguistics**
The cultural dimension of language has always been an important issue for Cognitive Linguistics (e.g. Palmer 1996; Langacker 1999b). One of the basic, and more philosophical, questions for cognitive linguists has been: How do individuals categorize entities in the world? Or more specifically, how are similar phenomena categorized in different cultures? In fact, one of the basic claims in cognitive linguistics is that language reflects general principles of categorization, such as the existence of prototypes (see e.g. Lakoff 1987, 58ff.). The kinds of prototype effects that have been most studied are asymmetries within categories and gradations away from a best example. For instance, on the basis of language acquisition data Bates and MacWhinney (1982) have proposed that prototype theory can be used to characterize the grammatical relation *subject* in the following way: *A prototypical subject is both agent and topic.*

In addition, the question of linguistic relativity, i.e. claims concerning the mutual influence of language and thought (e.g. Slobin 1996a; Sinha & Jensen de López 2000; Lakoff 1987) is an important issue in cognitive linguistics, with obvious implications for the impact of culture on language and vice versa. Different languages have different means of conceptualizing experience. This may be seen as an exclusively linguistic phenomenon, located e.g. in words, morphemes and grammatical constructions. However, it can also be claimed that such differences in linguistic construal may reflect, and/or influence, the realm of thought, and thereby the cultural identity of the individual. In fact studies such as Kay & Kempton (1984) have shown that words can impose categorizations that may also be applied in nonlinguistic tasks. Isolated conceptual differences relating to individual lexical items are not the most interesting variations; cf. the famous, and rather boring, discussion of the many words for snow in Eskimo and the supposed impact of this on the conceptual system of the Eskimos. The concept *snow* is not fundamental to the conceptual system, and words for snow are not part of the grammar. That there are many words for snow in Eskimo is no more surprising than that Americans have many names for cars (see also the discussion in Lakoff 1987, 308). More interesting is the kind of linguistic variation where the use of different grammatical constructions might be motivated by, or cause, systematic differences in conceptualization (e.g., Choi & Bowerman 1991; Lucy 1992, 1996). In the second part of the paper we will discuss an example of this in relation to the expression of motion events in the so- called satellite-framed languages (e.g. Danish and English) and the verb-framed languages (e.g. Spanish and other Romance languages).

The basic position in cognitive linguistics is that language, seen as one domain of human cognition, is intimately linked to other cognitive domains, such as the capacity for visualizing and reasoning. As such, it mirrors the interplay of psychological, cultural, social, and other factors (Talmy 1988, 2000). This implies that linguistic structure both depends on and influences our conceptualizations. These, on the other hand, are conditioned by our experience of ourselves and the external world. With this cognitive approach, it is impossible to separate linguistic knowledge from extra-linguistic knowledge, and studies of foreign languages must necessarily incorporate the cultural/social context as an integrated part of the representational system of language. For Langacker, the founder of cognitive grammar, this means that a language cannot be regarded as merely an instrument of communication in some culture. The language is also a fundamental component of that culture, with a special status: to some extent, the language internalizes the culture (see Langacker 1999b).

This implies that learners of a foreign language must study that language diligently to attain profound insight into the foreign culture and be able to communicate efficiently with individuals in the foreign culture. And from this cognitive view it follows naturally that the conditions under which we acquire another language must be understood in the cultural context of the foreign as well as the native language. Therefore, if the close relationship between language and culture is accepted, and in consideration of the basic scope of the network of language and culture, in this context we find it natural to discuss the contributions of cognitive linguistic frameworks to the study of SLA, and vice versa.

### Cognitive linguistics and the usage-based model

But from a more restricted linguistic point of view, it is the theoretical implications of the so-called usage-based model (Bybee 1985; Langacker 1987) that brings cognitive linguistics frameworks and SLA together. Recent theoretical and methodological advances have enabled the development of new approaches to grammatical formation, whose abstractions are not rule-based but rather grounded on actual usage events. Theoretically, the key is the recognition that linguistic competence is usage-based, in the sense that linguistic units are regarded as abstracted from usage events. Cognitive grammar, for instance, is a usage-based model of linguistic structure in which linguistic units are seen as abstracted from usage events via the schematization of recurring common properties (Langacker 1987; 1999a). As such, cognitive grammar is one among several versions of usage-based frameworks of grammatical representation.

The first point we wish to make is that as a usage-based theoretical framework, cognitive linguistics is destined to make an impact on various areas of research, such as language and culture, language in society and language acquisition (cf. Pütz et al 2001). It should therefore be emphasized that the usage-based perspective provides a theoretical underpinning for what we all know in practical terms, namely, the essential role of context and culture in the study of language, language use and language learning.

We must also remember that in cognitive linguistics lexicon and grammar are usually represented as forming a continuum, for example in cognitive grammar (Langacker 1987). It follows that all grammatical elements are considered to be meaningful. This view of grammar and lexicon is grounded on our cognitive ability to systematically conceive and portray the same situation in alternative ways. (Complex) events, situations, or reasoning are conventionally construed in different ways in a language, and across languages. In cognitive grammar such phenomena are covered by the notion of 'construal' (Langacker 1987; 1993; 1999a). One aspect of lexical construal is the level of specificity at which a situation is conceived and portrayed. In series such as: thing → object → vehicle → car → Fiat → Fiat Punto 60, each expression is schematic for the following, which instantiates it in the sense of providing a finer-grained characterization (Langacker 1999a, 206). With regard to grammatical construal, it is shown in Pedersen (2003) that the complicated distinction between the Spanish *aunque*-"subordinator", *aunque*-"subordinator/coordinator" and *pero*-"coordinator" can be accounted for as a complex variation of prominence assignment in the constructions of concessive reasoning (aunque /pero = although/but).

A further point we wish to make is that a usage-based approach is necessarily construction-based because of the implied ontological status of the linguistic units. In a construction-grammar framework, constructions are represented as complex symbolic units coupling form and meaning. The usage-based approach implies that constructions are basic rather than epiphenomenal, and that rules in grammar are nothing more than schematic constructions abstracted from usage, e.g. 'nominative (pronominal) case marking of subject' (**She** congratulated him; \***Her** congratulated he (Croft 2001)). Construction grammar builds on a few fundamental hypotheses:

A) The grammatical construction, which couples form and meaning, is the basic unit of grammatical representation.
B) The generalized notion of construction provides a uniform model of grammatical representation, ranging from "syntactic rules" (complex schematic constructions) to "the lexicon" (atomic substantive constructions).
C) The existence of constructions in grammatical representation is a function of frequency and similarity in form and meaning (Bybee 1985).

Cognitive grammar is only one among a number of versions of the construction-grammar framework. The main concern in Goldberg's (1995) version of construction grammar is to explore the types of linguistic information used to construct the meaning of a sentence. Most linguistic theories and psycholinguistic models of sentence-comprehension assume that the main determinant of sentence meaning is the verb. Goldberg's central argument, on the other hand, is that it is necessary to posit abstract constructions that exist independently of the words that instantiate them. This assertion is largely made to avoid the claim that the syntax and semantics of the clause are projected exclusively from the specifications of the main verb. In order to license a verb's multiple argument patterns, Goldberg therefore assumes that the semantics of some argument structure construction (e.g. the ditransitive construction) are fused with the verbal semantics encoded by the lexical entry of the verb (Goldberg 1995). In a recent study based on a sorting paradigm, Bencini and Goldberg (2000) actually showed that not only the verbal lexeme but also the argument structure construction has a strong influence on sentence interpretation. These results have been replicated in follow-up studies, and it has additionally been shown that L2 learners of English show progressively more reliance on the argument structure construction as their language proficiency increases (Goldberg et al 2003, 13f).

Most syntactic theories are essentially formal models for the representation of grammatical knowledge, and the result has been an endless cycle of new and revised theories of syntactic representation. The formal approach to syntax is simply incompatible with the grammatical variation found within and across languages. Croft's Radical Construction Grammar = RCG (Croft 2001), a critique of the formal approach which also emphasizes that more focus on syntactic form is desirable in cognitive linguistics, alters basic theoretical notions, in particular those concerning the constitution of the basic units of representation. In Croft's theory of grammar the primary status of constructions in grammar is taken to its logical conclusion: the categorical status of their elements is dependent on the construction(s) in which they occur, and not the other way around (e.g., Pedersen 2002a, 2002b, 2003). As a consequence, the only internal syntactic structure of constructions is the part-whole relations between a construction and the elements that compose it.

These principles of grammatical organization also apply to semantics, where it can similarly be proposed that semantic schemas, or situation types, are the primitive units of representation. The categories of the semantic schema components are correspondingly defined by their role in the schema. Semantic categories are thus dependent on the frames or situations to which they belong, just as syntactic categories are dependent on the constructions in which they occur (see e.g. Pedersen 2003).

Some of the strongest arguments for the construction-grammar model are actually found in recent empirical evidence from studies of language acquisition. In fact, complex grammatical constructions, rather than categories, have proved to be the basic acquisition units in language development (Tomasello 2003). Thus, as we have seen, there is in fact important experimental support for a constructional approach, not only on the basis of comprehension and production studies, but also of acquisition studies.

Up to now, the focus has mainly been on evidence from the acquisition of first languages. There is no reason not to believe, however, that evidence from SLA would also underpin the construction-grammar framework, at least to some extent.

In the next section we will focus in more detail on the reciprocal contributions of cognitive linguistics and SLA, and present some recent cases in which the cognitive framework has been applied in SLA. Important elements of these applications rely precisely on the usage-based nature of Cognitive Linguistics.

### Cognitive Linguistics and SLA: Mutual contributions

Cognitive Linguistics is considered to be a promising linguistic paradigm for the study of SLA since it can offer us insights that other linguistic approaches of a formalistic nature cannot (Achard, 1997; Cadierno & Lund, in press):

A) detailed contrastive analyses of the semantic structures of the learners' L1 and L2, where meaning is understood as encyclopedic in scope, as subjective, i.e., consisting of a human interpretation of the world, and as reflecting dominant cultural concerns and culture-specific modes of interaction as well as features of the world "as such" (Langacker, 1987, 1991);

B) an explanation of how semantic structure is related to general cognitive abilities (e.g., the ability to categorize, to impose figure/ground organization, and to conceive of a situation at different levels of specificity). This contrasts with formal approaches such as that of Chomsky, where a separation is posited between the linguistic faculty and other aspects of cognition;

C) a more thorough understanding of the role of L1 transfer in the acquisition of a foreign language, given the possibility of offering cognitive-plausible explanations for why L1 structures are or are not transferable into the learners' L2;

D) a satisfying conceptual integration of the structural and social/ cultural aspects of L2 acquisition, given that many of the constructs used in Cognitive Linguistics literature (schemas, metaphors, Idealized Cognitive Models and cultural models) are socially and culturally rich, and lend themselves well to cross-linguistic comparisons in foreign language teaching (Achard in press). This again contrasts with formal approaches to language, where emphasis is placed on the structural aspects of language rather than on its social and cultural aspects, as these are not considered to be directly relevant to the acquisition of grammar; and finally;

E) a more unitary picture of the learners' interlanguage, given that all linguistic expressions (i.e., lexical, morphological and syntactic) are viewed as an interconnected continuum of symbolic structures influenced by common cognitive principles and processes (Langacker 1987).

Consequently, Cognitive Linguistics can constitute the basis for theoretically grounded and testable hypotheses on the way language learners acquire specific structures in the L2. However, it is not only the case that research into SLA can benefit from Cognitive Linguistics; Cognitive Linguistics can, in its turn, also benefit from SLA studies in that empirical data from L2 learners makes it possible to test hypotheses about the linguistic analyses provided by the Cognitive Linguistics framework.

*Traditional vs. Cognitively-based contrastive analyses.*
As indicated above, Cognitive Linguistics can constitute the basis for contrastive analyses of learners' L1 and L2 linguistic systems. However, it is important to emphasize that this type of cognitively-based contrastive analysis differs in some fundamental ways from the traditional contrastive analyses which have been carried out since the 1960s:

A) Whereas traditional contrastive analyses are very restrictive in their scope, given their structuralist perspective on language and their emphasis on examining purely linguistic factors, cognitively-based contrastive analyses assume a broader perspective of language, given the Cognitive Linguistics emphasis on examining the semantic structure of language as well as its relation to general cognitive abilities.

In the literature this has been referred to as the "cognitive commitment" (Langacker 1987; Lakoff 1990); that is, the commitment to provide linguistic descriptions and explanations which accord with what we know about human mental processing. In Langacker's (1998, 1) own words, linguistic structure is as far as possible "analyzed in terms of more basic systems and abilities (e.g., perception, attention, categorization) from which it cannot be dissociated." A natural consequence of this cognitive commitment is that Cognitive Linguistics can offer us the possibility of providing cognitively plausible explanations of why foreign language learners acquire specific L2 constructions the way they do.

B) Whereas traditional contrastive analyses are based on a behaviorist learning theory in which language learning is equated with habit formation through practice and positive or negative reinforcement, cognitively-based contrastive analyses are based on a cognitivist learning theory (Achard 1997) in which L2 acquisition is viewed as partially similar to L1 acquisition in the sense that both make use of general cognitive capacities. From this perspective, L2 learning means learning the specific L2 mappings between the grammatical forms and the situations they code, i.e. learning the conventional coding of social functions by linguistic expressions. As indicated by Achard (1997, 170), the working construct responsible for SLA can be expressed in terms of schema formation: "As the learner starts to receive input in the L2, s/he starts to make generalizations about that input, and hypothesize constructional schemas. These schemas sanction the use of novel expressions. As additional input is received, the schemas get more entrenched according to connectionist principles. This process represents the CG equivalent of the learning of grammatical rules."

C) Whereas traditional contrastive analyses generally assume a behavioristic explanation of the nature of L1 transfer, i.e. transfer is viewed as a process of replacing old L1-habits with new L2-habits, cognitively-based contrastive analyses view transfer as a process of overcoming L1 schemas and conceptualizations. As indicated by Dirven & Verspoor (1998, 268), "...foreign language learning must take into account ... previously established linguistic categories. A learner dealing with new linguistic data inevitably must revise old categories, schemas and prototypes... This revision means adapting an old mental situation to specific data from a foreign language"; and finally,

D) Whereas traditional contrastive analyses tend to view L1 transfer as a simplistic and mechanistic process in which differences between the L1 and the L2 are considered as automatically causing learning difficulties, and similarities between the L1 and the L2 are considered as automatically making learning easier, cognitively-based contrastive analyses view transfer as a cognitive mechanism underlying SLA. This, in turn, is in agreement with the prevailing contemporary view on transfer adopted in SLA research, which stresses the importance of examining the constraints/factors determining the transfer of L1 patterns. According to Cognitive Linguistics theory, a key factor in the transferability of L1 patterns is the mapping between semantic functions and linguistic realizations. A transfer will thus be likely to occur when the L1 has a different mapping between form and function than the L2 (either a similar form with a different function, or a similar function coded by a different form). As indicated by Achard (1997), even though we may expect a considerable overlap in the conceptual structure of the learner's L1 and L2, these conceptual structures may be coded in the two languages by different linguistic expressions; and even if these expressions are structurally similar, the appropriate social range of the L2 expressions might be different from that of the L1-expressions, and this will have to be learned.

In sum, we believe Cognitive Linguistics to be a fruitful linguistic paradigm for the study of SLA. Furthermore, the contrastive analyses of learners' L1 and L2 that this paradigm affords are closely related to practices in foreign language departments.

In the following section, we will discuss two concrete examples of possible contributions made by Cognitive Linguistics to the study of SLA.

*Motion events in SLA*
As instances of the contributions which Cognitive Linguistics can make to the study of SLA, we will discuss a series of research projects (Cadierno & Lund, in press; Cadierno, in press; Cadierno & Ruiz 2003) conducted within cognitive typology. The aims of these projects have been: (a) to examine the uses which can be made in SLA research of Talmy's (1985, 2000) typological framework and of Slobin's empirical work on L1 acquisition (1996a & b, 2000) and his 'thinking for speaking' hypothesis; and, more specifically, (b) to investigate how adult language learners come to express motion events in an L2 that is typologically different from their L1 (e.g., Danish learners of Spanish and Spanish learners of Danish), and to compare this with learners whose L1 and L2 belong to the same typological pattern (e.g., Italian learners of Spanish).

As indicated above, these projects are based on Talmy's (1985, 2000) typological framework for motion events. A motion event, which is defined by Talmy (1985) as a situation containing movement or the maintenance of a stationary location, is composed of the following universal semantic components: (a) Motion: the presence *per se* of motion; (b) Figure: the moving, or conceptually movable, entity; (c) Ground: the object with respect to which the Figure moves; (d) Path: the course followed by the Figure with respect to the Ground; (e) Manner: the manner in which the motion takes place; and (f) Cause: the cause of its occurrence. However, languages differ in the way they map these semantic components onto linguistic forms, that is, they differ in the grammatical constructions typically used by their native speakers to speak about motion. Talmy (1985, 2000) distinguishes between two broad types of languages with different lexicalization patterns: satellite-framed languages (S-languages) and verb-framed languages (V-languages). In the former (e.g., English and Danish), the verb typically conflates Motion and Manner/Cause, while Path is encoded by a satellite (verb particle), as in *The bottle* (Figure) *floated* (Motion + Manner) *out* (Path) *of the cave* (Ground). In the latter (e.g. Spanish and Turkish), the verb typically conflates Motion and Path, while Manner and Cause, if expressed, are typically encoded separately, i.e., with an adverbial or a gerund, as in *La botella* (Figure) *salió* (Motion + Path) *de la cueva* (Ground) *flotando* (Manner).

Talmy's typological framework has been investigated within L1 acquisition by Slobin and his colleagues (e.g., Berman & Slobin, 1994, Slobin, 1996a; b; 2000). The findings of these empirical investigations show that the typological patterns described above have an impact on the rhetorical style used by the native speakers (both children and adults) of the two language types. Thus there is a higher degree of elaboration of the semantic components of path (e.g., more frequent use of ground adjuncts) and manner of motion in S-languages as compared to V-languages. Furthermore, whereas native speakers of S-languages tend to pay relatively more attention to the dynamics of movement along paths (e.g., *The deer threw them off over a cliff into the water*), the speakers of V-languages tend to pay relatively more attention to scene setting and static descriptions (*Lo tiró. Por suerte, abajo, estaba el río. El nino cayó en el agua* –Slobin, 1996b, 204). In the English example, the speaker provides a detailed and elaborated description of the trajectory involved, which allows for the setting to be inferred (i.e., that the cliff is over the water); in the Spanish example, on the other hand, the speaker provides stage-setting information, which allows for the details of the trajectory to be inferred (i.e. that the trajectory went from some elevated place down into the water).

These systematic differences found in speakers of typologically different languages have been explained by Slobin (1996a, 2000) as reflecting different patterns of 'thinking for speaking'. According to Slobin, the lexicalization patterns of a language may influence its speakers' thinking patterns, i.e., the thinking carried out in the process of speaking, listening, reading, writing or signing. Given its emphasis on the influence of language on the mental processes involved in language comprehension and production, this hypothesis constitutes a modified and weaker version of the Whorfian hypothesis on linguistic relativity and determinism. According to Slobin (1996a), each language trains its native speakers to pay different kinds of attention to particular details of events when talking about them. Consequently, the child acquiring its native language learns particular ways of 'thinking for speaking'. Slobin further suggests that this childhood training could be very resistant to restructuring in adult SLA.

Talmy's typological framework and Slobin's 'thinking for speaking' hypothesis have important implications for the study of SLA. A plausible hypothesis would be that learning an L2 involves learning another way of 'thinking for speaking' (Cadierno & Lund, in press; Cadierno, in press), that is, learning how the semantic components of a motion event are mapped into L2 surface forms, and which particular details of a motion event must be attended to in the input and expressed in the L2. In this respect, it can be expected that learners' L1-'thinking for speaking' patterns would be the point of departure for the interpretation and production of L2 patterns. More specifically, the following hypothesis can be logically posited: (a) given that in S-languages there is a higher degree of elaboration of path and manner of motion, Danish learners of Spanish can be expected to exhibit a higher degree of complexity and elaboration of these semantic components than both Italian learners of Spanish and Spanish NSs; and (b) given that in S-languages there is relatively more attention to the dynamics of movement along paths, Danish learners of Spanish can be expected to show relatively more attention to these dynamics, and relatively less attention to scene setting and static descriptions, compared to Italian learners of Spanish and Spanish NSs. These theoretically motivated hypotheses constitute the basis for empirical investigations such as those of Cadierno (in press) and Cadierno & Ruiz (2003), whose results will not be reported here owing to space constraints and the fact that the rationale behind presenting this line of research was simply to show how Cognitive Linguistics based research can be fruitful for the investigation of how adult learners acquire specific L2 constructions (e.g., motion constructions).

*On the L2 acquisition of Gustar vs. Kunne lide.*
A second example of a research project where the linguistic framework of Cognitive Linguistics is applied to the study of SLA is that of Marras (2003) and Marras & Cadierno (submitted, 2003). The aim of this project is twofold: (a) to provide a contrastive cognitive analysis of the Spanish intransitive construction involving dative experiencers (i.e., *Me gusta el chocolate* 'Me-OBJ likes the chocolate-SUBJ') and the corresponding Danish transitive construction involving subject experiencers (i.e., *Jeg kan*

*lide chocolade* 'I-SUBJ like chocolate-OBJ'); and (b) to examine the implications of this analysis for SLA, i.e., whether the results of this analysis can explain the possibly different levels of difficulty in the acquisition of the equivalent L2 construction by Danish learners of Spanish and by Spanish learners of Danish. The contrastive analysis of the two grammatical constructions is based on categorization and prototype theory (Rosch 1978; Taylor 1995), cognitive grammar (Langacker 1987, 1991; Maldonado 2002) and Figure / Ground segregation (Talmy 1978; Langacker 1991).

Even though it is beyond the scope of this paper to report on the different analyses based on the theories mentioned above, their results show that: (a) the categories of subject and dative object, and of transitive and intransitive constructions, do not have clear-cut boundaries, that is, the experiencer involved in the two constructions and the situation coded by the verbs *gustar* and *kunne lide* respectively share characteristics of both category sets; (b) the situation of *kunne lide/gustar* is coded in the two languages by different clause types, each representing a metaphorical extension (from physical processes to mental interactions) from a different prototype, i.e., transitive in the case of Danish and intransitive in the case of Spanish; and consequently, (c) languages such as Spanish and Danish profile different aspects of the same objective situation: in Spanish the experiencer is not the initiator of the verbal situation but the participant affected by it, whereas in Danish the experiencer is the participant with the highest level of activity which, in turn, leads to a higher level of prominence, manifested in the syntactic function of subject.

The results of this contrastive analysis have important implications for SLA. A higher level of acquisitional difficulty can be posited for Danish learners of Spanish than for Spanish learners of Danish: whereas in the Spanish construction there is a conflict between the natural level of prominence of the dative experiencer and the syntactic prominence of the subject (i.e., *Me gusta el chocolate* 'Me-OBJ likes the chocolate-SUBJ'), in the Danish construction there is a correspondence between the natural prominence of the experiencer and its syntactic function of subject (i.e., *Jeg kan lide chocolade* 'I-SUBJ like chocolate-OBJ').

As was the case with the research projects detailed earlier on the expression of motion events in SLA, the theoretically motivated hypothesis mentioned above can constitute the basis for empirical investigations (Marras & Cadierno 2003; Marras 2003) of whether Danish learners of Spanish and Spanish learners of Danish exhibit different levels of difficulty in the acquisition of the equivalent L2 construction.

### Cognitive Linguistics and SLA: Pedagogical implications

The Cognitive Linguistics framework can also have pedagogical implications for the teaching of foreign languages. Space will permit the mention of only two instances. One important implication, which has also been discussed by Achard & Velázquez-Castillo (1996), is that given the Cognitive Linguistics view of lexicon and grammar as a continuum of symbolic units consisting of form – meaning mappings, the often cited distinction between focus on form vs. focus on meaning in language teaching becomes irrelevant. Linguistic form cannot be dissociated from linguistic meaning. This perspective is in full agreement with the general "focus on form" approach to language teaching advocated by Long & Robinson (1998), in which attention to both meaning and form is encouraged in language instruction, and with one particular pedagogical proposal within this approach, that of processing instruction (e.g., Cadierno 1992; VanPatten & Cadierno 1993a, b; Cadierno, 1995), where the emphasis is placed on establishing appropriate form-meaning connections on the part of the L2 learner when processing incoming L2 input.

A second pedagogical implication of Cognitive Linguistics (also discussed in Achard & Velázquez-Castillo 1996) is the superiority of inductive over deductive language teaching methods, since this type of instruction permits the natural processes of schema extraction and formation. This implication is thus derived from the conception of usage-based linguistic competence discussed in the first part of this paper, namely, from the conception of constructional schemas extracted from usage events, i.e. from naturally occurring expressions in the language. This proposal is likewise in agreement with some recently proposed pedagogical practices, such as the "garden-path approach" advocated by Herron & Tomasello (1992). This consists of guided inductive grammar instruction, where learners are presented with particular constructions embedded in contextualized samples of the L2 and are encouraged to arrive at their own generalizations of how these constructions might work, through the processes of hypothesis formation and testing. The proposal is likewise in agreement with the approach of processing instruction mentioned above, which advocates the use of an input-based approach to language teaching. It is important to emphasize here that both pedagogical proposals – the garden-path approach and processing instruction – have received empirical support from investigations which have compared these methods with alternative ones: a deductive approach in the case of the former, and a production-based approach in the case of the latter.

Cognitive Linguistics thus provides a theoretical linguistic framework that is compatible with existing discussions on the role of grammar instruction in the acquisition of a second language and with specific well researched pedagogical proposals on the teaching of grammar.

## Conclusion

As indicated in the introduction, it has been the main aims of this paper to outline the overall role of Cognitive Linguistics in the study of language and culture and to discuss the contributions of usage based cognitive theories of language to the study of adult second language acquisition by presenting some concrete instances of research. We hope to have shown that Cognitive Linguistics is indeed a promising linguistic paradigm for both the study of SLA, i.e., for examining how learners go about the process of learning an L2, and for the teaching of foreign languages.

## References

Achard, Michel: 1997. "Cognitive grammar and SLA investigation". *Journal of Intensive English Studies, II*, 157-176.

Achard, Michel: In press. "Grammatical instruction in the Natural Approach: A cognitive grammar view". In: M. Achard & S. Neimeier (eds.), *Cognitive linguistics, second language acquisition and foreign language pedagogy*. The Hague, Mouton de Gruyter.

Achard, Michel & Maura Velázquez-Castillo: 1996. "Functional linguistics and communicative grammar instruction". *Studi Italiani de Linguistica Teorica e Applicata, 2*, 313-336.

Bates, Elizabeth & Brian MacWhinney: 1982. "Functionalist approaches to grammar". In: E. Wanner & L. Gleitman (eds.), *Language acquisition: The state of the art*. New York, Cambridge University Press.

Bencini, Giulia M. L. & Adele Goldberg: 2000. "The Contribution of Argument Structure Constructions to Sentence Meaning". *Journal of Memory and Language* 43, 640-651.

Berman, Ruth A. & Dan I. Slobin (eds.): 1994. *Relating events in narrative: A crosslinguistic developmental study*. Hillsdale, N.J.; Lawrence Erlbaum.

Bybee, Joan L.: 1985. *Morphology: a study of the relation between meaning and form*. Typological studies in language, vol 9. Amsterdam/Philadelphia, Benjamins.

Cadierno, Teresa: 1992. *Explicit instruction in grammar: A comparison of input based and output based instruction in second language acquisition*. Unpublished Doctoral Dissertation. Champaign, IL, University of Illinois at Urbana-Champaign.

Cadierno, Teresa: 1995. "Formal instruction from a processing perspective: An investigation into the Spanish past tense". *The Modern Language Journal, 79* (2), 179-193.

Cadierno, Teresa: In press. "Expressing motion events in a second language: A cognitive typological approach". In: M. Achard & S. Neimeier (eds.), *Cognitive linguistics, second language acquisition and foreign language pedagogy*. The Hague, Mouton de Gruyter.

Cadierno, Teresa & Lucas Ruiz: 2003. "Motion events in Spanish L2 acquisition". Paper presented at the 8th International Cognitive Linguistics Conference. Logroño, July 20-25.

Cadierno, Teresa & Karen Lund: In press. "Motion events in a typological framework". In: J. Williams, B. VanPatten, S. Rott & M. Overstreet (eds.), *Form – Meaning connections in second language acquisition*. Hillsdale, N.J., Lawrence Erlbaum.

Choi, Soonja & Melissa Bowerman: 1991. "Learning to express motion events in English and Korean: The influence of language-specific lexicalization patterns". *Cognition, 41*, 83-121.

Croft, William: 2001. *Radical Construction Grammar.* Oxford, Oxford University Press.

Dirven, Rene & Marjolijn Verspoor: 1998. *Cognitive exploration of language and linguistics.* Amsterdam, John Benjamins.

Goldberg, Adele: 1995. *Constructions.* Chicago, University of Chicago Press.

Goldberg, Adele, Devin M. Casenhiser & Nitya Sethuraman: 2003. "The role of prediction in construction-learning". Submitted paper.

Herron, Carol & Michael Tomasello: 1992. "Acquiring grammatical structures by guided induction". *The French Review, 65,* n.5.

Kay, Paul. & Willett Kempton: 1984. "What is the Sapir-Whorf-hypothesis?". *American Anthropologist 86,* 65-79.

Lakoff, George: 1987. *Women, Fire, and Dangerous Things.* Chicago/London, The University of Chicago Press.

Lakoff, George: 1990. "The invariance hypothesis: Is abstract reason based on image-schemas?" *Cognitive Linguistics, 1* (1), 39-74.

Lakoff, George & Mark Johnson: 1999. *Philosophy in the Flesh.* New York, Basic Books.

Langacker, Ronald W.: 1987. *Foundation of Cognitive Grammar Vol. 1: Theoretical prerequisites.* Stanford / California, Stanford University Press.

Langacker, Ronald W.: 1991. *Foundation of Cognitive Grammar Vol. 2: Descriptive Application.* Stanford/California, Stanford University Press.

Langacker, Ronald W.: 1993. "Universals of construal". Proceedings of the Annual Meeting of the Berkeley Linguistics Society 19, 447-463.

Langacker, Ronald W.: 1998. "Conceptualization, symbolization, and grammar". In: M. Tomasello (ed.), *The new psychology of language: Cognitive and functional approaches to language structure.* London, Lawrence Erlbaum.

Langacker, Ronald W.: 1999a. *Grammar and Conceptualization.* Mouton de Gruyter, Berlin/New York.

Langacker, Ronald W.: 1999b. "The Contextual Basis of Cognitive Semantics". In: J. Nuyts and E. Pederson (eds.), *Language and Conceptualization.* Language, Culture and Cognition 1. Cambridge: Cambridge University Press, 229-252.

Long, Michael H. & Peter Robinson: 1998. "Focus on form: Theory, research, and practice". In. C. Doughty & J. Williams (eds.), Focus on form in classroom second language acquisition (pp. 15-41). Cambridge, Cambridge University Press.

Lucy, John: 1992. *Grammatical categories and cognition: A case study of linguistic relativity.* Cambridge, Cambridge University Press.

Lucy, John: 1996. "The scope of linguistic relativity: An analysis and review of empirical research". In: J. J. Gumperz & S. C. Levinson (eds.), *Rethinking linguistics relativity* (pp. 37-69). Cambridge, Cambridge University Press.

Maldonado, Ricardo: 2002. "Objective vs. subjective datives". *Cognitive Linguistics, 13* (1), 1-65.

Marras, Valentina: 2003. *Gustar vs. Kunne lide: Un análisis cognitivo de las dos estructuras y sus implicaciones en la adquisición de una segunda lengua.* Unpublished Master Thesis. Odense, University of Southern Denmark.

Marras, Valentina & Teresa Cadierno: Submitted. "Spanish *gustar* vs. English *like*: A cognitive analysis of the constructions and its implication for second language acquisition". In: A. Tyler (ed.), *Cognitive approaches to language and language acquisition.* Georgetown, Georgetown University Press.

Marras, Valentina & Teresa Cadierno: 2003. "Dative vs. Subject experiencers in the L2 acquisition of Spanish and Danish". Paper presented at the 8th International Cognitive Linguistics Conference. Logroño, July 20-25.

Palmer, Gary: 1996. *Toward a Theory of Cultural Linguistics.* Austin, University of Texas Press.

Pedersen, Johan: 2002a. "The Spanish impersonal se-construction. Agreement, case and word order: constructional aspects of the diachronic development". Paper presented at the International Conference on Construction Grammar, Helsingki, september 2002.

Pedersen, Johan: 2002b. "Kategorien refleksiv i spansk. På tværs af sprog og på tværs i sproget". In: *Ny Forskning I Grammatik 9*, SHF. Odense Universitetsforlag, Odense, 223-242.

Pedersen, Johan: 2003. "La base discursiva de la oración compuesta". In: N. Delbecque (ed.), *Aproximaciones cognoscitivo-funcionales al español.* Ámsterdam/New York, Rodopi, 107-117.

Pütz, Martin, Susanne Niemeier & Rene Dirven (eds.): 2001. *Applied Cognitive Linguistics I: Theory and Language Acquisition.* Berlin/New York, Mouton de Gruyter.

Rosch, Eleanor: 1978. "Principles of categorization". In: E. Rosch & B. B. Lloyd (eds.), *Cognition and categorization.* Hillsdale, N.J., Lawrence Erlbaum, 27-48.

Sinha, Chris & Kristine Jensen de López: 2000. "Language, culture, and the embodiment of spatial cognition". *Cognitive Linguistics*, Vol. 11-1/2, 17-41.

Slobin, Dan I.: 1996a. "From 'thought and language' to 'thinking for speaking'". In: J. J. Gumperz & S. C. Levinson (eds.), *Rethinking linguistics relativity* (pp. 70-96). Cambridge, Cambridge University Press.

Slobin, Dan I.: 1996b. "Two ways to travel: Verbs of motion in English and Spanish". In: M. Shibatani & S. A. Thompson (eds.), *Grammatical constructions: Their form and meaning* (pp. 195-219). Oxford, Clarendon Press.

Slobin, Dan I.: 2000. "Verbalized events: A dynamic approach to linguistic relativity and determinism". In: S. Niemeier & R. Dirven (eds.), *Evidence for linguistic relativity* (pp. 107-138). Amsterdam, John Benjamins.

Talmy, Leonard: 1978. "Figure and ground in complex sentences". In: J. Greenberg et al. (eds.), *Universals of human language*, vol.4. (pp. 627-649). Stanford, Stanford University Press.

Talmy, Leonard: 1985. "Lexicalization patterns: Semantic structure in lexical forms". In: T. Shopen (ed.), *Language typology and syntactic description. Volume 3: Grammatical categories and the lexicon* (pp. 36-149). Cambridge, Cambridge University Press.

Talmy, Leonard: 1988. "The Relation of Grammar to Cognition". In: B. Rudzka-Ostyn (ed.), *Topics in Cognitive Linguistics.* Amsterdam, Benjamins, 165-205.

Talmy, Leonard: 2000. *Toward a cognitive semantics. Volume II: Typology and process in concept structuring.* Cambridge, Mass., The MIT Press.

Taylor, John: 1995. *Linguistic categorization. Prototypes in linguistic theory.* Oxford, Clarendon Press.

Tomasello, Michael: 1998. *The new psychology of language: Cognitive and functional approaches to language structure.* London, Lawrence Erlbaum.

Tomasello, Michael: 2003. *Constructing a Language: A Usage-Based Theory of Language Acquisition.* Harvard University Press.

VanPatten, Bill & Teresa Cadierno: 1993a. "Input processing and second language acquisition: A role for instruction". *The Modern Language Journal, 77* (1), 45-57.

VanPatten, Bill & Teresa Cadierno: 1993b. "Explicit instruction and input processing". *Studies in Second Language Acquisition, 15,* 225-243.

# Challenging the Boundaries:
## Exploring the Interface of Linguistics and Literature

by
Nina Nørgaard

1. Introduction

To many people, challenging the boundaries between the traditional disciplines in foreign language studies means doing cultural studies. The aim of this article is to pull in a different direction by suggesting how the interface between linguistics and literature may be another fertile field to explore in the study and teaching of foreign languages. Not only may linguistics and literature be employed to shed light on each other[1], the insights gained may furthermore prove useful in a broader context in our foreign language studies. The article will begin with a brief introduction to literary linguistics in general and to Hallidayan linguistics in particular. The theoretical framework thus laid out, I will exemplify how Halliday's theory of language may be employed in the analysis of literature, and will conclude by considering the possible status of literary linguistics in a broader perspective within our foreign language studies[2].

2. Linguistics and literary analysis

If we want to make a close reading of a literary text, language is a dimension that cannot be ignored. This does not mean that literature cannot be analysed without a knowledge of linguistics, but since the concern of lin-

---

[1] In this article, my focus will be on the contribution of linguistic theory to the analysis of literature. For examples of how the linguistic analysis of literature may in turn throw light back on the linguistic theory employed and suggest adjustments of it, see Nørgaard (2003a) and Nørgaard (2003b).

[2] Parts of this article are based on my Ph.D. on Hallidayan linguistics and literary analysis, and certain passages stem directly from that work. For a more detailed exploration and discussion of the interface of linguistics and literature, see Nørgaard (2003b).

guistics is the way meaning is created through language it seems obvious that linguistic theory may provide the literary critic with an understanding of the way meaning is created through language in literature, and with a systematic way of dealing with this aspect of the text. Nevertheless, linguistic approaches to literature, known as 'stylistics' or 'literary linguistics', are often frowned upon. The scepticism is probably based on what Toolan (1992, xiv) describes as "the myth that stylistics entails a fundamental separation of text from context, linguistic description from linguistic interpretation, or language from situation." Myths seldom emerge out of the blue. A glance at the history of stylistics reveals that the hostility towards the discipline probably springs from a tendency – particularly among its early proponents – to heap up large amounts of linguistic detail from literary texts without seriously combining this practice with interpretation. While illuminating in other ways, many formalist stylistic analyses such as those presented by Roman Jakobson, for example, and by various proponents of Chomskyan linguistics, often display this tendency[3]. In contrast, and for reasons that will be sketched below, Halliday's Systemic Functional Linguistics appears to be a useful model for bridging the gap between linguistics and literary criticism because it combines text with context, linguistic description with linguistic interpretation, and language with situation, and thus goes against the 'myth' mentioned by Toolan above.

### 3. Systemic Functional Linguistics
Unlike formal theories of grammar, Systemic Functional Linguistics is a descriptive theory of language which focuses on language in use rather than a more abstract concept of language competence. Of fundamental importance to the theory is the conception that language is purposeful behaviour and that the purpose of using language is to make meanings. The object of a systemic functional investigation of language is therefore the question of how language is structured to make meaning in context.

As indicated by its name, the theory is systemic – and thereby paradigmatic – in orientation. This means that it views a text as a large system of choices made from different paradigms and that the chosen wording receives part of its meaning from that which could have been chosen instead. This combines with the functional – and thereby pragmatic – orientation of the theory, which makes it particularly interested in the function of the chosen wordings and gives emphasis to the status of texts as functional acts of communication between interlocutors. Together, the systemic and the functional aspects of the theory invite us to examine a literary text as a large system of meaningful linguistic choices made by the

---

[3] See e.g. Taylor (1981) for a critique of Chomskyan stylistics.

author – choices which get part of their meaning from that which could have been chosen instead.

Another important feature of Halliday's theory is its broad concept of semantics. When we ask "what does the text mean", we usually refer to experiential meaning, i.e. meanings relating to how we represent experience/the world. According to Halliday, however, language is structured to express not just one but essentially three different major types of meaning – and to do so simultaneously. In addition to making experiential meanings (i.e. representing experience in terms of who is doing what to whom, where, when, why, and with what), language also expresses interpersonal meanings (i.e. meanings to do with the relations between the interlocutors; what we use language to do in relation to other people) and textual meanings (i.e. meanings relating to our organization of texts). These are the three metafunctions of language: the experiential, the interpersonal and the textual metafunction. For each kind of meaning, systemic functional linguists employ different grammatical systems of analysis – systems that give priority to semantic function over form. It is in this connection important to note the emphasis given to the concept of 'construal' in Hallidayan thinking, that is, the conception that language *construes* (i.e. creates) meaning, rather than *represents* meaning which is already there, waiting to be conveyed through language in terms of a given one-to-one relationship between the world and the word.

When it comes to the object of analysis, Systemic Functional Linguistics also has a broader scope that many other linguistic theories. Where linguists traditionally tend to look at sentences in isolation, the Hallidayan approach is geared to the analysis of whole texts, which would seem to make it more suitable for literary analysis than most other linguistic theories.

Unlike many of these theories, Systemic Functional Linguistics is furthermore largely context-oriented. Language is seen as being functional within a particular context, and the utterance as being influenced by the specific situation in which it is created. Not only does the text occur in context – the context is *in* the text, it is claimed. The theory operates with three layers of context: the context of the immediate social situation in which the text is made, termed 'register', and the two larger contexts of culture, ie 'genre' and 'ideology'. Register, genre, and ideology are all socio-cultural factors which influence the linguistic choices people make when communicating. This, in turn, means that to various degrees the choices made – and thereby the texts produced – all reflect such socio-cultural factors.

Finally, Halliday insists that there is a close connection between grammar, semantics and pragmatics which must be reflected by our linguistic analysis. This insistence sees to it that if we make a Hallidayan analysis of a literary text, this analysis will be firmly anchored in the lexis and grammar of the text[4] so that we avoid the tendency to separate linguistic description and interpretation.

It should be mentioned that the various elements of Systemic Functional Linguistics listed above are not in themselves unique to the theory, yet an important strength of Hallidayan linguistics is the way it brings together the various kinds and levels of meaning in language and demonstrates how they interact in the construal of the overall meaning of a given text.

### 4. Systemic Functional Linguistics and literary analysis

To illustrate how Halliday's theory of language may be of use in the analysis of literature, the following pages will illustrate how the three kinds of meaning (i.e. experiential, interpersonal and textual meaning) are made in a short story by James Joyce. It should be noted that what follows is by no means a fully-fledged Hallidayan analysis of the story, but is merely intended as exemplification.

Joyce's "Two Gallants" is a short story about degenerate gallantry, written in the literary mode of realism. It is an inverted romance about two young Irishmen, Lenehan and Corley, who exploit a servant girl's affection for the latter to make her give them money. The plot of the story is fairly simple: after a walk through Dublin, during which Corley's many exploits are discussed, Corley walks off with the girl, leaving Lenehan to wander aimlessly around the streets of Dublin until his friend's return. On returning, Corley makes his girlfriend fetch him a gold coin, which she has either taken out of her own savings or stolen from her master. The story may be seen as reflecting the situation of Ireland around the turn of the century, with the political, economic and spiritual debasement of the country as some of its areas of concern[5].

### 4.1. Experiential meaning.

According to Halliday, we understand – and in turn construe – experience in terms of processes, participants, and circumstances. When analysing a literary text from the experiential perspective, we hence examine how the author construes his or her fictional universe through choices of these three basic semantic functions, i.e. of who is doing what to whom under what circumstances. It is obviously of consequence for the characterization of a given character whether she is frequently construed as the participant of Material processes of doing or of Mental processes of thinking, for

---

[4] What Halliday calls "lexico-grammar".

[5] Despite the interesting nature of such interpretations, my focus here does not allow them a central place in the present article.

*Exploring the Interface of Linguistics and Literature* 173

instance, or whether she seldom (or never) occurs in these participant roles.[6]

An examination of the experiential metafunction in "Two Gallants" proves particularly interesting when it comes to patterns of Mental processes of perception, since Lenehan occurs often and with great variety as the participant of such processes and is thereby construed linguistically as someone who tends to observe things, while Corley is construed experientially as a character who acts. In this connection, Kennedy (1982) observes from a Hallidayan perspective that not only is Lenehan frequently construed as the participant of Mental processes of perception, very often it is furthermore his eyes rather than Lenehan himself that occur as the actual participant of these processes. In cases like this, the value of considering texts as sets of paradigmatic choices is evident. As demonstrated by the diagram below, a comparison of actual choices of wording with their possible, yet unchosen, alternatives often reveals what is obtained by the selection of one type of construction instead of another:

| Actual choice of wording | Alternative choice of wording |
| --- | --- |
| His eyes [...] glanced at every moment towards his companion's face (43.19-21)[7] | He glanced at every moment towards his companion's face |
| Lenehan's gaze was fixed on the large faint moon (46.1) | Lenehan fixed his gaze on the large faint moon |
| His bright small eyes searched his companion's face (47.26) | He searched his companion's face with his bright small eyes |
| His eyes made a swift anxious scrutiny of the young woman's appearance (49.20-22) | He made a swift anxious scrutiny of the young woman's appearance |
| Lenehan's eyes noted approvingly her stout short muscular body (49.30-31) | Lenehan noted approvingly her stout short muscular body |
| His eyes took note of many elements of the crowd (50.23-24) | He took note of many elements of the crowd |
| His eyes searched the street (53.19-20) | He searched the street (with his eyes) |

---

[6] For clarity, I simplify matters here. One should, of course, be careful with generalizations across entire texts, which may in actual fact reveal very little, and instead look out for local rather than global patterns of participant, process and circumstance structures.

[7] My references to "Two Gallants" have the following format: (page.lines).

This paradigmatic mapping of constructions with respectively Lenehan's eyes and Lenehan himself as participant clearly supports Kennedy's claim that Joyce's selection of the former creates an image of a character who is somewhat distanced from the processes in question. Readers do, of course, know that ultimately Lenehan is the one who is glancing and gazing. However, the systematic exclusion of this character as the participant of Mental processes of perception where he might be expected to fill in this role participates in the construal of the image of a relatively passive character. Not only does Lenehan perceive things rather than act, often he is not even presented as the explicit participant of the given processes of perception.

*4.2. Interpersonal meaning.*
In the analysis of interpersonal meaning, i.e. of what we use language to do in relation to other people, central aspects to consider are: the distribution of speech roles (i.e. who is speaking and for how long), the speech functions employed (e.g. does a character ask a lot of questions or state things as given facts), the grammatical realization of speech functions (i.e. the significance of congruent and incongruent choices[8]), the use of modality (who expresses attitude in terms, for instance, of certainty/uncertainty), and vocatives and naming (encoding attitude of characters as well as narrators).

An analysis of these aspects of "Two Gallants" reveals how Lenehan is construed as a polite, attentive and insecure speaker – which is certainly not the case with Corley. Through his constant questioning, Lenehan is construed as a character who signals interest in his addressee, is anxious to keep the conversation going to maintain a good atmosphere and is desperate for reassurance that Corley will make it. Corley, in turn, first demonstrates his power by talking at great length about himself and the girls he has been with, but later changes his communicative strategies and manifests his power by being silent. A good example of this – which is also a good example of the usefulness of a paradigmatic approach to text analysis – occurs when Corley is leaving Lenehan in order to meet the girl:

> Corley had already thrown one leg over the chains when Lenehan called out: "And after? Where will we meet?"

---

[8] While the congruent – i.e. the grammatically prototypical – way of expressing a command, for instance, would be by means of an imperative construction (e.g. "Close the door!"), an interrogative may be employed instead with interpersonal implications of politeness (e.g. "Would you mind closing the door?"). The latter choice would be considered an incongruent one in the given context. It should be noted that 'incongruent' does neither mean unusual nor inappropriate, but rather refers to a grammatically atypical choice.

"Half ten," answered Corley, bringing over his other leg.
"Where?"
"Corner of Merrion Street. We'll be coming back." (49.1-7)

The fact that Corley answers Lenehan's question about *where* to meet afterwards by stating the *time* of meeting may seem a minor detail, yet it is nevertheless curious and seems worth considering. Why this discrepancy? Some may explain Joyce's wording as a means of creating verisimilitude, since interlocutors often get something wrong in real life conversations and hence answer accordingly. Others may argue that the misunderstanding between the two characters (provided that this is what it is) indicates that Lenehan and Corley are physically so far apart at this point that Corley simply cannot hear Lenehan's question properly. Prompted by the systemic functional approach to language, I will argue that the function of this particular verbal exchange may involve the interpretations above, yet is more complex than they imply. In the exchange, Lenehan asks a question, namely the question of where to meet later. The expected reply to such a question is one that provides the information requested, whether in a positive form as in "Corner of Merrion Street", or negatively as in "We won't meet afterwards". These and similar wordings are the likely paradigmatic options available to Corley, but none of them is chosen. Instead, he chooses to break the paradigm of likely answers, which has a powerful effect. It is uncertain whether Corley does not care enough about Lenehan to pay attention to what he says, deliberately chooses to mishear Lenehan's question, or mishears Lenehan's question because he is simply walking away without an appointment. In all these cases, however, his (linguistic as well as physical) reply has interpersonal implications in that it indicates how little Lenehan and their conversation mean to him. By breaking the paradigm of likely responses, Corley manifests his position of power in a subtle, yet very effective way. We understand this because we recognize the tension between Joyce's actual wording and more predictable wordings of the same passage. Ultimately it is, of course, the author who breaks the paradigm, thereby construing Corley as a character who behaves contrary to our expectations.

*4.3. Textual meaning.*
While simultaneously representing the world and expressing dimensions of the interpersonal relations between interlocutors, language furthermore involves the expression of a third kind of meaning to do with the organization of texts. In the English language, as well as in Danish and many other languages, there are two main resources for the creation of textual

meaning – Theme structures and cohesion – of which the limited space available here allows me to focus only on the latter[9].

When we tie sentences together to form a text, cohesion is the most important linguistic resource involved in that process. Cohesion refers to the way a text is 'glued together', so to speak, by means of the text-internal ties of conjunction, reference, ellipsis and lexical organization. Some texts display a large number of cohesive ties, while the 'texture'[10] of other texts is of a looser nature. Altogether, "Two Gallants" is a highly cohesive text, which clearly helps construe it as a text belonging to the mode of literary realism and make it relatively easy to decode. Against this background of smooth texture, cohesive markedness draws our attention to the passage where Joyce uses the indefinite article in connection with what appears to be a known entity when Corley and the slavey return from their evening out:

> They talked for a few moments, and then the young woman went down the steps into the area of a house. Corley remained standing at the edge of the path, a little distance from the front steps. Some minutes passed. Then the hall-door was opened slowly and cautiously. A woman came running down the front steps and coughed. Corley turned and went towards her. His broad figure hid hers from view for a few seconds and then she reappeared, running up the steps. The door closed on her, and Corley began to walk swiftly towards Stephen's Green. (54.3-13)

A possible reading of the indefiniteness would be to claim that the woman referred to must be someone else than the slavey, who has been referred to as "the woman" ever since she was first introduced as "a young woman" on page 48. Although such a reading would make sense at the level of the lexico-grammar, it does not seem to do so at other levels of the analysis, however. Who would this other woman be? And why would she give Corley money after his walk with the slavey? For reasons of coherence, the slavey who has previously paid Corley's tram fare and provided him with cigarettes and cigars must be the one who gives him the golden coin, and the motivation for the selection of the indefinite article should therefore be sought for elsewhere. The logical explanation for Joyce's choice of wording must consequently be related to perspective, in that the indefiniteness reflects the fact that this is how Lenehan perceives things. From a distance, Lenehan simply cannot see who the woman is, hence the indefinite expression, which, in turn, encodes the perspective.

---

[9] For a discussion of Theme-structures in "Two Gallants" see Nørgaard (2003b) sections 8.2 and 8.3.

[10] The term employed by Halliday and Hasan (1976/1997) about the 'textness' of a text as compared to strings of unrelated sentences.

Besides adding to our sense of focalization on Lenehan, the choice of the indefinite article may furthermore be seen as a subtle way of establishing an aspect of setting, namely that of darkness, which appears to be of symbolic significance in the story. This is in truth a dark moment in the history of gallantry – no matter whether gallantry is understood literally in terms of the behaviour of men to women, or symbolically in terms of that of the English (and the English-friendly) to the Irish.

*4.4. Literature as functional acts of communication between author and reader.*
With the brief analysis of the examples from "Two Gallants" above, I hope to have indicated – though in a rather sketchy manner – some of the ways in which Systemic Functional Linguistics enables us to describe and interpret how the fictional universe of characters, settings, actions, etc is created linguistically through the selection and combination of material from the three metafunctions. In addition to creating a fictional microcosm, however, writers furthermore encode in their writing a particular relationship between themselves and their readers. With its aim of seeing texts as functional acts of communication between senders and addressees, systemic functional theory invites us also to consider this aspect of literature[11].

A contrastive examination of "Two Gallants" and Joyce's later writings such as *Ulysses* and *Finnegans Wake* soon reveals that the communication that takes place between the author and his readers (via the narrator) varies considerably in these texts. In "Two Gallants", as in literary realism in general, the author appears to give priority to the characters' fictional context of situation over the context of situation in which the author and the readers participate. But even though attention is drawn away from the communication that takes place between the author and his readers, this does not mean that this particular aspect of the text is of no importance to the analysis of literary realism. On the contrary, Halliday's theory may help us see and describe how the 'toning down' of this aspect of the text is, in fact, the result of careful linguistic organization and revision, created by means of linguistic choices made within the three metafunctions – choices which are largely conventional and therefore relatively easy for the reader to decode.

In *Ulysses* it is clearly not Joyce's aim to ease the reader's way through the fictional universe. Instead, he constantly constructs this text in ways which are likely to puzzle and frustrate readers. The status of the text *as text* is often foregrounded, with the result that our attention is partly moved from a mimetic understanding of the fictional microcosm of the novel (i.e. of the experiential, interpersonal and textual meanings made at character-

---

[11] Even if such an approach is seldom made by Hallidayan stylistitians.

level) to the meanings encoded at the level of the text as an interpersonal act of communication between author and reader. This, of course, comes as no surprise to literary critics, yet a Hallidayan approach to the novel may help us understand and describe how these meanings are encoded linguistically. Thus an awareness of the concept and mechanisms of cohesion, will provide us with a more thorough understanding of – and a consistent terminology for explaining – the linguistic construal of perspective and the way Joyce's extensive use of unresolved cohesion[12] encodes a much more subjective reality than the seemingly objective reality of "Two Gallants".

Another aspect of *Ulysses* which seriously impacts on the nature of this text as communication between author and reader is Joyce's use of genre in the novel. Since systemic functional theory does not limit itself to analysing sentences or texts in isolation, but – at least ideally – considers texts within their larger contexts of immediate situation, genre and ideology, the theory also offers tools for dealing with genre in literature. Genre may be regarded as a paradigm on a very general level of the text – a paradigm which in turn involves choices from various sub-paradigms such as typographical form, schematic structure, narrative perspective, diction, etc. which are all encoded by selections of linguistic material within the three metafunctions. What is particularly interesting about the systemic functional approach to genre is hence the claim that this layer of context can be traced in the lexis and grammar of a given text, so that a description of genre from this perspective will be firmly rooted in the actual wording of the text. Another advantage lies in the model's functional view of genre, which motivates us to move beyond description to considerations of the functionality of the generic choices made by the author. Furthermore, the broad applicability of the theory to all kinds of genre means that in our analysis of *Ulysses*, for instance, we can equally well employ it for the examination of genres engaged in by the characters of the text, Joyce's use of genre at chapter-level, and the overall genre of the text[13].

Throughout *Ulysses*, Joyce makes a large number of genre signals, yet rather than adhering to the conventions of the chosen genres, he constantly undermines them, or selects genres unusual for a literary context. In chapter 13, for instance, the linguistic choices he makes within the three

---

[12] In terms of definite references to a context of situation with which the reader is often not familiar, which helps construe this very context as the inner psychological reality of the consciousness of a character.

[13] While the overall genre of *Ulysses* in a transformed manner mirrors that of Homer's long heroic epic, almost every single chapter of the novel adopts (and transforms) genres as diverse as journalism, encyclopaedic prose, trivial romance, drama and music.

metafunctions produce a configuration of meanings typical of trivial literary romance. At the outset of the chapter, Joyce provides enough genre-signals for readers to recognize the genre. In particular, interpersonal meanings of modality and evaluation play a prominent role in this respect, which makes the chapter a far cry from the preceding part of the narrative where narratorial evaluation, for example, is typically minimalized. When he has established the paradigm, however, Joyce begins to exaggerate the use of modality, evaluative items and cliché, i.e. some of the linguistic elements that helped construe the genre in the first place. The effect of this is a certain subversion of the genre which makes us notice the hollowness and deceitful nature of it and the world view it usually promotes. This is supported, of course, by the marked clash between form and subject matter in that what the romance narrator attempts to present as virtuous romantic love, actually turns out to be Bloom masturbating while watching a girl on the beach.

In several ways Joyce's aim in *Ulysses* appears to be exactly that of frustrating his readers' expectations and thereby make us reconsider the validity of these expectations and the literary conventions on which they are based. What we see in this novel may, in fact, be described as a thematization of Halliday's three metafunctions of language – i.e. of the three kinds of meaning that language has evolved to express. By means of defamiliarizing the familiar, the novel thus foregrounds and problematizes meanings to do with the representation of experience in literature, meanings to do with the interpersonal relations involved at the author-reader level of the text, as well as textual meanings to do with the role language is playing in the interaction. If not exactly self-reflexive, the novel is at least distinctly self-conscious in ways which induce us to consider what a literary text is and to recognize the nature of literature as acts of communication between the author and ourselves.

## 5. Literary Linguistics in a broader perspective

Let me make it quite clear that my intentions here are not to proclaim the supremacy of Hallidayan linguistics when it comes to the analysis of literature and pass over all other approaches as insignificant. In this respect, I agree in principle with Halliday's observation (1964/1970, 70) that "Linguistics is not and will never be the whole of literary analysis, and only the literary analyst – not the linguist – can determine the place of linguistics in literary studies". I am furthermore aware that some of the observations made about Joyce's writings above can be and indeed have been made without Systemic Functional Linguistics. What I would like to suggest, however, is that the Hallidayan model of language can be seen as a richly equipped linguistic tool kit that literary critics and others may draw upon when they need linguistic substantiation of their analyses. For that purpose, Hallidayan linguistics seems particularly useful since its ability to cover the very large semantic spectrum of meaning comprised by the three metafunctions, as well as its ability to describe and interpret different dimensions of context in text, enable it to address a great variety of aspects of literary texts. In a literary context, another obvious strength of Hallidayan linguistics is the paradigmatic orientation of the theory which sees to it that its application is not limited to texts which fit nicely into conventional paradigms of different genres and modes, but also enables us to deal with texts that stretch conventional paradigms to their outmost as done, for instance, by *Ulysses*.

In my presentation above, I have referred to the breadth of Hallidayan linguistics as a positive trait which makes it particularly attractive in a literary context. The other side of the coin is a prevalent tendency to drown in detail when attempting to acquire the theory and when employing it for analysis. A good example of the latter is Halliday's otherwise illuminating article on Golding's *The Inheritors* which clarifies significant aspects of Golding's novel by means of an analysis of experiential meaning in central passages of the text, yet at the same time appears to lose itself somewhat in its minute analysis of detail. As for the question of acquiring the theory without drowning in detail, it is important to constantly keep in mind the overall ideas of the theory about the three types of meaning and their function in context. For this purpose, relatively simple introductions to the theory like Butt et al. (1999), Thompson (1996) and Eggins (1994) are recommendable, while Halliday's own introduction (1994) tends to scare away newcomers to the field and should preferably be reserved for later perusal.

It is often argued, as in one of Halliday's early enquiries into the language of literature (1964/1970), that a linguistic approach to literary texts will provide the literary critic with a fairly objective method of analysis. To some extent, the linguistic approach to literature may seem to contain some sort of objectivity in so far as such analyses will be closely tied up with the actual wording of the text, yet to believe that the linguistic analysis of literature is inherently more objective than most other approaches is a fallacy that should be avoided. As a matter of fact, an important consequence of Hallidayan thinking is that all uses of language must be seen to encode some kind of ideology – thus also linguistic theories, including the systemic functional model itself. It hence seems likely that our selection of material for analysis, as well as the analysis itself, will be influenced by our theoretical approach which may cause us to give priority to some elements of the text while disregarding others. So rather than striving to approach literature from the perspective of some kind of ideal "objective linguistic scholarship" (Halliday 1964/1970, 71), it is essential that we acknowledge and make explicit possible biases of our approach.

All this being said, there are in my view several advantages of approaching literature from a linguistic perspective – the most immediate one, of course, being the way this kind of approach provides students and teachers alike with a more pronounced understanding of the ways in which meaning is created through language in literature. It enables us to make literary analyses that are firmly anchored in the actual grammar and wording of the text and provides us with a consistent metalanguage for doing so plus a conscious knowledge of language that may open our eyes to aspects of meaning-making in literary texts that might otherwise pass unnoticed.

Without doubt, the understanding and skills obtained within the field of literary linguistics will furthermore prove useful in other contexts, too, since they apply equally well to texts other than literary ones. In particular, the concept of 'construal', which takes up a central place in Hallidayan thinking, is a good point of departure for making students and others aware how language actively construes rather than neutrally represents meaning. If we introduce the Hallidayan model of language to our students within the context of literary analysis, we thus simultaneously provide them with an approach to language that may be drawn upon for the analysis of a possibly unlimited range of texts – stretching from sms-messages and gossipping to political speeches and the ten o'clock news.

In addition to providing students with tools for analysing literary as well as non-literary texts, another advantage of Hallidayan stylistics is the likely impact on students' own text-production of their increased conscious knowledge of how language works. In the writing of essays and other types of text, recurring problems typically concern textual organization (i.e. Halliday and Hasan's 'texture') and a weak sense of genre. Texture and genre are aspects of language use that are specifically addressed by Hallidayan theory and are therefore aspects of text and text-production that a familiarity with this particular approach to language will almost automatically help students master more competently.

Furthermore, literary linguistics – and text linguistics more generally – appear to be useful supplements to the knowledge of language students typically achieve from their traditional grammar courses. With their focus on text, these disciplines train students in analysing entire texts rather than sentences in isolation, which ultimately resembles the kind of work with text they are likely to encounter outside the class room.

Last, but not least, literary linguistics is, in my view, of great relevance to the current debate about the status and nature of foreign language studies. By working with the interface of linguistics and literature – and possibly also linguistics and other disciplines – we automatically create a larger sense of continuity between the traditional pillars of our foreign language studies – at university level as well as at lower levels of the educational system. It is no secret that when students move from one lecture to another of what is considered the 'core disciplines' of our foreign language studies (i.e. language, literature and history), they often have the feeling that these disciplines have virtually nothing to do with each other. By becoming more explicitly aware that – and how – meaning is construed through language in literature, historical documents, media texts, etc., students may come to see their foreign language degrees as more coherent wholes of which the various disciplines are both relevant and interdependent.

To me, the tendency to keep linguistics and other disciplines apart seems unnecessary and artificial. If we want to bridge the traditional gap between them, Halliday's theory of language and its application to the analysis of literature seem a good place to begin.

## References

Butt, D., et al.: 1999. *Using Functional Grammar*. Sydney, Macquarie University.

Eggins, S.: 1994. *An Introduction to Systemic Functional Linguistics*. Great Britain, Pinter.

Halliday, M.A.K.: 1964/1970. "Descriptive Linguistics in Literary Studies." In: D. C. Freeman (ed.), *Linguistics and Literary Style*. New York, London, Sydney; Holt, Rinehart and Winston, Inc.

Halliday, M.A.K.: 1971/1973. "Linguistic function and literary Style: an enquiry into the language of Willian Golding's *The Inheritors*." In: *Explorations in the Functions of language*. London, Edward Arnold.

Halliday, M.A.K.: 1994. *An Introduction to Functional Grammar*. London, New York, Sydney, Auckland; Arnold.

Halliday, M.A.K. & R. Hasan: 1976/1997. *Cohesion in English*. London & New York, Longman.

Joyce, J.: 1914/1992. *Dubliners*. London, New York, Victoria; Penguin.

Joyce, J.: 1922/1993. *Ulysses*. London & New York, Vintage Books.

Kennedy, C.: 1982. "Systemic Grammar and its Use in Literary Analysis". In: R. Carter (ed.), *Language and Literature. An Introductory Reader in Stylistics*. London, George Allen & Unwin; 83-99.

Nørgaard, N.: 2003a. "Halliday og Hasans kohæsionsbegreb i en litterær kontekst." In: C. Bache, M. Birkelund & N. Nørgaard (eds.), *Ny Forskning i Grammatik 10*. Odense, University Press of Southern Denmark; 153-165.

Nørgaard, N.: 2003b. *Systemic Functional Linguistics and Literary Analysis. A Hallidayan Approach to Joyce – A Joycean Approach to Halliday*. Odense, University Press of Southern Denmark.

Taylor, T.J.: 1981. *Linguistic Theory and Structural Stylistics*. Oxford, Pergamon Press.

Thompson, G.: 1996. *Introducing Functional Grammar*. Great Britain, Arnold.

Toolan, M.: 1992. *Language, Text and Context. Essays in Stylistics*. London and New York, Routledge.

Toolan, M.: 1998. *Language in Literature. An Introduction to Stylistics*. Great Britain, Arnold.

Weber, J.J.: 1996. *The Stylistics Reader. From Roman Jakobson to the present*. Great Britain, Arnold.

# Narratives of Natives
## The construction of the Other as object of aid

by
Jan Gustafsson

Introduction
This paper deals with the construction of identities within epic-narrative schemes of cultural self, and other issues resulting from development aid. More specifically, it addresses the question of Latin America and Latin Americans as objects of aid[1] financed and administered by Danish governmental institutions and/or NGOs. Special attention will be given to current strategies developed during the 1990s, according to which the main objects of such aid are indigenous peoples (and women and children). The aim of the paper is to put forward the view that the very idea of development aid as expressed in different types of texts and contexts tends to posit mutual identities of 'Us as givers' and 'the Others as recipients', as, respectively, an active subject and a passive object. Elements of structural narratology will provide the main theoretical instrument; however, structural narratology will not be regarded as a general theoretical frame for the study of texts, but rather as one possible instrument for the detection of fixed or limited readings (interpretations) of non-fictional texts.

'Aid-construction' is one of the basic mechanisms in the production of images of 'Us' and 'the Others'; in the case of Denmark, Danes and Third World peoples, respectively. Exploring this question in depth would require the consideration of a number of contextual spaces, which is not possible given the limited length of this article. I do, however, consider it plausible to suggest that a basic representation by most Danes of any Third

---

[1] Currently and officially this aid is often called 'development aid' or 'development assistance' although the traditional development perspective has changed, at least to a certain point. Cf. Danida 2001.

World individual would be of a 'poor person'[2]. Furthermore, development aid and related NGO activities are very visible in the Danish public sphere – in schools, publicity, fund raising activities etc. – and I therefore believe it relevant to suggest that the constructions of self and Other discussed in this article are not specific phenomena of the texts examined, but rather part of a generalized context.

Due to limitations of space and the preliminary importance of presenting general issues, this article will mainly be of an introductory and general character, with examples for the analysis taken from a variety of texts: a deeper exploration of the subject with more extensive textual analysis are projected for future works.

### Theoretical approaches: Narratology and narragraphies

This paper draws partly on identity theories in general, with a special interest in relational theories of identity construction and boundary mechanisms (cf. Jenkins 1996, Barth 1969 and Gustafsson 1999/2000). Its other – and probably most visible – theoretical approach is derived from semiotics and textual theories, especially narratology (cf. Ricœur 1994, Greimas 1973, Bal 1985/97).

The analytical models developed on the basis of these latter theories have been criticized for focussing too narrowly on narrative patterns and structures. In doing so, these theories have helped to elucidate general structural elements in literature, but they have not always been successful in accounting for the more specific and individual aspects of signification in the actual literary work. This is not the place for a discussion of the relevance of such structurally oriented approaches to literature. The purpose of using, or recycling, these theoretical constructs as methodological instruments in non-literary studies like this one is to show how narrative-epical structures tend implicitly to form and perpetuate the cultural self and Other in certain pre-conceptualized positions; these are not only images or signs of mutual others, but also contribute to maintaining the actual patterns of interaction, i.e. the social, political and economic relations between the actual individual and collective actors. In other words, narratives are not only expressions of power relations, they also contribute to creating them.

Furthermore, even if narratological models have failed to account for the complex textual reality of aesthetic representations, they might all the same help to indicate certain instruments of *ideological* perceptions of

---

[2] In a survey made in 1996 among students of the Copenhagen Business School concerning their perception of Latin America and Latin Americans, the words 'poor', 'poverty' and related expressions were by far the most frequent (cf. Gustafsson 1999).

social life. A discussion and definition of the concept of ideology would extend the intentions and scope of this article[3], but I will propose to see ideology as a conceptual frame that constrains or influences social representations. Amongst these are what could be called 'intercultural representations', i.e. the representations of selves and Others defined according to 'cultural' (e.g. national, ethnic, racial, religious, gender and other) categories. There is no doubt that representations of such categories are subject to different kinds of ideological constraints. What I intend to show is that one such ideological limitation of the representation of self and Other in a concrete case of intercultural representation is the narrative scheme(s) in which the roles of both parties are defined.

As already mentioned, narratology suggests a structural approach, and this will be the case in part: certain generalized narrative structures will be seen as meaning-generating mechanisms and, at the same time, as ideological constraints in the construction of mutual identities. The function of the basic elements of epic-narrative texts, i.e. space, time and actors, will be related to identity construction as explicit or implicit manifestations functioning in a broader context. However, they should not be regarded as simple intra-textual configurative elements, but mainly as mechanisms of boundary and translation, in particular between the concrete spatio-temporal *moment* of reception and re-production of the (specific) textual meaning and the (more or less) generalized contextual situation. Thus, time and space might be explicitly manifest in a specific text, but they are always inserted into, and the result of, a specific context of spatio-temporal configuration of identities, reproduced by the text. In the case of the actors, something similar happens. In some of the texts various named actors are present, and their mutual relations can be analyzed; but whether these actors are expressly manifest or not, there will be a constant and contextual presence of ready-made identities taken for granted by a majority of the 'members' of the given contextual sphere[4].

As indicated, the instruments of narratology can help to identify more or less fixed mechanisms of meaning according to which certain narrative schemes are repeated within a discursive context, creating what might be termed *narragraphies*, i.e. certain epic, narrative and semantic models constituted by ideas of fixed relations between specific actors (for instance 'Us as givers' and 'the Others as recipients'). These actors are (and are experienced as) 'real' actors in a 'real world', but tend to act discursively within the constraints of specific narragraphies.

---

[3] For a general discussion of the concept, see Haslett 2000. A recent classic work is that of Zizek (1989).

[4] For a given contextual or semiotic 'sphere', I propose the term 'semiosphere', following Lotman (1990).

## Hypotheses

In this general approach to the analysis of the relation between self and Other in some mainly official Danish documents concerning development aid, I will discuss the following points:

- The Other is inserted in a spatio-temporal position of exteriority or marginality (vs. 'centre') and of past and fixed originality (vs. a dynamic and developmental 'now').
- Self and Other are given more or less specific roles that influence the constitution, conception and (probably) actual interaction of the implied parties.
- Applying semantic-structural narrative models, the Other is seen as the *object* of *our action*. As a consequence, the Other is passive (vs. 'Us' as active) and an inferior *recipient* (vs. the active *giver*);
- This construction of the Other, and various strategies and conceptions of the aid policy, lead to contradictions and aporias on a general ethical and/or ontological level as well as on specific and empirical levels.

## Elements of the narrative

The activities taking place within the 'actual' world of development aid depend on the actions of 'actual' actors, i.e. individuals belonging to different national, cultural and institutional contexts. These 'actual actors' are physically embodied and have names, professions, gender and other means of identification. They act within certain formal institutional frames and are constrained by other forms of relations of which power is an aspect to a greater or lesser extent. But a very important aspect of the 'frame' for this (as well as any other) activity is its semiotic, textual or symbolic dimension[5]. My thesis is that one very important element in this semiotic-textual dimension is the fact that most 'texts' constitute and (or) are constituted within narrative models. Texts can actively posit their elements in a more or less explicit narrative frame, constituting space, time and actors, but they are also very often part of a context that explicitly or implicitly deals with a narrative frame into which the actual or specific texts are inserted. In this case, both factors are in play. A large number of texts dealing at different levels (formal and informal, for instance) with the question of development aid establish specific actors (normally defined as

---

[5] Although the three concepts are not completely synonymous, they are closely interrelated aspects of that basic dimension of any human activity that can be called the symbolic or semiotic dimension, i.e. the sign- and sense-making part of human life. The word 'text' in this context implies a broad definition, according to which 'text' can be any meaningful or sense'-giving compilation of signs. Any text will always refer to a 'context', which can be, e.g. 'genre', and (more extensively) 'semiosphere' (cf. Lotman 1990 and Bakhtin 1997).

collective subjects and institutional entities) and more or less specific temporal and spatial dimensions. At the same time, these texts belong to different contexts, more or less definable, examples of which are: *genre* (typically these texts belong to an institutionalised context of official or NGO-papers, or are news texts), *genealogy* (these texts have a history and origin), *discursive position* (they are inserted in national and international discursive systems of development, cf. Escobar 1995) and others. A more general type of context is that termed the *semiosphere*, defined by Lotman (1990, 125) as "the result and the condition for the development of culture". A discussion of the question of the semiosphere is not possible here (see Lotman ibid), but the concept could tentatively be defined as the cultural *context* in which a text 'takes place' as an actual event. In this concrete case, we are dealing with texts that pertain to, and contribute to the reproduction of, relatively specific cultural semiospheres, such as national (in this case Danish) and regional (European). As such, one of their basic roles is the constitution of *identities* of cultural selves and Others.

It is today a widely accepted theoretical position in human and social studies that identities are constructed as relational phenomena (cf. Jenkins 1996). But when inserted as actors into a narrative construction, identities tend to relate to each other in patterns that contribute to giving them specific roles, sometimes more or less independent of the actual acts of actual actors. In other words, the thesis is that implicit or explicit narratives tend to constrain and define the roles of the intra-textual actors, and that these textual-narrative roles or characters cannot be separated from our interpretation of the extra-textual actors.

The basic elements of any narrative, as of any other 'thing' that happens (i.e. an actual event, a performance or a dramatic play)[6], will be the dimensions of *space* and *time* and the *actors* who act in them. Regarding the first elements, it can be relevant to distinguish between an internal time and space of a given narrative and the relation between these and the external world. In the case of the third element, the actors, the principal question is not the specific characteristics of the individual actors, but the *relations* between them. A well-known contribution to the study of relations between actors is the actantial model of Greimas (1973, Barthes et al. 1994, Bal 1997), which establishes six basic 'actantial'[7] functions: *subject*,

---

[6] A basic idea in narratology is that the structural elements of an epic or a narrative correspond to the elemental structures of language, especially the sentence (with a subject, an object etc.). Cf. Greimas 1973, Ricoeur et al. 1994.

[7] This terminology indicates clearly that 'actants' and 'actantial model' represent abstractions for certain generalized functions of narrative schemes, and not narrative 'actors' (persons, personified animals, animated machines etc.) as such (cf. Bal 1990).

*object, giver/sender/power, receiver, helper, opponent*[8]. Depending on the type of narrative, these actantial functions can be fulfilled by different types of actors, of which individual subjects (whether human or not) constitute only one. Institutions, natural or supernatural entities, collectives etc. are other examples. Completely abstract phenomena might also fulfil an actantial function. The object, for instance, is often an inanimate or abstract phenomenon, such as knowledge, love, richness, liberty; or, as in this case, the abolition of poverty.

As stated above, the very designation of the different actantial roles indicates that we are dealing with relational definitions. These relations have three basic characteristics, or are centred around three relational axes. First, a subject desires an object, creating the relation or axis of *desire* or project. Second, a giver or sender gives the object to the receiver, corresponding to the relation or axis of *communication,* and third, there is a relation of *conflict,* in which the helper (normally) assists the subject in his project, while the opponent tries to impede it. As indicated, these different functions are abstractions, and do not necessarily correspond to actual or personified actors of a narrative; for this reason there might be coincidence of identity between different functions. A subject might very well be the same actor or person as the receiver. This is typically the case in a traditional love story, in which a hero (subject) struggles for and gains the love of another person.

*Time, space and otherness.*
The representation of cultural self and Other implies a 'mise en scene' based on implicit or explicit discursive constructions that tend towards narrative structures. I will not go into the question of the general positioning of the Other in such narratives (see Gustafsson 1999/2000), but limit the discussion to the problem of the positioning of the 'indigenous peoples', who are a main focus object in Danish development aid (Danida 1994, 7).

The spatio-temporal configuration of 'Indigenous Peoples' is of particular interest, as a general tendency of exteriorization of the Other is especially manifest in this case, which also becomes obvious with regard to the question of development aid. A discussion of 'who the indigenous people are' can be found in Danida (1994, 9). This discussion stems from the ILO

---

[8] 'Giver'or 'sender' seem to be the most common terms used in English (for the original French 'destinateur'). Cf. The Literary Encyclopedia (www.LitEncyc.com) et al. However, Bal (1985/1997) prefers the term 'power', mainly because " 'sender' suggests an active intervention [...] and this does not always apply". But the Bal's proposal does indeed also imply the idea that the sender/giver/power is in many cases a powerful entity which very often "has power over the whole enterprise" (ibid).

Convention No. 169 from 1989. Recognising that it "will probably never be possible to find a clear-cut definition", it is proposed that most of these characteristics will probably apply to groups of indigenous peoples:

- members of the group "feel" that they belong to the indigenous peoples and wish to maintain their special identity;
- the group consists of descendants of people who lived on their land before the colonization or invasion which subsequently subjected them to an alien political system;
- in terms of language and culture, the group differs from other people living in the country, e.g. because it lives in geographically marginal areas;
- the group has a close bond with nature, which can be observed in its economy and ways of using nature [...] and
- the community is locally oriented with respect to political, financial and cultural institutions, resulting in social marginalisation. (Danida 1994, 9)

The first criterion differs from the others in pertaining to the question of auto- or self-identification, while the other elements aim at an external categorization, establishing criteria for 'indigenousness' that can be used in self- as well as hetero-identification. The first criterion would indeed be very interesting to discuss due to its obviously tautological character, but as my focus here is on the construction of Otherness, I will limit my remarks to the other four, or rather to some of their specific aspects, focussing on the ways in which the criteria for 'indigenousness' posit the 'indigenous peoples' as actors within a narrative or epical scheme. Problems such as the historical, political, economic and other possible issues related to the discussion and justification of the category of indigenous peoples will not be discussed here[9].

Basically, these criteria point to the 'indigenous peoples' as an actor loaded with *difference*. They are different not only from the geographically distant (Danish) 'us', but also from other people of the same nation-state or geographical area. This difference can be expressed in terms of *space*, *time* and (narrative or dramatic) *relations* (to other actors).

The spatio-temporal difference is that of exteriority: they belong to a temporal past and a spatial periphery. They "wish to *maintain* their special identity" (my emphasis). In other words, the indigenous identity is not

---

[9] The problem of Latin America as an object of Post Colonial studies is discussed by Jeppesen and Henriksen in another article of this book. Other questions which might be relevant are: the problem of 'boundaries' (who are and who are not 'indigenous'); tradition and the re-invention of tradition; classification and economic convenience etc.

dynamic, but static, related to a time and a space that were "*before* the colonization or invasion" (my emphasis). Furthermore, they live in "geographically *marginal* areas" (my emphasis) and their "community is *locally* oriented", resulting in "social marginalization".

Thus these basic criteria define the indigenous peoples as decentred in space and time, oriented to nature and to the past. This interpretation has been part of European representations of the exotic Other, especially the American exotic Other, since the 15th century[10]. The idea of the noble savage has been essential in these constructions. What is interesting is that the orientation of the development discourse has engaged in a sort of cultural ecology, according to which the conservation of certain species becomes an essential problem.

We have seen that "the group differs from *other people*" due to the criteria mentioned, and possibly others. But these 'other people' tend to a play a particular role, especially as invaders and colonizers, because the indigenous peoples are "descendants of people who lived on their land before the colonization or invasion" (second criterion). This opposes two actors: the 'indigenous peoples' who descend from the original inhabitants (those living there before invasion or colonization took place), and the 'other people', who logically must be descendants of those who participated in the 'invasion' or 'colonization'. This construction places two actors vis-à-vis each other: the ones who (descend from those who) originally lived in 'their' space and the ones who (descend from those who) 'invaded' or 'colonized' this space. The notion of 'invasion' especially has the connotation of injustice, and in relation to this the same can be said of 'colonization'. In the textual narration or dramatization of the situation, the indigenous subject is victim and passive, the object of unjustified acts committed by the 'other Other', those natives of another country.

In any narrative or epic construction, such a situation of imbalance – in this case injustice – can be a basic motif of the text (cf. Ricœur 1994, Bal 1997 and Barthes et al. 1996). Something is lacking or has been lost, in this case the rights and identity of the indigenous peoples. But as these peoples do not seem capable of handling the situation themselves, they cannot be the protagonists (in this construction) of their own redemption: someone else has to act for them, hence the role of 'us who help'. From the actantial point of view, this suggests an abstract and almost implicit object of 'justice', sought by a (collective) subject, namely the indigenous peoples, with the intervention of a helper (the 'aid' or the donor of the aid) and the opposition of an opponent that might be identified as the 'other of the

---

[10] In Gustafsson 1999/2000, I discuss this question and some of the vast literature on the subject, of which can be mentioned the works of Anthony Pagden, Antonio Gerbi, Stelio Cro and others.

Other', i.e. the descendants of 'invaders' or 'colonizers'. However, the passiveness of the given (indigenous) subject points to the possibility of bestowing this role on another, stronger, actor, in this case the aid donor and protector of indigenous peoples and human rights, i.e. the giving 'Denmark'. The 'ecologization' of the indigenous peoples stresses the passiveness of this subject and the role of the helper: the Other is the victim of former crimes and the ('indirect') object of our redemption. The narrative of a subject struggling for justice becomes a story of an 'us' helping the Other. This question will be further discussed in the next section in relation to the general construction of actantial roles in the texts of development aid.

*Subject, Donor and Receiver – Self and Other in the general context of development aid.*
I now intend to look at the probable or logical narrative actants of the discourse of development aid in general, seen from the point of view of the donor entity. First, I propose to consider the *object*, i.e. the project or goal pursued by a subject. According to Danida 2001, "the overriding goal" of Danish development assistance is to "reduce poverty". Furthermore, the "aspects of gender, the environment, and democracy and human rights are integral concepts in all development activities which receive Danish support". The text clearly shows an 'object' for the narrative, i.e. the 'overriding goal' and 'integral concepts'. The basic idea is that in the context of development assistance/aid this object is by its very nature something that can be 'given' or 'donated'. This implies that the actantial role of the 'giver' or 'donor' is particularly important in this discursive-narrative construction, and that the communicational axis, with a 'giver' or 'donor', is essential to it as well. The actual giver is the Danish Agency for Development Aid (Danida), which is also the author and sender of the text as such. But in several texts (Danida 2001, 1996 and 1994), there seems to be an extension of this specific giver identity to a less specific, and more ideologized,[11] national identity. In Danida 2001 it is expressed in this way: "Denmark is one of the countries in the world contributing the largest percentage of GNP to international development co-operation. With its population of 5 million, Denmark is the 8$^{th}$ biggest donor in the world". The actual entity – author, sender and giver – tends to hide in the background, transferring the honourable role of 'donor' to the national identity.

---

[11] To extend a specific actor – a person or institution – to a general national actor is a common feature of national(ist) (i.e. a specific type of ideological) discourse. See Wodak 1999, Billig 1995 et al.

The consequence of this is that the economic transactions implied in the activities of Danida and the NGOs (which mainly receive their funding from Danida) appear as relations between *Denmark* (and not specific Danish entities or persons) and the 'receivers' of the assistance. In this way, the text becomes clearly *intercultural*, defining relations between (assumed) national (or other collective) identities. The development assistance thus appears not as a series of economic transactions and other kinds of working relations between specific persons and institutions, but as relations between nations or similar collective entities, in which one has the role of the donor and the other(s) that of the receiver.

I have maintained the term 'giver' or 'donor' for the actantial function termed 'destinateur' by Greimas. Bal's proposal that this function be termed 'power' (see above and note) is, nevertheless, quite interesting in this context. Bal (1997, 201) suggests that the 'power' "has power over the whole enterprise" and that it is "often abstract". In the present case, Danida – as well as the generalized 'Denmark' – being the donor with full control over the resources, has the effective power over the whole enterprise, whether this is seen in general as the development aid as such, or more concretely as specific projects in the 'developing' or 'receiving' countries. This suggests that on the actantial level of the 'communicational axis', the relation between donor and receiver in the context of development aid can be seen as a relation between a powerful and a (more or less) powerless actant.

In a narrative relation centred round an object ('reducing poverty', 'human rights', 'gender rights' etc.) defined as a 'gift', 'giver' and 'receiver' become central actors, while in various other kinds of narratives these roles would be more peripheral. This suggests the possibility that the 'giver' in this case tends to be the central actor, i.e. the 'subject'. In other words, the presumed general actantial model for 'reducing poverty' could be the following: object/project: to reduce poverty (and violation of human rights, gender rights et al); subject/protagonist: the poor (and victims of violations of rights); opponent: socio-economic structures, illiteracy, opposed social actors, international relations etc. (depending on the socio-economic or political analysis applied); helper: social or political organization, education, new international economic order, reforms, (depending on the analysis); giver: national government, reforms, revolution, international aid, or, for instance, the poor organizing themselves and changing the conditions etc. (again depending on the actual interpretation or analysis); and receiver: the poor. This actantial model would place the development aid as a circumstantial element and the donor as a secondary actor in the narrative. In some contexts (and texts) this is the case. But, as proposed, in the context of development aid and from the point of view of the giver, the actants are posed differently. Having the aid or the 'gift' as the immediate and main object, the narrative of development assistance tends to place the donor as protagonist of the action, i.e. the subject of the narrative construction. This becomes manifest in specific texts on the theme, like the ones studied here, but it can be suggested that it is also part of a general 'Danish' semiosphere, where a construction of a 'Danish' and 'developed' 'we' vis-à-vis an 'underdeveloped', 'Third World' 'them' depends partly on the idea that 'we' help 'them' by giving part of 'our riches' to 'those poor people'.

The general cultural construction of a 'we' as a powerful donor and a 'them' as a powerless receiver can be seen in other texts (newspapers, TV, Internet sources), political debates on all levels (from the Parliament to the dinner table) and in the texts of NGOs working in the development sphere, to mention some examples.

Among such texts are the advertisements of Danida and various NGOs such as Save the Children, Red Cross and others. These advertisements appear typically as posters in public spaces and as newspaper ads. Normally they consist of a photograph or some other image and a verbal text. The image will typically depict one or more persons whose impoverished living conditions are manifest in some way. There is a preference for children and women (whose situation is of special concern to Danida and some NGOs), and a tendency to show people whose phenotype does not correspond to the 'Caucasian'. I believe that this choice of images will tend to stress the 'othering' of the (potential) receiver of the help. Whether or not this is part of a conscious communicative strategy, it is plausible to assume that an average middle-class Dane who receives such messages will interpret the difference between herself and the people in the photograph as a radical otherness. The verbal part of the message is normally an invitation to give money to an NGO, adopt a child in a Third World country or to engage in some other kind of activity to contribute to 'our' helping action. In this example, there are two mutually reinforcing elements, or signs, related to the 'receiver': firstly, the general narrative construction of the Other as a receiver, and secondly, the image showing an *ideal type* of such a person. The general idea would point to a person like the one in the image, and the image would in itself lead to the idea of a Third World person needing assistance. In other words, a 'receiver', a person in need of help, is a Black, a South American Indian or a dark-skinned Asian child or woman; and vice versa, a Black, an Indian or dark-skinned Asian (especially if the person is a child or a woman) is somebody in need of help.

This help is presented as a good deed done by an active subject that can be regarded as a general 'we' (meaning that any member of this 'we' might feel like a 'giver' without actually having done anything specific), which in this case corresponds to 'Denmark'. When individual subjects engage in actions of help, for instance by giving a donation to a fund or an NGO, this subject will be acting both as a 'good' individual and as a concrete manifestation of the general 'we'.

Regarding the role of the receiver, it has already been said that it implies a powerless position. It is also by definition more or less passive, thus turning the receiver into a kind of *object* for 'our' action. This becomes manifest at the syntactical and semantic levels. In the phrase "I give you a gift", an elementary syntactical analysis shows that 'I' is subject, 'gift' direct object and 'you' indirect object. In the previous discussion, I have tried to show that this syntactical relation also works at the semantic level: we see the receiver of the aid as a relatively passive object of 'our' action. The Other is an object of our subjectivity – i.e. conscious and intentional acting – and not a subject acting upon her or his own situation.

**Concluding remarks:**
To conclude this initial approach to the narrative construction and relational schemes implied in the 'story' of development aid in general, and more specifically in the reading of some Danida texts, it has been suggested that analytical conceptions derived partly from structural narratology can help to reveal the semantic mechanism of texts related (in this case) to the question of development aid. Although the analysis is brief, I believe it has been satisfactorily argued that in these texts the 'Other' – the general or more specific object of aid, especially indigenous peoples of Latin America – is constructed as a more or less passive and powerless 'indirect' object of 'our' Western help, and as a decentred identity.

Basically, I assume that such a construction is of an ideological character (cf. Zizek 1989, Haslett 2000). It could be analyzed as a Barthian myth (Barthes 1994, 199 ff), i.e. as a 'second semiological system' or a 'metalanguage' that constitutes a semantic context for the concrete linguistic (or other) signs. In this article it has been suggested that such 'myths' or ideological constructions also have a narrative or epical dimension within which the actors are positioned in temporal, spatial and relational schemes that are interpreted as 'real' by the reproducer of a given text. As suggested above, such schemes can be termed 'narragraphies'. A 'narragraphy' is a narrative scheme of 'writing', which tends to perpetuate relatively fixed significations and interactions of a given 'theme'. In the case of the identity constructions related to development aid, the 'writing' of the 'Western' (in this case, Danish) 'Us' as givers and 'the Others' as recipients is fixed in predetermined positions. The 'narragraphy' of development aid is bound to certain actantial schemes (as discussed above) and to the idea of certain spatio-temporal positions. Just as historiography is a 'model' for what can be said in the writing of history, a 'narragraphy' limits the semantic possibilities for how to 'write' (and 'read') the relations between social actors.

In the first part of this article I have suggested another idea or hypothesis, which can only be mentioned briefly in this final remark: namely, that such a construction of the Other might lead to contradictions or aporias on an epistemological, ontological or ethical (including political) level. The question is very complex, and I will restrict myself to two basic problems. The first is the question of what might be called the *conceptualization* of the Other: i.e. the Other seen as a *type* or model and not as a real individual situated in 'my' space and time; the conceptualization of the Other can thus be said to be an antidialogical mechanism. This idea is present in Levinas (1969) as a basic philosophical problem: the conceptualization is an obstacle to seeing the *face* of the Other; and it can also be found in the social phenomenology of Schütz (1980).

In the 'development aid construction' of the Other, the Other is not only a semi-passive object, but is also conceptualized as 'poor', 'ill', 'child', 'woman', 'indigenous' etc., which excludes the Other from being an individual self who is not inferior to the producer or re-producer of the text. Though this conceptualization simply appears to reflect a banal social fact, in fact it stands in opposition to the conception of the 'Western' individual self, recognized as such in legal rights and duties, in psychology and sociology, and in the elemental idea of human rights. Such a critique might be seen as a purely abstract problem which is scarcely relevant to actual political action within the field, but whether this is in fact so will depend on further analysis at different levels.

A second problem (closely related to the first) is that epistemological, ethical and political conflicts may appear between Danida's different declared goals, for instance in the co-existence of such parallel objectives for aid as 'human rights' and 'indigenous peoples'. Here two opposed concepts of a human being are in play. One (indigenous peoples) implies a vision of the person as a (literally) anonymous member of a community, whilst the other sees the individual as the fundamental human reality. This epistemological contradiction between two declared goals might very well translate into ethical and political aporias.

## References

Bajtin (Bakhtin), Mihail: 1997. *Estética de la creación verbal*. México D.F., Siglo XXI.

Bal, Mieke: 1997 (1985). *Narratology. Introduction to the Theory of Narrative*. Toronto, University of Toronto Press.

Barthes, Roland et al: 1996. *Análisis estructural del relato*. México D. F., Diálogo.

Barthes, Roland: 1994 (1980). *Mitologías*. México D. F., Siglo XXI (English version: *Mythologies*, London, Grant & Cutler).

Barth, Fredrik. 1969. "Introduction". In: F. Barth (ed.), *Ethnic Groups and Boundaries: The Social Organisation of Difference*. Oslo. Universitetsforlaget.

Billig, Michael: 1995. *Banal Nationalism*. London, Sage.

Escobar, Arturo: 1995. *Encountering Development – The Making and the Unmaking of the Third World*. Princeton, N.J., Princeton University Press.

Greimas, Algirdas J.: 1973. *Strukturel semantik*. Copenhagen, Borgen.

Gustafsson, Jan: 1999. "Figuras de la alteridad: visiones danesas de América Latina". In: Cristoffanini (ed.): *Identidad y otredad en el mundo de habla hispánica*. México D.F., Universidad Nacional Autónoma de México & Universidad de Aalborg.

Gustafsson, Jan: 1999/2000. *El salvaje y nosotros – signos del latinoamericano. Una hermenéutica del otro*. Copenhagen, Copenhagen Working Papers.

Haslett, Moyra: 2000. *Marxist Literary and Cultural Theories*. London, Macmillan Press.

Jakobson, Roman: 1956. "Two Aspects of Language and Two Types of Aphasic Disturbances". In: *Fundamentals of Language*. The Hague, Mouton.

Jenkins, Richard: 1996. *Social Identity*. London, Routledge.

Lévinas, Emanuel: 1969. *Totality and Infinity: An Essay on Exteriority*. Pittsburgh, Duquesne University Press.

Lotman, Yuri: 1990. *Universe of Mind. A Semiotic Theory of Culture*. London, Tauris.

Ricœur, Paul: 1994. *Relato: historia y ficción*. México, D.F., Dosfilos Editores.

Schütz, Alfred: 1980 (1967). *Phenomenology of the Social World*. London, Heinemann.

Tvedt, Terje: 1990. *Bilder av 'de andre'. Om utviklingslandene i bistandsepoken*. Oslo, Universitetsforlaget.

Tvedt, Terje: 1998. *Angels of Mercy or Development Diplomats? NGOs and Foreign Aid*. Oxford, James Currey.

Wodak, Ruth et al: 1999. *The Discursive Construction of National Identity*. Edinburgh, Edinburgh University Press.

Zizek, Slavoj: 1989. *The Sublime Object of Ideology*. London, Verso.

# Narrating Postcolonial Nations: Reading Homi Bhabha's Notions

by

Heidi Bojsen and Ingemai Larsen

This contribution deals with the relationship between the various narrative strategies which authors and writers employ in their texts and the representations of the nation expressed by those strategies. Our intention is thus to engage with a problematic directly related to the continual struggle between different discourses on nation, a struggle which takes place on the periphery of already existing nation states and is intensified by the many border crossings stemming in particular from the history of (post)colonialism and globalisation.

The focus of this paper will be on such narrative strategies as the overall structure of texts, the genre to which they belong, the authors' use of specific linguistic registers and markers of time, which constitute together a series of elements also applied in the analysis of enunciation, thus contributing to the (re)negotiation of a collective national self-understanding.

In our analysis we will draw on a few of the theoretical concepts formulated by Homi Bhabha, whose work has had a decisive impact on postcolonial and cultural studies in general. Following a brief introduction to the definition of these concepts two analyses will be presented, first of a text written by the Martinican politician Garcin Malsa, and next of a novel by the Mozambican author Mia Couto. Finally, the disentangled threads will be tied together, forming we hope, a harmonious interdisciplinary knot.

### From cultural difference to the differentiating of culture
The title of Homi Bhabha's collection of essays *The Location of Culture* (1994) alludes to the author's conception of the main project of postcolonial theory, namely an attempt to "reconstitute the discourse of cultural difference" (ibid. 171). This phrase implies a theoretical stand in opposition to both cultural relativism and essentialism. Instead, Bhabha proposes

to start cultural theory and the literary analysis pertaining to it one step further back, in the place where these entities come into being (hence the mention of location). In language theory this place is most often conceptualised as the level of 'enunciation', to which we will return shortly.

Edward Said's influential work *Orientalism* (1978) set off a critical reading of the colonial and postcolonial experience and of its textual and discursive representations. This critique, which remains very heterogeneous despite its unifying label of 'postcolonial theory', has been developed on the grounds of what Bhabha names the "…historical necessity for elaborating empowering strategies of emancipation, staging *other* social antagonisms" (Bhabha 1994, 171), thus other than those conveyed by the canonical references of the historical, literary and sociological disciplines and of political science. Put more simply, the 'empowering strategies' become 'empowering' in the sense that they pave the way for the concept of 'knowledges' and for new ways of conceptualising history and differentiating cultural formations. The shift from cultural difference to a study of the differentiating of culture and of various epistemologies prepares the development of a "postcolonial contramodernity", a notion which Bhabha explores on the basis of the historian Partha Chatterjee's work. Bhabha emphasises how this shift prevents the concept of contramodernity from working as a notion of anti-modernity or as a celebration of the lost traditions of the past (Bhabha 1994, 175).

Bhabha stresses repeatedly that cultural identity is a discursive sign. The meaning of the sign of cultural identity and its impact on people and other signs depend not only on historical, social and economic factors, but also on enunciation. Who pronounces the words and within what ideological and ontological framework? What happens to the signification of the sign 'nation' and to its meaning as a concept, once it has been enunciated in this or that (con)text?[1] Does the sign 'Denmark' convey the same meaning and, more importantly, does it signify in the same manner, when pronounced in relation to sport events, in a letter to the editor composed by a politician from the extreme right-wing party *Dansk Folkeparti*, or when given as nationality by black Danish school pupils travelling in England?

Bhabha's evocation of time as a fundamental parameter in the discourse of cultural difference is central to his argument in the article "DissemiNation" (1990), in which he aims to display the "disjunctive temporality" of the sign 'nation' (ibid. 299; Bhabha 1994, 148). Temporality here means the linguistic representation of time and space, and we are thus entering an

---

[1] The sign of the nation refers both to the geographical borders, the criteria of citizenship and residency and to legal, language and cultural policies and norms, etc. It encompasses meanings pertaining to the modern idea of nationalism as well as to what certain historians qualify as 'national sentiment', which has been expressed in written sources as far back as the early Middle Ages. (Bell 2001.)

interdisciplinary field drawing on semiotics, philosophy and theories of enunciation. Theories of enunciation often set out the ways in which the perspective of the speaker (meaning his or her positioning in relation to time and space) is connected to the temporality expressed in the text through the means of specific temporal markers, in particular the so-called shifters. In that sense, temporal shifters in any text are connected not only with the author's personal outlook on the world (time and space) but also, and more principally, with the social temporality, i.e. the normative and conventional mode of conceiving time and Being (in the Heideggerian sense) to which authors must adhere if they wish to *make sense* – to signify meaningfully – to their readers[2]. The fact that fictitious people act as subjects of the enounced does not change this but only activates the specific rules of fiction as they have been theorised by Genette, Bakhtin or others. Saussure is aware of the significance of the context with regard to the speech act, as are Emile Benveniste and Oswald Ducrot. As a supplement to (not an abolishment of) these linguistic approaches, Bhabha adds the significance of the "discursive embeddedness" as well as the "cultural positionality" of the enounced (Bhabha 1994, 36), inviting the historiographic and philosophical disciplines to participate in the conceptual investigation of enunciation and signification. This leads us to propose that in our current cultural embeddedness we expand the repertoire of the temporal shifters connecting the level of the enunciated to the level of enunciation, to include words such as 'old-fashioned', 'originary', 'progress', 'development', 'modernity', 'backward', 'antediluvian'. The signified of these words can only be named when considered in relation to their context, which also includes what we call social temporality, that is, the discursive conception of time and place implemented through different institutions and norms. It does not merely refer to our conception of time (as being, perhaps, chronological and progressive) but comprises the pragmatic premises on which, according to Benveniste, the enunciation must work for the enunciated to make sense[3].

### Pedagogical and performative temporality

The definition of cultural identity as a discursive sign implies that it must be narrated in order to come into being. Thus, national and cultural identities do not simply acquire specific meaning via statements from

---

[2] See also Bhabha's comment on social temporality (Bhabha 1994, 171).

[3] One brief comment on the *we* used in this paragraph. We have refrained from any specification for two reasons. A) the *we* should be perceived as a universal generic in its function as a *pronoun*. It is open to the identification of any collective subject. B) the *we* refers of course also to our own positioning which ought to be quite clear from the editorial details of this volume as well as from our intertextual references.

political authorities but are also formed by institutionalised narratives in the shape of historiographic, literary, philosophical disciplines, not forgetting political science, ethnology, etc., as well as by the modes of mediating these narratives both in the institutions they derive from and in the media. Coming from national institutions, they can be seen to represent the pedagogical intent of certain ideological agendas of a given society. But the narration of cultural identity also encompasses the quotidian, performative formulation and practice of cultural identity as it is lived through everyday life. This 'performative discourse', appearing in *medias res* of the national chronological history and embracing various views and norms, may convey a renegotiation or opposition to the institutionalised tales, though it may indeed support the *status quo*. This can best be described as two temporalities, i.e. two alternative modes of narrating time and space (Bhabha 1990, 304-305). The fact that both temporal modes of narrating time and place are at work in national communities, and thus within the sign of the nation, leads to the notion of 'disjunctive temporality'.

It is important to understand that this temporal splitting (which is not a separation) is not merely a characteristic of the meeting of differently empowered social groups. Rather, it is immanent in the national social temporality, i.e. in our way of transferring our conception of time and space into language and action.

> ...[T]he people are the historical 'objects' of a nationalist pedagogy, giving the discourse an authority that is based on the pre-given or constituted historical origin or event; the people are also the 'subjects' of a process of signification (...) The scraps, patches, and rags of daily life must be repeatedly turned into the signs of a national culture. (Bhabha 1990, 297)

The calendar is a classical example of a constituent in the discursive formation that places society in what Walter Benjamin calls 'homogeneous empty time' (Benjamin 1992, 245-255). Walter Benjamin reads the calendar of the French revolution in close relation to its historical context. The new talk of universal human rights demanded a new positioning of the speaking subject in relation to time, and the inauguration of the new calendar embodied what Benjamin sees as the most important task of the translator, namely to provoke so-called ruptures in the ongoing logic of empirical history and thereby create what Bhabha reads as a 'strange stillness' (Bhabha 1994, 224), in which the pertinence of the past to the immediate moment of enunciation (what Benjamin calls *Jetztzeit*) is re-evaluated (Benjamin 1992, 252-253)[4]. But we have other and more recent examples of the same mechanism: Germany's *Stunde nul*, signalling a new

---

[4] To be precise, Bhabha also connects this 'stillness' with the negotiation of cultural difference that occurs in the process of (cultural) translation. See also Benjamin 1992, 75.

start after the Second World War, and *Ground Zero* in New York. The latter has been and continues to be inscribed in narrations that also talk of a 'new era', 'war of religion', and 'crusades', all examples that support our earlier suggestion that the word 'medieval' should also be considered as a temporal shifter bearing on social temporality.

As we read Bhabha's reading of Benjamin, this temporal stillness occurs when the temporality presented in the text, and the temporality (or temporalities) it refers to and is part of, represent radically different ontological and epistemological views. The reader is thus forced to reflect on the premises at play, to consider not only the cultural differences displayed in the text, but also the modes (including her or his own) of differentiating culture.

## Garcin Malsa and the narration of independent Martinique

Garcin Malsa has been the mayor of the Martinican town St. Anne since 1989 and belongs to the MODEMAS-party. He advocates an independent Martinican nation in which environmental concerns are given very high priority. His essay *La Mutation Martinique* (1992) explains his political and ideological visions for Martinique in some detail even if the language and style have the characteristics of a manifesto. Garcin Malsa's plea for a Martinican nation can be seen as a moment of temporal stillness as his texts open up for a different writing of the Martinican present and history from the one produced in the French institutions which govern the island. Malsa performs a rupture within the pedagogical tale of the French nation, whilst at the same time reproducing a nationalistic pedagogical discourse in his description of the Martinican space.

At the enunciative level, the pedagogical sign of the Martinican nation relies on a temporality of *continuum*. This temporality is evoked repeatedly by the use of the future tense in describing the nation, and is apparent in the recurrent discussion of development. As an example of this, Malsa states that a people takes a departure from one point and strives towards another which it alone must determine, thereby causing a positive modification of its prior situation (1992, 26). Malsa believes that the edifying claim of tradition is indispensable in any process leading to modernity.

His text is filled with traditional nationalist arguments, often drawing on such Romantic-nationalistic values as the beauty of the countryside and the *genie du peuple*; yet in this moment of translating the idea of nation into the Martinican reality there is a certain disturbance of the received nationalist ideas. In naming this reality, Malsa is confronted with the people acting as "subjects of a process of signification," as Bhabha puts it in our quote above. They are subjects through their use of the Creole language and their concern with local problems such as water supply, land repartition, unemployment, extended dependency on financial aid from France, etc. The following examples will demonstrate the disseminating complexity of this process.

At the beginning of the essay, Malsa writes *Savoir* (Knowledge) with a capitalised S as if aligning it with a Romantic transcendent concept. This forms a contrast to Bhabha's discussion of 'knowledges' in *The Location of Culture* (1994, 22, 163) and suggests ideological standardisation, at least at a discursive level in Malsa's text. However, a certain plurality is permitted when he goes on to talk about different sorts of know-how (Malsa 1992, 10-11). Small enterprises and family businesses are vital assets combining technological knowledge with local know-how and practical craftsmanship, their small size keeping them flexible. At this point Malsa's terminology takes a turn, and he concludes the chapter with a plea for the "production and mobilisation of Knowledges" (*Savoirs*) (ibid. 12)[5]. It is as if the economic and structural realities of the island and the ensuing performative enactment of being Martinican impose on the text the notion of 'knowledge' in the plural.

As another example, we will briefly mention Malsa's plea at the beginning of his text for Martinicans to stick to their own ways and only apply knowledge and know-how from the outside when these are "mastered" (*maîtrisé*) (ibid. 10). Yet towards the end of the essay he introduces the French sociologist Edgar Morin's notion of 'meta-nation' in a plea for the creation of "harmonisation of economics and cultural policies" (ibid. 21) with other communities, once the nation is "*affermie*"(ibid. 20-21). Again, the realities of the small Caribbean island force themselves upon a logic conceived in larger and economically stronger European countries, and create fissures in Malsa's Romantic-inspired ideals. Martinique is too small to turn its back on the world.

These observations lead to the question of agency in the process of signification described above. We propose to answer this question by suggesting that agency here can be defined as the subject of enunciation, knowing that this 'subject' is never personified or connected to one concrete figure in the theories of enunciation. However, by applying Bhabha's notions, we may be able to say something very precise about the nature of the subject of enunciation, exactly through its contextual and historical embeddedness. In our context, agency is the fact that the sign 'knowledge', in the singular and embedded as it is in narrations of national values and traditions, cannot readily be translated into the Martinican reality: agency is the fact that Martinique does not possess the (national and pedagogical) discursive formations (in Foucault's sense) that could turn the many into one. The answer we are proposing, but have not the space to explore

---

[5] All translations of Malsa and Couto are our own.

thoroughly in this article, is that Foucault's notion of discursive formations might have a decisive role to play in our quest for a specification of agency in the process of signifying.

The sign of the nation becomes the unifying emblem of the multiple possibilities and potentials of Martinican cultural and economic life, but Malsa's cumulative description of Martinique's identity and possibility as a nation is supplemented, through the concrete examples he presents in the text, by an iterative temporality that appears in and through the phenomena and events described. This disjunctive temporality offers an obvious opportunity to rethink what it actually *means* to be Martinican and how to *signify* that meaning. However, in the process of signifying created in his text, Malsa excludes the French and European identity-claims that are widely present in the Martinican public. The opponents of independence and the faction demanding assimilation with French conditions are described as the exponents of a "spiral of dependency," who are thus working within a temporality without progress (ibid. 15). Here, it is quite obvious how the 'wrong kind' of social temporality suffices to disqualify the argument for a given claim of identity. Consequently, Malsa misses out on the theoretical parliamentary and democratic potential of the double time of the national sign (i.e. the dynamics of the performative and the pedagogical), a potential that is evoked implicitly in Bhabha's recurrent use of the concept of 'negotiation'.

Through our reading of Bhabha's notions we can see that Malsa's revolt against Martinique's current status within the French nation could have been an opportunity to outline some sort of contra-modernity with a deliberate infusion of new meanings into the pedagogical intent of the nation. Malsa does present ideas about 'eco-civism' and 'eco-citizens' which might have lead to such an investigation, but they are not resolved in relation to their underlying Romantic ideals. There is no reflection on what it means to *master* outside knowledge or on the historical difficulties of distinguishing between what is outside and what is local.[6]

### Mia Couto: *Somnambulist land*

Mozambican written literary history primarily comprises two genres, poetry and the short story. During the second half of the 20th century, and particularly during the years of anti-colonial struggle, poetry was the dominant literary genre, mainly because poems were more likely to escape censorship than other forms of writing. The esteem of the short story, however, has been growing for the past twenty years. Mia Couto's *Som-*

---

[6] In fact, the Martinican authors Édouard Glissant and Patrick Chamoiseau, who also advocate Martinican independence, seem more successful in rethinking the sign of the nation through their literary and philosophical works. (Bojsen 2002, 230-242).

*nambulist Land*[7] is however a special case. It has been singled out as one of the first novels, or at least novel-like works, published in Mozambique, and the critical confusion concerning its classification is well founded.

As will appear from the following, the problematic of genre is central to our analysis both because this problematic constitutes a prism through which the close relation between literature, language and politics is highlighted, and consequently because this focus will serve to exemplify an empowering strategy as conceptualised by Homi Bhabha.

With regard to the overall narrative structure of the text, *Somnambulist Land* consists of two parallel stories, the life story of a young man, Kindzu, and a frame story set in the recent civil war, in which the main characters, a boy and an old man, become friends and together set out from a refugee camp in order to find the boy's parents. The two stories intersect when the main characters of the frame story find the young man's diary, and reading it aloud are taught about the past of their country and its cultural values which the war has devastated and almost consigned to oblivion. Nevertheless, these values prove themselves capable of being revived through the very *spoken* 'act'. The author of the diary recounts his journey, which he felt called upon to make in order to become a Naparama warrior, one who fights under the protection of a medicine man. His goal, or rather his search for identity, is in fact accomplished, making his death less tragic, also because he dies at the place where the two friends set out on *their* journey, taking with them his diary as their legacy. Thus the story comes full circle, the symbolism transparently indicating that the boy metonymically represents the hope of a future Mozambique, a country with a fulfilled identity.

In spite of the brevity of this summary it should be clear how the principle of circularity is combined with a linear or chronological principle of narration[8], and also how plot and narrative structure work hand in hand. This brings us back to the question of genre, since we read the text as a performative practice, an attempt to create a new genre or rather to consolidate the genre known in Mozambique (and the other Luso-African ex-colonies) as '*estória*', which has its own traditions and requirements of form.

---

[7] Mia Couto, of Portuguese origins, was born in Mozambique in 1955. With *Terra Sonâmbula* he gained international recognition. Mozambique became independent in 1975 after 12 years of colonial war and a democratic revolution in Portugal. Until the first free elections in 1994 the country was ruled by a marxist-leninist regime.

[8] It may be argued that the story contains linearity to a very limited degree, but focusing on the history of Kindzu we may justly say that the two principles are indeed combined.

What are the characteristics of this genre, and why do we suggest that in its challenge to the institutionalised genres (which in an African postcolonial context correspond to the genres of the West) it brings about a meeting of temporal stillness between a pedagogical and a performative discourse, at the same time displaying the disjunctive temporality of Mozambican society?

First of all the written *estória* must be understood as the textualisation of the oral *estória*. Thus it gives a representation of a storytelling *process*, since by its nature the *estória* is always intended to be handed down by transmission to other persons, to be retold by numerous other voices in numerous variations. Hence what we are dealing with here is, in the words of Eco, an explicitly open text almost yelling out for interpretation, contradiction, correction, expansion; and thus, according to Bhabha, a performatively defined practice taking place *in medias res*.

Secondly, a characteristic of the oral *estória* is a circular or mythical perception of time, whereas in the written *estória* this circular or mythical perception of time alternates with a linear temporal perception, and this is easily recognized one of the narrative strategies of Couto's text. Certain chapters of the diary may be read as independent and completed *estórias*, though as a sequence they make up a chronological history of the young man's journey. At times the frame story shows a circular movement, whilst at others it is forwardly progressive, and this combination of a 'homogeneous empty time of ongoing progress' and 'an iterative time of moving forward', (to use Benjamin's expressions) is symbolised in various ways, for example when the boy and the old man proceed along a road yet end up in same place as they started.

The presence the two time perceptions and temporalities and the way they are mediated constitute the *leitmotiv* of the text. The same mediation is thus repeated, in relation to its epistemological and ontological implications. Magic and prophecies form part of the fictive universe side by side with 'rational' forces[9]; however, it is interesting that Kindzu, who keeps the diary, is perfectly able to discriminate between his father's true prophecies

---

[9] This mediation is also recognizable at the level of narration of events; for example the civil war is represented as having been equally destructive to the country as the colonial war.

Couto's mediation between a Western and African style should not to be understood in the sense of 'modern' versus 'traditional'. Establishing such a dichotomy would imply that tradition was considered the 'reverse' of modernity, conceding a hegemonic status to the temporality of the West rather than realizing that an interplay between the two takes place in every culture. Thus it is not contradictory to say that the book is modern in literary terms and at the same time deeply influenced by African mythology.

and those that derive from madness. Here, for example, Kindzu's mother calls the children because their father has had a dream:

> – Come here, Father has had a dream!
> And then we crowded, every one of us, to listen to the truths that had been revealed to him. Taímo received revelations about the future through his ancestors. (...) *This time* the old man [the father] was wearing tie, suit and shoes with soles. His voice did not run away with him and it wasn´t delirious. It predicted an event: The Independence of the Country. (Couto 1992, 14. Our italics)

The novel contains few direct references to the history of Mozambique. We understand that the war has obliterated people's memory of an earlier life, but this does not mean that the past is thought of as dead; on the contrary, to the extent that it is recognized, it is considered alive in a concrete and even normative sense, and this contributes to adding a didactic and moralizing dimension to the text. An example of this is when Kindzu follows the advice his late father gives in his dreams. The same holds true for the future as it is revealed through dreams, where it is represented as a time which up to now has been materialized 'only' in this way. All in all, the dream seems to function as a recurring metaphor for the ability to survive and create, which in its turn is closely tied to the language. This is also reflected in the title of the romance, which refers to the tribe Matimati, known to Mia Couto, and to its belief in the magical power of sleep and dreams.

Above, temporality was related to language, and this leads to the third characteristic of the *estória*: its oral nature. Apart from functioning as a metaphor, throughout the entire text language represents a moral and aesthetic value in the form of a collective repository of inherited experiences. Until written literature emerged in Africa this found its condensed expression in the oral and mythic story telling, handed down from generation to generation[10]. Precisely this oral tradition is omnipresent in *Somnambulist land*, in the loan words from regional Bantu languages in the Portuguese, but also in the numerous new verbs, adjectives, puns and nouns, creating rhythmic effects and semantic enlargement, and as syntax and morphology that transgress Portuguese norms, on the model of the far more flexible Brazilian usage. With this strategy for linguistic autonomy Mia Couto draws on a tradition familiar in a number of postcolonial countries in its valorisation of the oral story-telling tradition, which is alive even today, and not only in Mozambique. In this novel the oral manifestations function diachronically as the vehicle of a return to the forgotten

---

[10] Cf. Ashcroft: "In the language of oral cultures, words are *sacred*. They have the power of the things they signify because they *are* the things they signify. Rather than representation, language is closer to *presentation* (Ashcroft, 2001, 79-80)

magic, the fantastic, the beliefs, the traditions and the divine space and time, and synchronically as the medium of communication between the (few) literate, such as the boy, and the (many more) illiterate, in this case the old man. In this horizontally and vertically open nation-space, orally transmitted experiences are as authoritative as those transmitted textually.

The language transformations and inventions which until a few years ago would have been called subversive operate homologically to the Portuguese currently spoken in the major cities of Mozambique. Thus the non-hierarchical language of *Somnambulist land*, as one of the very first novels in the history of the country's literature, represents a rupture with the period in which Portuguese was a stratifying and repressive element of colonialism whose retention was not negotiable under the subsequent Marxist-Leninist regime either[11]. What the two regimes had in common was an essentialist national discourse that in the name of modernity would exclude from influence the cultures and languages of the tribes. *Somnambulist land* threatens the dichotomy between tradition and modernity; it includes the victims of the hegemonic pedagogical discourse, inviting them to re-negotiate the content of the sign of the nation. Seen from that perspective, it also exemplifies what Homi Bhabha calls a postcolonial contramodernity, that is neither a celebration of lost traditions of the past nor an anti-modernity, but a representation of a different historiographic temporality.

Conclusion

Our analysis has shown us how the specification of the context of a given subject-matter can prove to be analytically productive, in the present case as illuminated by the concepts of Homi Bhabha, and in particular the concepts of performative and pedagogical temporality. In other words, it is absolutely legitimate to object that the strategies of the *estória* are comparable with those of the European experimental novel or Latin-American magical realism, and that consequently it cannot be considered a new genre. However, when the work is examined in its proper contexts of enunciation, including the oral tradition which until recently was disregarded and contained by an inflexible language policy, the assertion of it being a distinct genre holds true.

Speech acts, but also words, are influenced by the context of enunciation, and in this case we have opted to focus on the social temporality because it has a considerable impact on the conceptualisation of national

---

[11] Even though the new rulers' prediction that the language of the former colonizers would be transformed into a language of emancipation was very controversial at the time, the consensus was to retain the Portuguese norm (Larsen 2003).

identity. This Mozambican novel provided us with an example of how a linguistic repository may generate myth, while also depending on a performative 'presence' in the shape of an oral statement, and as such new meaning is created within a specific social temporality.

Garcin Malsa represented his nation through the use of temporal markers, thus reinforcing the impression of a progressively developing country where political adversaries seemed to constitute the main obstacles to progress. Malsa may appear to be an eco-romantic nationalist, so why, it may be objected, should we include his writing as empirical material for our analytical work? Attending to the level of enunciation, i.e. reading him through the concepts of Homi Bhabha, we see how his attempt to formulate an empowering strategy for Martinican politics is entangled in the contextual premises in which the enunciation of the text functions. This cultural embeddedness refers amongst other things to the inheritance of European Romantic nationalism and ecology, as well as to the material and conceptual realities of contemporary Martinican life. Malsa fails to see the disjunctive temporality of the nation, and this partly explains some of the contradictions and awkwardnesses of his text, which seems to impose a common identity on the Martinican population. His arguments appear awkward because he does not recognise the performative temporality as an immanent element of the sign of the nation *and* of its enunciation. Instead he focuses solely on the enunciated, which he either rejects (as in the case of the assimilationists) or seeks to incorporate in the Martinican nation.

By including the concept of temporality and the analysis of enunciation we avoid labelling Garcin Malsa as an 'essentialist eco-romantic', or Mia Couto as a 'modern' nation-builder, which would imply a politically normative judgement on our part, and an ignorance of the social temporality of both our own enunciation and that of the authors. Instead, we may begin one step earlier, by observing how the two texts enunciate the sign of the nation in relation to the concepts of time and space and how they deal with the circumstances in which those concepts are embedded. Furthermore, we may use our analysis to acquire knowledge of the workings of language in relation to the context of enunciation. In both texts the meeting between language and reality has called for neologisms and adjustments, hence the play of signification also takes place at the semiotic level. In *Somnambulist Land* new words are created in order to represent a new experience of reality and the discrepancy between linguistic norms: in Malsa's text we observed the shifts of *Savoir* (Knowledge) from singular to plural, from nation to meta-nation, shifts that have been developed in much Caribbean literature and theory. Both texts provide examples of how the implementation of a national discourse in a new context provokes an ontological and linguistic re-evaluation of the content of the sign of the nation.

To consider the possible effects of the empowering strategies of narration we would have to analyse such aspects as the whole question of reception, something that postcolonial studies are increasingly interested in doing. In this case it has not been possible. However, we would like to draw attention to one incident: in the recently published *Moçambicanismos – towards a lexicon of usages of Mozambican Portuguese* (Lopes et.al., 2002), which among other things must be considered an institutionalised attempt to create an autonomous discourse on oneself, it appears that part of the corpus has been taken from the work of Mia Couto.

Our contribution to this volume should be considered as an invitation to consider the interrelatedness of literary, political and historical source material. Reading this material in relation to its context of enunciation, we take account of knowledge, terminology and methodology drawn from the disciplines of literature, linguistics, history, and philosophy. We would like to conclude by stating that the iterative processes both of writing and of reading and critiquing this paper must also be regarded as manifestations of a performative temporality that permits the re-negotiation of a number of problems in the on-going process of translating notions from one discipline to another, from one context of enunciation to another.

### References

Ashcroft, Bill: 2001. *Post-Colonial Transformation*. London, Routledge.

Benjamin, Walter: 1992. "The Task of the Translator" (1923). In: H. Arendt (org.) *Illuminations*. London, Fontana Press. (1973).

Bell, David A.: 2001. *The Cult of the Nation in France: Inventing Nationalism, 1680-1800*. Cambridge MA / London, Harvard University Press.

Benjamin, Walter: 1992. "Theses on the Philosophy of History" (1940). In: H. Arendt (org.) *Illuminations*. London, Fontana Press. (1973).

Benveniste, Émile: 1966. *Problèmes de linguistique générale* (Vol. I, II). Paris, Gallimard.

Bhabha, Homi: 1990. "DissemiNation: Time, Narrative, and the Margins of the Modern Nation". In: H. Bhabha (ed.), *Nation and Narration*. London, Routledge.

Bhabha, Homi: 1994. *The Location of Culture*. London, Routledge.

Bojsen, Heidi: 2002. "L'hybridation comme tactique de résistance dans l'œuvre de Patrick Chamoiseau". *Revue de littérature comparée*, 2.

Couto, Mia: 1992. *Terra Sonâmbula*. Lisboa, Caminho.

Ducrot, Oswald:1984. *Le dire et le dit*. Paris, Éditions de Minuit.

Foucault, Michel: 1971. *L'ordre du discours*. Paris, Gallimard.

Foucault, Michel: 1975. *Surveiller et punir : naissance de la prison*. Paris, Gallimard.

Larsen, Ingemai: 2003. "O império português responde por escrito ou *estamos numa nice* – sobre a situação luso-africana na perspectiva dos estudos de pós-colonialismo". *Folha de Linguística e Literatura*, nr. 5, Maputo.

Lopes, Sitoe & Nhamuende: 2002. *Moçambicanismos – Para um léxico de Usos do Português Moçambicano*. Livraria Universitária, Universidade Eduardo Mondlane.

Malsa, Garcin: 1992. *La Mutation Martinique: Orientations pour l'épanouissement de la Martinique*. Fort-de-France.

Morin, Edgar: 1987. *Penser l'Europe*. Paris, Gallimard.

# Studies of postcolonialism and the Latin American tradition: National Identities and Indigenous struggles

by

Anne Marie Jeppesen & Ken Henriksen

Introduction
Since the 1980s the area known as Postcolonial Studies has gained in prominence and has now become a challenge to important fields within the social sciences and the humanities[1]. Significant new insights have emerged from the postcolonial critique of former studies of the impact of colonialism, as well as of history writing, cultural studies, and studies of gender and ethnicity. It has brought clarification of the cultural embeddedness of the ideas applied in research and the consequences of the cultural blindness pervading many concepts and studies. Furthermore, it has also suggested new ways of conducting research and of examining the relationship between empirical studies and theory.

Although broad in scope, postcolonial studies have almost exclusively been limited to the former British colonies in Africa and Asia. Surprisingly, works on the former French and Portuguese colonies have only recently started to appear, and studies on the American continent (both North and South) have until now been rare[2].

Since the late 1970s discourses of indigenous identities and rights have become increasingly salient throughout Latin America. But although there have been many successful struggles, and rights and entitlements have been formally recognized, the politics of indigenousness seems not to have

---

[1] The first contribution within this field is considered to be E. Said's *Orientalism*, from 1978.
[2] One contribution to Latin American postcolonial studies is *El debate de la postcolonialidad en Latinoamérica*, edited by Alfonso and Fernando de Toro (1999, Frankfurt Am Main).

gained ground as a basis for alternative post-colonial discussions. It is remarkable that pre-conquest cultures and identities have mainly come to the fore in secluded 'ethnic settings' and only included to a minor degree in post-colonial projects advanced by Latin American intellectuals. In this paper we argue that owing to historical processes the term *indigenous* and its linguistic equivalents have been loaded with a range of negative and inferior connotations, to such an extent that it is hard to imagine any post-colonial project along indigenous lines. Although Indian groups have been empowered by the global focus on indigenous rights, the dominant perception of the Indian population continues to be one of inferiority and backwardness.

The aim of this paper is to discuss possible reasons for the apparent lack of interest in the term 'postcolonial' and postcolonial theories among Latin American researchers and intellectuals. It is not the intention here to give conclusive answers. Rather the aim is to explore what concepts have been developed and to analyse and discuss the complexities and contradictions in the way identity has been constructed in Latin America in colonial and postcolonial times, and finally to suggest areas in which postcolonial theories may become especially relevant in the future. Our hypothesis is that the orientation towards Europe, including the identification with European culture and tradition in the identity construction of non-indigenous groups in the Latin American populations, has distinguished the discussion of the colonial past in this part of the world from present-day discussions in other post-colonial areas. Another hypothesis is that the time factor in the processes of colonization and of independence is of crucial importance. However, we can make no claim to be exhaustive in our discussion[3].

The following items will be considered in this article:

1. The era of Spanish and Portuguese colonization, with the time phase and duration of the colony and the character of the colonial administration;
2. The historical epoch of the independence movements and the construction of the post-colonial/post independence identity of Latin America;
3. The relationship between Latin America and Europe and the exclusion of the indigenous Other in colonial and post-colonial time, adducing the example of the Miskitu Indians on the Nicaraguan East Coast to demonstrate the use of ethnicity to confront state repression and exclusion.

---

[3] In our discussion of these points we will focus especially on Spanish-speaking areas, since our knowledge of Brazil is very limited.

## The Spanish Empire

The Spanish kingdom covered large areas of the present-day USA, (i.e. California, New Mexico, Texas), Mexico, Central America, and the whole South American continent except for Brazil. The colonial administration of this enormous empire was in many ways decisive for the later creation of the independent states. One crucial characteristic has been the administrative distinction between urban and rural areas. Where the Spanish colonisers could benefit from indigenous labour, i.e. in the areas where highly developed civilisations like those of the Incas and the Aztecs had prevailed, they were able to delegate some of the administrative burden to the indigenous leaders and authorities. These were obliged to provide work gangs for the mines and to collect taxes, as well as to function in a number of other ways as mediators between the Spanish colonisers and the indigenous rural population. In the cities, on the other hand, indigenous costume was not permitted, and life was organised more or less as in Europe. This bifurcated state led to the development of two very different but at the same time closely interrelated and interdependent societies in the colonies[4]. The cities were the administrative centres where the highest posts were reserved for Spaniards born in Spain, the so called *peninsulares*; whilst the indigenous groups lived neglected in the rural areas, often at the mercy of local landowners, but also able to preserve some of their original practices, values and languages.

Spanish colonization was a demographic catastrophe for the original population of Las Indias. The figures at which researchers have arrived tell a tale of genocide[5]. Larraín refers to investigations into demographic development in America which estimate that the indigenous population of Mexico declined from 25 million to one million in the course of the first century following colonization (Larraín 2000, 45). About 10 million African slaves were transferred to the continent to alleviate the effects of the labour shortage, especially in the costal regions and the plantations.

At the same time, colonization brought the settlement of Spaniards, although their numbers far from corresponded to the decrease in the Indian population[6]. The lack of European women during the first decades

---

[4] The term *bifurcated state* originates from the South African M. Mamdani's analysis of the British colonial rule.

[5] See Burkholder & Johnson (2001), or Lockhart & Schwartz (1983) for discussions about the calculations and further references about the problem.

[6] The exact number of Spanish immigrants is unknown. Calculations have been made on the basis of the passenger lists of the ships, and it appears that 156.637 persons of Spanish origin remained on the continent between 1506 and 1699. The Spanish state kept strict control over passages to the colonies. Protestants, descendants of Jews, and gipsies were banned (Burkholder & Johnson, 2001, 113).

led to an increase in the numbers of *mestizos*[7], and at the end of the colonial period this group had grown so much that they outnumbered the Spaniards[8].

The settlement of Spaniards led to the creation of important intellectual institutions, for example the University of Lima and the University of Mexico City, both founded in the 16$^{th}$ century and financed by the Spanish Crown. However, only an absolute minority of *peninsulares,* or *criollos*[9], were permitted to study, and the list of books allowed into the colonies was heavily censored by the Inquisition, as was also the case in Spain. According to Lockhart & Schwartz, higher education was meant to benefit the sons of local Spaniards who wanted to enter the professions (Lockhart & Schwartz 1983, 160). A few schools were also established with study programmes that were identical to those followed in Spain. All in all, access to formal education was extremely restricted. This situation was not very different from that in Europe at this period, but it was perhaps even more unequal since indigenous forms of knowledge were completely excluded (Quijano 1999). There were of course large private libraries and a market for books which also included literature from other European countries, but the inhabitants of the colonies were only permitted to write and publish on very local matters. All the same, there are many examples of important writers and intellectuals from the period[10].

What we see developing during the colonial period is a society that becomes gradually increasingly complex in racial, cultural and social terms. Larraín characterizes it as a period:

> [I]n which modernity could not penetrate. It was excluded by the Spanish and Portuguese construction of a cultural identity in which traditional Catholicism played a central role and which tried to maintain and defend a situation of Christendom which was being challenged by the Reformation and by modernization processes in the rest of Europe. (Larraín 2000, 66)

Larraín thus makes it clear that Iberian domination created special characteristics and therefore special problems. We have highlighted two interconnected effects of the colonial administration: 1) Spain established a

---

[7] Mestizo means mixture, in this case of the Indigenous and European populations, very often the result of rapes of Indian women.

[8] According to Lockhart & Schwartz (1983) at the end of the colonial period the part of the population in Peru of Spanish origin was 18,0%, the mixed group 29,2% and the indigenous people 58,2% (p. 342).

[9] *Criollo* (Creole) was the term used for the sons and daughters of Spaniards born in the Indies. During the first centuries both groups were referred to as *Spaniards.*

[10] See Lockhart & Schwartz for a discussion about the intellectual life of the colony.

bifurcated order whereby Latin America was spatially, politically, and culturally divided into two societies, and 2) through the use of control and a coercive colonial regime Spanish America was kept from the advance of modernity. As will be made clear below, these factors have exerted decisive influence on the construction of independent states and national identities in the post-colonial era.

## Independence

According to the Mexican writer, Carlos Fuentes, the population in 1810, when the Wars of Independence broke out, was 18 million. Of these, 8 million were considered to be Indians, one million were black African slaves, five millions were *Mestizos,* and four million were of Spanish or European descent. Of the last group only one in nine was actually born in Spain, and it was this small group, maybe less than 400,000 persons, who dominated the administration in the colonies, the military and the church – but not the economy to the same degree! The local Creole elite had gathered significant wealth, especially in the form of land, and eventually wanted political power, in the first place to be able to trade with other countries than Spain, especially with Great Britain, the emerging world power that was already trying to consolidate and expand its powers overseas at the beginning of the 19$^{th}$ century.

The Latin American Creoles were close observers of the situation in Europe, on which they were very dependent. When in 1808 the Iberian Peninsula was finally invaded by Napoleon Bonaparte, who also named his brother king of Spain, the Creole elites in the American colonies began to wonder to whom they should be loyal. If the Spanish king was no longer a Spaniard, then what were the colonies? Groups of Creoles met and declarations of independence were written (Rodríguez 1998). What started as sporadic peaceful attempts to take charge of the local administration, the so-called *cabildos*, very quickly developed into real conflicts because the Spanish administration of course resisted these take-overs.

According to Fuentes, the surprising thing about Latin American Independence is not so much the speed and the simultaneity of events but much more that it could happen at all (Fuentes 1992). The Spanish colonial empire lasted relatively long; there was a widespread sense of loyalty to the Spanish Monarchy, habits of living and organization were maintained by inertia, and the colonial elite was bound to Spain by family and business ties.

This point of view is confirmed when we read the famous letter "Carta de Jamaica", written by Simón Bolívar, one of the most important liberation heroes, when he was exiled in 1815 following his defeat in Venezuela by the Spanish army. Obviously struggling with his former loyalties, Simon

Bolívar gives an emotional account of the reasons why be believes it is necessary to separate the colonies from Spain:

> The bonds that formerly tied it (America) to Spain have been disrupted... what formerly united now separates; the hatred we now feel for the Peninsula is greater than the ocean that separates us from her; it would be less difficult to unite the two continents than to unite the people in both countries. The habit which meant obedience... religion, a mutually positive climate; a gentle love for the cradle and the honour of our forefathers; all that which was earlier our hope came from Spain...today the opposite is taking place...we have to suffer everything from this unnatural stepmother. (Bolívar 1815; translated from the Spanish by the authors)

The Spanish colonial power not only monopolized trade with other countries, it also controlled most of the production, and not the least, as we have already stated, the whole administration. Consequently in his legendary letter Simón Bolívar also laments the fact that the Creoles were forbidden the right of entry to all administrative posts of any importance. When the Spanish Monarchy was finally defeated in 1826 the construction and formation of the independent nations was gradually initiated. Although the first decades were marked by economic decline, political instability and *caudillos* – military strongmen – who dominated many regions, with time nation states developed whose populations had a sense of belonging and identity, although maybe one that was fragile and complex.

The creation of the Latin American nations thus took place more or less at the same time as the consolidation of European nationhood, as described by Benedict Anderson, although under very different circumstances. As will become evident below, the guiding fictions of the new nations were built on contempt and exclusion, and in some countries narratives able to include all groups in society have never been developed (Schumway 1991).

The Creole elite from the cities led the independence movements. These were wealthy young men many of whom, like Bolívar, had travelled and studied in Europe and were inspired by the literature and philosophy of the period, as well as by the French revolution and the North American War of Independence. They were to become the creators of some of the images and guiding fictions of the independent nations. The new constitutions were drawn up on the model of that of the North American republic, praising the ideas of an unregulated economy, freedom, the rule of law, democracy and representative constitutional government.

But as in Europe the project was restricted to a very small part of the population. The Creole victors were not interested in sharing power with the largest section of the population, the indigenous groups, whom they considered to be inferior and uncivilized. Larraín calls this first project of modernization oligarchic because of its restricted nature (Larraín 2000). The elite applied their liberal ideas in societies that were extremely divided both socially and racially, with an underdeveloped economy and deeply rooted centralized state domination (ibid).

The same circles that favoured freedom and independence were also ready with arguments justifying their contempt of the indigenous population. Contemporary European philosophy taught European racial superiority. As stated in 1824 by Comte de Buffon, one of the creators of the modern approach to the natural sciences:

> The reproductive organs of the savages are weak and small; they have no hair in their bodies or beards, nor are they attracted to females. Although lighter than the European, due to his habit of running more, he is nevertheless much less strong in his body; and is also much less sensitive and yet much more fearful and cowardly; he lacks vivacity, and he has no life in his soul; the activity of his body is less an exercise or willing movement than an automatic reaction to his needs; deprive him of hunger and thirst, and the active cause of all his movements will be destroyed at the same time; he will remain stupidly standing or lying during days. (Quoted by Larraín 2000, 54, c.f. A Gerbi, *The dispute of the New World; the history of a polemic 1750-1900*, University of Pittsburgh Press, 1973)

Since the Creole elite would identify with the Europeans of whom they were descendants, these statements were not understood as being about themselves but about the rural population of the Americas, i.e. the peoples who because of the bifurcated state had been kept at a distance from the civilized cities, very often in deep poverty, and who had preserved their languages and special costume, working methods, and social organization. The very foundation of the new independent states was thus based on a profound contempt for the non-European elements in these societies. This is reflected in both the economic sphere, where indigenous costumes and communal ownership of land were widely abolished, and in the political sphere, where in many places the indigenous population was not given the right to vote until well into the 20$^{th}$ century[11].

The contempt for everything indigenous is clearly reflected in almost all 19$^{th}$-century writings[12], and in many from the 20$^{th}$ century. The first signs of a positive non-European identity can be seen in writings about the *Mestizo* after the Mexican Revolution at the beginning of the 20$^{th}$ century,

---

[11] In Bolivia, one of the countries in South America with a majority of indigenous origin, the right to vote was not given to the indigenous peasants until 1952.

[12] One example is the Argentinean Domingo Faustino Sarmiento, who in his famous book from 1845 about the Argentinian *caudillo* Facundo makes the distinction between civilization (the cities) and barbarie (the countryside and the people living there) which has become a cornerstone in Argentinian identity and has also been highly influential in identity construction in other Latin American countries.

and in the *Indigenista* writings[13]. Both of these intellectual currents were nevertheless of urban 'white' origin and reflect the fact that Latin American identity was never stable or fixed, but also that the bifurcated state remained culturally effective. The imagined communities of the Latin American nations were created on the basis of narratives that effectively excluded the indigenous peoples, except maybe in the cases of the Incas or the Mayas and the Aztecs, who could be used on special occasions to exemplify a glorious past for the region[14].

Unfortunately this silencing of the indigenous past and the uncritical identification with European culture is a double-edged sword. As becomes clear when reading one of the greatest Latin American writers and philosophers of the 20$^{th}$ century, the Mexican writer Octavio Paz, the price is a feeling of solitude (Paz 1950). But in more recent writings too, the Latin American identity is problematized on the background of the European. Carlos Pérez sees the cultural history of Latin America as the history of a 'non-identity'. Perez considers Latin America as belonging to a tradition which it cannot itself address legitimately because its bodies of knowledge are European. He sees the Latin American as "a kind of European who is not the owner of his identity", "he is nothing more than the recognition, under European form, of his non-European being". (Pérez 1991, cited in Larraín 2000, 186). Although this might not be exactly the point of what Pérez is discussing, he denies that the indigenous bodies of knowledge are part of Latin American knowledge[15]. Below we will discuss other consequences of this denial of the indigenous groups.

**An ethnic revival**
It has been argued that no Latin American nation has experienced sustained ethnic political mobilization, as have, for example, India, Malaysia and South Africa (Lebaron 1993)[16]. Nevertheless, in a publication from 1994 the Mexican anthropologist Rodolfo Stavenhagen has presented some considerations on this issue. He argues that in Latin America the term

---

[13] See for example Larraín, 2000, for a discussion of *Indigenismo*.
[14] See Carbó (1997) for a discussion of the Mexican case.
[15] A much more positive, although highly critical, contribution is made by Néstor García Canclini in his *Hybrid cultures, or Strategies for entering and leaving modernity*, even though this book is also based on European theories.
[16] According to Lebaron, the Inca rebellion led by Tupac Amaru in 1780 and the Maya Totonicapán revolt of 1820 are two interesting exceptions. It is beyond the scope of this paper to discuss whether Lebaron's claim indicates a lack of historical knowledge about such manifestations rather than simply the absence of such political activities. A tentative argument would be that Lebaron's claim in fact reflects the disdain for everything indigenous in Latin America, which has also resulted in an official silencing of indigenous political activities.

*indigenous* has gone through a process of modification whereby the once discriminatory connotations have been transformed into a symbolic appeal to resistance, the defence of human rights and the transformation of society (Stavenhagen 1994, 14-15). In the same paper he claims that the discourse of 'indigenousness' has led to a denunciation of injustices and to the formulation of specific rights that derive from the injustices suffered and from the very quality of being indigenous (Ibid. 17).

Since the beginning of the 1980s a large number of indigenous insurrections, protests and ethno-political mobilizations have confirmed Stavenhagen's point. Apart from the Coast peoples' struggle for autonomy and self-determination in Nicaragua, other examples are the neo-Zapatistas of Chiapas, Mexico, and organizations of lowland indigenous peoples in Ecuador who combine a struggle for recognition with a fight for democracy. In addition, as we are writing, groups of indigenous peasants in Bolivia are fighting against privatisation and the neo-liberal world order[17]. Moreover, the fact that these groups have actually achieved improved constitutional conditions and growing recognition as peoples illustrates that indigenous political mobilization has often had a social and political pay-off. However, most of the accomplishments have not yet transcended the formal constitutional arena. Despite formal advances, the indigenous population continues to struggle against exclusion, poverty and racism.

In what follows we will address the question of whether this ethnic revival contributes to the construction of new post-colonial identities in Latin America that challenge not only the discourses of exclusion and marginalization but also the sense of solitude that is the result of the self-denying glorification of European culture.

Nicaragua is an interesting case in point. In July 1979, when the Sandinista Revolution brought an end to more than four decades of dictatorship, many Nicaraguans saw this as the dawning of a new epoch. Initiatives were taken to construct a just socio-political framework aiming at economic redistribution, and the state started to exert direct responsibility for social welfare, health security, education and poverty eradication (Walker 1997; Sollis 1989). But firmly rooted in the social realities of Mestizo Nicaragua, the Sandinista policy adopted a top-down integrationist approach on the Atlantic Coast (Hale 1994). Accordingly, what government officials saw as benevolent political interventions, the Coast population, and the still more powerful ethnic organizations, interpreted as racist attempts to colonize and hispanicize the Atlantic Coast. Familiar with the emerging global focus on the Fourth World and on aboriginal populations worldwide, these organizations started to promote indigenous rights. One

---

[17] See for example Jeppesen 2002, for an analysis of identity construction among the indigenous peasants of Bolivia.

of the leading organizations, MISURASATA (Miskitu, Sumu, Rama and Sandinistas Working Together), expressed solidarity with the Sandinista program. But the nature of MISURASATA's demands rapidly radicalised (Vilas 1990, 237ff). The ideas of a Nicaraguan nation-state had been accepted in the first announcements of this organization, but gradually discourses of indigenous nations and territorial independence became still more salient (Henriksen 2002, 140). The contradictions between FSLN's integrationist approach and the discourses of indigenous rights were still more apparent, and at the beginning of 1981 Indians started to mobilize against the Sandinista state.

**The construction of indigenous identities on Nicaragua's Atlantic Coast**
Unlike most of the western highlands of the Central American isthmus, what is today known as Nicaragua's Atlantic Coast was never under the direct influence of Spain. Instead, the region was under British colonial rule from roughly 1745 until 1894, when Nicaraguan troops enforced a violent annexation of the territory. Since then many members of the five ethnic minorities living in the region have interpreted Nicaraguan presence as a continuation of foreign colonial rule. But whereas people have a positive remembrance of British rule, the attitude towards Nicaraguan influence can best be described as one of distrust and hatred of anything 'Spanish', the word most often used when talking about things or people of west-Nicaraguan origin (Hale 1994; Gordon 1998).

The multi-ethnic make-up of the Atlantic region is the outcome of this historical trajectory under different colonial masters. After the Incorporation, heavy eastward migration meant that today the majority population on the Atlantic Coast are Spanish-speaking Mestizos. Apart from the three Indian groups, the Miskitu, Sumu and Rama populations, two other minorities started to make their presence felt under British Rule: the Garífunas, who are of Caribbean origin, and the English-speaking black Creoles[18], who descended from African Slaves[19]. The Atlantic Coast can

---

[18] In this paper we have hitherto used the term "Creole" about Europeans born in Latin America. Nevertheless, in Nicaragua this term mainly refers to black people of African descent born in Nicaragua. In order to avoid misunderstanding we have chosen to use the prefix "black" about Creoles of African descent

[19] Because of defective means of registration and heavy in- and outward migration any demographic estimation is bound to be questioned. Moreover, whereas government censuses tend to understate the numbers, the ethnic organizations often exaggerate. The indications below rely on a study made by CIDCA, an independent Center for Research and Documentation about the Atlantic Coast (Hale & Gordon 198, 726): Mestizos (Spanish speaking) 180.000; Miskitu-Indians (Miskitu-, Spanish or English speaking) 70.000; black Creoles (English speaking) 25.000; Sumu-Indians (Sumu- and Spanish-speaking) 5.000; Rama-Indians (English-speaking) 1.000, Garífunas (English-speaking) 1.500.

therefore be described as a multiethnic field in which differing and shifting ethnic boundaries (Barth 1969; Jenkins 1997) are constantly drawn and redrawn. The legacy of Nicaraguan domination has nevertheless resulted in a stable boundary between the ethnic minorities and the Spanish-speaking Mestizos. This boundary has been the driving force in shaping ethnic identities on the Atlantic Coast (Hale 1994; Henriksen 2002).

During the 20$^{th}$ century, the state consolidated what has been called a "myth of a Mestizo Nicaragua", a collective belief that Nicaragua is an ethnically homogeneous society (Gould 1997, 16). One of the implications of this myth is that the indigenous traces have completely vanished from official histories of the nation. In their place, the Mestizo – understood as the victory of civilization over barbarism (Gould 1997, 16) – has come to stand as symbol of Nicaraguan identity. Located at the margins of common Nicaraguan Mestizo destiny, the *Indio*, on the other hand, has become synonymous with backwardness and ignorance (Gould 1997, 17). This means that the post-colonial formation of the Nicaraguan nation-state reflects the above-mentioned pattern of ethnic divisions in Latin America (see also Wade 1997; Lebaron 1993). Moreover, this fixation on civilization and cultural homogeneity at the expense of indigenous traces is also a sign of the general obsession with progress and evolution in Latin America, which has resulted in the pursuit of a European-styled modernity and an associated exclusion of 'irrelevant' identities. In Nicaragua, contemporary textual representations of the Coast population, as expressed in ordinary parlance and in national newspapers, are contributing to the reinforcement of this binary structure of a traditional 'them' and a modern 'us'. Whereas ordinary Mestizos depict the Atlantic Coast as a black otherness populated with ignorant, irrational savages (Lancaster 1992), national newspapers have produced an image of the minorities as passive recipients of development and assimilation (Hale 1994; Gordon 1998; Henriksen 2002). This means that two different but closely interrelated discourses contribute to the exclusion of Atlantic Coast minorities. If the Coast population is not to be doomed to perennial inferiority, their salvation will rest upon a unidirectional movement whereby 'they' become 'us'. In both cases the discourses are unequivocally exclusive, portraying the Coast as an isolated region populated with enigmatic Others. The result is a relatively stable hierarchical ethnic edifice with the Mestizos uniformly on the top (Henriksen 2002).

Not surprisingly, the connotations of inferiority have historically been internalised in the Coast people's self-perceptions. Some of the ethnographic and historical research on the Atlantic Coast observes that until the 1980s the ethnic minorities were ashamed of their ethnic status and afraid to publicly remember their collective history or to speak their native languages outside of their homes (Gabriel 1996, 168; Gordon 1998, 183).

Nevertheless, a recent fieldwork study on a Miskitu community on the Atlantic Coast has observed a renewed ethnic pride which contrasts with previous self-denigrating perceptions (Henriksen 2002). In this community townspeople express deep-felt pride of their ethnic identity, and are aware of their regional, even national, reputation as one of the ethnic communities which are most vigorous in defending their rights and safeguarding land and local territory. Self-denigration has to a large extent been replaced by ethnic pride. Perhaps as the result of the loss of the Miskitu language, there is today a high level of attention to alternative indications of cultural survival and historical continuity. The endurance of traditional livelihood practices, communal ownership of land, and the widespread use of mutual aid and other types of political and economic organization have been constructed as important ingredients in a moral link with the past in general and in a retrospective affiliation with the Miskitu ancestors in particular. In addition, the recent establishment of a council of elders in this and other communities on the Coast adds another dimension to the "invention of tradition" (Hobsbawn & Ranger 1983) and to the creation of an indigenous way of life.

More immediate threats add another dimension to this shift. In recent years an increasing pressure on land has exacerbated the situation. With poor Mestizo peasants, Pacific elites and international logging firms staking out claims to huge tracks of land for subsistence or speculation, one of the political strategies of ethno-political organizations and ordinary people alike is to combine indigenous discourses with claims about land rights and historical grounded privileges. In this situation, the construction of historical continuity and the demonstration of moral and cultural links with pre-conquest ancestors and their ways of life are being used as means to strengthen identities in the negotiations and conflicts. The argument is that "we" have lived here since "our ancestors' time", dating back to before the arrival of the Mestizos, the black Creoles and the Garífunas. From this point of view the three last-named ethnic groups have either very limited or no rights to communal lands. This step has led one observer to argue that "[black] Creole identification as Miskitu [is] a potentially important strategic move" (Gordon 1998, 263). The underlying rationale of this position is that the combination of indigenous identity and historical rights represents a powerful device in political and social conflicts over access to scarce resources. In a situation where international donors and human rights organizations are increasing pressure on Third World countries to make them respect the rights of the ethnic minorities, an indigenist strategy seems to be an attractive option, though perhaps only at first glance.

## The localization of global ideas about Indigenous Rights
With the global flow of terms, ideas and images, even people who remain in familiar ancestral places find the nature of their relation to these places increasingly changed. It is, however, a central paradox that as these places become ever more blurred, *ideas* of culturally and ethnically distinct identities and places (countries, regions or villages) prove to be even more salient (Gupta & Ferguson 1992). A quick survey of the world demonstrates that ethnic and national identities are often fixed upon a cultural interpretation of descent which assumes a primordial given of social existence and an essential connection with ancestral societies. According to Arjun Appadurai, we have here the paradox of 'constructed primordialism' (Appadurai 1997, 28). Whereas primordialists argue that ethnic and national identity derive from birth and are thus prior to human experience and interaction, constructivist approaches hold that ethnicity is formed and re-formed by human beings. The juxtaposition of the terms *constructivism* and *primordialism*, therefore, connotes the idea that aboriginal sentiments do not result from cultural 'givens' but from the work of the imagination.

It is not necessary to point out that the flow of these terms and images across the world should not be conflated with homogenisation. Appadurai argues that they have "loosened the internal coherence that held them together in a Euro-American master narrative" providing instead dissimilar meanings and social significances in different contexts (Appadurai 1996, 36). He goes on to argue that problems of both a semantic and a pragmatic nature are involved: semantic, to the extent that the terms require translation from context to context, and pragmatic to the extent that the political use of these words may be subject to different sets of conventions and purposes (ibid. 36).

Below we will indicate one of the ways in which images associated with indigenousness go through a process of semantic and pragmatic translation in Latin America. It follows that political organization along indigenous lines reproduces existing power relations and thus endangers postcolonial projects that seek to construct new and more just multi-cultural societies.

## Indigenous identity as a source of inferiority
Among ethnic minorities in Latin America, primordial attitudes are often created in a retrospective relation to pre-colonial societies and cultures, and may thus come to stand in opposition to the national identities that have dominated the formation of post-colonial states. As argued above, these national identities are built upon a modernist interpretation of social evolution whereby indigenous traces are viewed as having been exterminated and then replaced by civilization and progress. The result is a social

division between two types of identity constructed on the basis of two different sets of values and ideas: a socially weak indigenous identity built on ideas of cultural survival in opposition to a dominant national identity founded upon ideas of modernization and an associated denial and repudiation of pre-colonial traces.

This suggests that in Latin America indigenous political strategies are not always unproblematic, and that a full understanding of indigenous politics must be based on an awareness of the historical and cultural context in which ideas of aboriginality are supposed to be active. According to Stuart Hall, it must be recognized that the roots of identity are located in historical and marginalized experiences (Hall 1995).

This means that the extent to which indigenous identities function as cultural and political resources in specific negotiations and interactions is constrained by existing power relations and by experiences of exclusion and marginalization.

As mentioned above, in Nicaragua as well as in many other Latin American countries a post-colonial historical trajectory of exclusion has resulted in a dominant interpretation of the Mestizo identity as the victory of civilization over barbarism, and a concomitant understanding of the Indian groups as undesirable relics of the past. The proliferation of indigenous identities based on ideas of cultural survival and aboriginality can perhaps enable improved access to land and other resources, as in the Nicaraguan case. But the indigenous groups are in fact claiming moral and cultural affinities with a distant, pre-colonial past, which stand in contrast to dominant national identities constructed on the basis of self-images in which traditional and indigenous traces are synonymous with backwardness, and thus erased. Resistance along indigenous lines therefore constitutes a two-edged sword whereby ethnic pride and the recognition of rights are achieved at the cost of reproducing the initial positions of inferiority. Though constituting a platform for oppositional politics, indigenous strategies are also deflected so as to strengthen the dominance of the Mestizo population.

## Concluding remarks

Since the politics of indigenousness is still in an early phase as a basis for alternative post-colonial projects, it is difficult to make any judgments on the longer-term political and social implications of the indigenous revival. Despite their formal recognition as peoples with specific rights, the initial domination of a European-oriented population over inferior, 'backward' minorities remains mostly intact. In Nicaragua, the indigenous population was granted formal political autonomy in 1987, and different ethnic communities have successfully demanded titles to land, but the discursive denigration of everything indigenous has not been assailed by these changes. Instead, dominant discourses continue to represent the indigenous population as passive, underdeveloped objects of governmental benevolence. Their indigenous status is constructed as a retarded Otherness which can by rectified by progress and education (Henriksen 2002, 104-130).

In this paper we have argued that the principal explanations for the limited success of indigenous strategies can be found in a Latin American context. Among the hypotheses that have guided the analysis is that of the time factor, and the fact that five centuries of colonial and post-colonial political realities have resulted in 'bifurcated states'. By this we wish to indicate the establishment of an extremely stable dichotomy between, on the one hand, a European-oriented Spanish-speaking Mestizo population which understands itself in terms of civilization, progress and modernity, and on the other, a poor, excluded ethnic population which is interpreted as exactly the opposite: backward, inferior, anachronistic, and unmodern.

We claim that along with the oligarchic nature of the political administrations, the time factor is a peculiarly Latin American phenomenon which differs from the colonial and post-colonial processes that took place in Africa and Asia. The fact that the dominant national identities have steadily looked towards Europe and categorized the ethnic minorities as undesired Others is a painful reality that few other ethnic minorities have to struggle with in other parts of the so-called post-colonial world.

This implies that post-colonial projects based on indigenous discourses and strategies are doomed to confront a stable and powerful conception of Indian cultures as merely relics of the past. We dare to argue that this is part of the explanation of why the post-colonial critique has been relatively limited in scope in Latin America.

The foreign language departments in Denmark that, as in other places, have been structured according to modern European perceptions of national and linguistic boundaries, have been slow to recognize the existence of the multiplicity of languages and texts stemming from alternative bodies of knowledge within the geographic boundaries of their languages. These have been left to the anthropologists, or maybe to the historians. Latin America has in fact only recently been integrated into the curricula of the Spanish departments in Denmark. Today the challenge is to recognize this as part of the post-colonial heritage. Post-colonial theories offer us the possibility of an interesting future collaboration between the different language departments on the basis of the common colonial past of the European countries and the ethnic revival throughout the post-colonial world.

# References

Anderson, Benedict: 1996. *Imagined Communities*. London, Verso.
Appadurai, Arjun: 1996. *Modernity at Large. Cultural Dimensions of Globalization*. University of Minnesota Press.
Barth, Fredric 1969: "Introduction". In: F. Barth (ed.), *Ethnic Groups and Boundaries: the Social Organization of Culture Difference*. Oslo, Universitetsforlaget.
Bólivar, Simon: 1815. "Carta de Jamaica". In: *Escritos del Libertador, vol 8*, Caracas, Sociedad Bolivariana de Venezuela, 1972.
Burkholder, Mark A. & Lyman L. Johnson: 2001. *Colonial Latin America*. Oxford, Oxford University Press.
Carbó, Teresa: 1997. "Who are they? The Rhetoric of Institutional Policies toward the Indigenous Population of Post-revolutionary Mexico". In: Riggens (ed.), *The Rhetoric of Othering*. London, Sage.
Díaz Polanco, Héctor: 1997. *Indigenous Peoples in Latin America. The Quest for Self-Determination*. Westview Press.
Freeland, Jane: 1989. "Nationalist Revolution and Ethnic Rights: The Miskitu Indians of Nicaragua's Atlantic Coast". *Third World Quarterly*. 11, 4.
Fuentes, Carlos: 1992. *El Espejo enterrado*. México, Fondo de Cultura Económica.
Gabriel, J: 1996. "UNO.....What Happened to Autonomy? Politics and Ethnicity on Nicaragua's Atlantic Coast". *Ethnic and Racial Studies*, 19, 1.
Gordon, Edmund T: 1998. *Disparate Diasporas. Identity and Politics in an African-Nicaraguan Community*. University of Texas Press.
Gould, Jeffrey: 1997. *El Mito de 'la Nicaragua Mestiza' y La Resistencia Indígena 1880-1980*. Editorial de la Universidad de Costa Rica.
Gupta, Akhil & J. Ferguson: 1992. "Beyond "Culture": Space, Identity, and the Politics of Difference". *Cultural Anthropology 7 (1)*.
Hale, Charles. R: 1994. *Resistance and Contradiction. Miskitu Indians and the Nicaraguan State, 1894-1987*. Stanford, California.
Hale, Charles & Gordon Edmund: 1987. "Costeño Demography: Historical and Contemporary Demography of Nicaragua's Atlantic Coast". In: CIDCA/Development Study Unit, *Ethnic Groups and the Nation-State. The Case of the Atlantic Coast in Nicaragua*. University of Stockholm.
Hall, Stuart: 1995. "Caribbean Identities". *New Left Review, No 209*.
Henriksen, Ken: 2002. *The Construction of Ethnic and Spatial Identities. Everyday Forms of State Mutation on Nicaragua's Atlantic Coast*. Copenhagen Business School. Ph.D. Series 26.
Hobsbawm, E. & T. Ranger: 1983. *The Invention of Tradition*. Cambridge University Press.
Jenkins, Richard: 1997. *Rethinking Ethnicity. Arguments and Explorations*. Sage.
Jeppesen, Anne Marie Ejdesgaard: 2002. "Reading the Bolivian Landscape of Exclusion and Inclusion: the Law of Popular Participation". In: N. Webster & L. Engberg Pedersen (eds.), *In the Name of the Poor*. London, Zed Books.
Lancaster, Roger: 1992. *Life is Hard. Machismo, Danger, and the Intimacy of Power in Nicaragua*. University of California Press.

Larraín, Jorge: 2000. *Identity and Modernity in Latin America*. Cambridge, Polity Press.

LeBaron, Alan : 1993. The Creation of the Modern Maya. In Crawford Young (ed.), *The Rising Tide of Cultural Pluralism. The Nation-State at Bay?* The University of Wisconsin Press.

Lockhart, James & Stuart B. Schwartz: 1983. *Early Latin America. A History of Colonial Spanish America and Brazil.* Cambridge, Cambridge University Press.

Paz, Octavio: 1950. *El Laberinto de la Soledad*. México. Fondo de Cultura Económica.

Rodríguez O. Jaime E.: 1998. *The Independence of Spanish America*. Cambridge, Cambridge University Press.

Quijani, Aníbal: 1999. "Coloniality and Modernity/Rationality". In: *Globalizations and Modernities*. FRN Report, 99, 5, Stockholm.

Schumway, Nicolas: 1991. *The Invention of Argentina*. Oxford, University of California Press.

Sollis, Peter: 1989. "The Atlantic Coast of Nicaragua. Development and Autonomy". *Journal Of Latin American Studies 21.*

Stavenhagen, Rodolfo: 1994. "Indigenous Rights: Some Conceptual Problems". In: Assies & Hoekema (eds.), *Indigenous Peoples' Experiences With Self-Government*. IWGIA and University of Amsterdam, Copenhagen.

Vilas, Carlos M: 1990. *Del Colonialismo a la Autonomía. Modernización Capitalista y Revolución Social en la Costa Atlántica*. Editorial Nueva, Managua.

Wade, Peter: 1997. *Race and Ethnicity in Latin America*. Pluto Press.

Walker, Thomas W (ed): 1997. *Nicaragua Without Illusions. Regime Transition and Structural Adjustment in the 1990s.* SR Books.

# African Literature Today: The Stakes in Teaching and Research

by

Bernard Mouralis & Heidi Bojsen

## Introduction

African literature, comprising both works written in Africa and writings from the diaspora, occupies an important place in the curriculum and research of numerous universities in Africa, America and Europe. Over the last thirty years real progress has been made in the knowledge of this literature, as the growing number of scholarly works on the subject and regular publications in the field testify.

In this article we will comment very briefly on the current status of research on African literature, and then embark on a discussion of a number of general issues, viewing this research as a point of departure for scrutinising the task of the academic critic and for investigating both the construction of the text corpus (as a research object) by critics, writers and society, and the premises underlying their conceptual and analytical tools. In using the term 'African literature' in the singular we refer to the generic conceptualisation of literature as an event, without of course denying it the pluralistic manifestations that sometimes lead critics to talk about 'literatures'.

Contemporary readings of African literature often suffer from a lack of analytical tools that can do justice to the complexities of the intertwined histories of the former colonies and Europe. Presenting a number of examples, we will argue that African literature requires a reading that acknowledges this complexity, while also considering the importance of intertextuality, the presence of universal themes of human concern, and the autonomy of the writer. Finally, we will apply some concepts from the work of the French sociologist Pierre Bourdieu in order to outline the ways in which the works of African writers can benefit the development of literary scholarship in general.

Considering the percentage of university courses on the subject, the number of theses presented and of jobs advertised in the discipline, there is no doubt that there has been a positive development in this area in many countries since the 1970's. However, despite such progress it cannot be ignored that there is still a certain degree of resistance to and reticence about teaching and critiquing African literature in some European and American universities. Firstly, in some instances university structures continue to affirm, implicitly or explicitly, the existence of a hierarchy in the field of literature, on the model of the centre versus the periphery. In France, for example, there is the opposition between 'French literature' and 'Francophone literature', and in the United States between the 'canon' and the 'minority'.

Furthermore, works on literary theory continue to focus for the most part on authors belonging to the literature of the centre, such as Dante, Miguel de Cervantes, Gustave Flaubert, Marcel Proust, Henry James, James Joyce, etc. Yet writers like Chinua Achebe, Ngugi wa Thiong'o, Wole Soyinka, Aimé Césaire, Edouard Glissant (from Martinique), and V.Y. Mudimbe have produced a theoretical corpus which must be analysed for its general literary value, and not only in relation to African texts.

In this respect, it is interesting to note that while the New Criticism in France represented an important innovation in method, it was still founded exclusively on a corpus of classical texts. Critics like Roland Barthes or Gérard Genette have not written a single line on writers from the Francophone perimeter. Even Kateb Yacine's famous novel *Nedjma*, published in 1956, has never captured the attention of specialists of the *nouveau roman*, despite its sophisticated narration.

### The duty to analyse
Teachers and scholars working on African literature must take into account both the progress in the field just noted and the resistances at work in the formulation of knowledge of African literature. It is quite possible to analyse this opposition without entering into polemics of little scientific merit, formulated as Western literature against African literature. Our task as teachers and critics is not to transmit or celebrate a European or an African heritage, even if this has been an important premise for the foundation of national literary historiographies, but to understand and explain certain types of literature and to underline the issues negotiated in the formulation of these types. In this respect, we should be well aware that the positions occupied respectively by the conservatives defending the Western canon, and radicals like Martin Bernal or Ivan Van Sertima who claim Africa as the origin of civilisation, are working within identical conceptual frameworks. We therefore find it worth investigating what Bourdieu describes as the need to accept "the realist representation of hu-

man action which is the first condition for scientific knowledge of the social world" (Bourdieu 1998, x-ix).

But what is a realist representation in this case? Our first difficulty is to select an unprejudiced bibliography of the literary texts produced in the field we intend to study. Therefore, before even using terms such as 'Anglophone literature', 'Francophone literature', 'Commonwealth literature', 'Black African literature', 'Postcolonial literature', we could simply talk about 'Literature in Africa' and on this basis deal with questions of text corpus, authorial usage of different languages, and biographical aspects. Moreover, our reading of European literature would benefit from the same conceptual scrutiny.

Literature everywhere contains an individual attitude whereby the writer positions her- or himself on the margins of society, even if she or he is not always fully conscious of this fact. Africa is no exception, even with regard to its oral literature. Consequently, our task must also be to elucidate this complex dialectic between social context and the paradoxical position which nurtures artistic activity.

## Literary production, colonisation and decolonisation

A simple but also very fundamental problem in the analysis of 'literature in Africa' is the fact that our present conceptual tools cannot do justice to the complexities either of the context of this literature or to the signifying processes which it exposes. An obvious example of this inadequacy is found within the critique that focuses on the relationship between the colonial situation and literary production in Africa. In fact, investigations of what is now broadly termed 'postcolonial criticism' can only be really innovative if they also provide specific and detailed analysis of what colonialism actually is and was in Africa[1].

Ever since René Maran published *Batouala* in 1921, colonisation has been a central theme in much of African literature (or better, 'Literature in Africa'!)[2]. The critical approach that was employed by many writers served to unmask and denounce not only the colonial system, but also, and maybe even more, the political, social, and cultural context in which this literature was created[3]. Due to the pervasive presence of a discursive and literary resi-

---

[1] For discussions of colonialism and historiography in the African space see the three volumes of *Histoire de la France coloniale*, 1991.

[2] For very practical syntactic reasons the term 'African literature' will occasionally be used here. It is our hope, however, that the phrase 'Literature in Africa' will remain as a ruminating supplement (as this Derridean notion is interpreted by Homi Bhabha) that 'adds to without adding up' (Bhabha 1990, 312-131; 1994, 163).

[3] As in Mongo Beti, *Perpétue et l'habitude du malheur* (1974), *Remember Ruben* (1974) and in Ngugi, *Petals of Blood* (1977) and many others.

stance to the colonial system in this literature, it became natural to label it political and anti-colonial. However, this label does not help us to elucidate what is in fact at stake in these often very sophisticated literary strategies of resistance. Did they merely express a deliberate intention to break with the European world, or did they represent an attempt to appropriate what the Europeans had refused to grant the colonised peoples of Africa?

This apparently simple question becomes much more powerful the moment it is asked in relation to the French colonial assimilation policy. If this notion carried with it specific intentions when it was launched by the French authorities, then what happened to those intentions the moment they were accepted as aims worth struggling for and embedded in African nationalism in several countries between 1930 and 1950, in particular in French territories during the era of what became known as the French Union (*Union française*)? This union came into being in 1946, at the time when the Fourth Republic was ratifying a new constitution whose charter was the result of the persistent efforts of the African deputies in the two constitutional assemblies. These African politicians (L. S. Senghor, Gabriel d'Arboussier, F. Houphouet Boigny, Lamine Gueye, Ouezzin Coulialy, etc.) had already participated in the passing of a series of fundamental laws within the French overseas territories (*Territoires d'outre-mer*). The new constitution would establish one code of citizenship and a single electoral college within the French Union, including France as well as the overseas territories. Furthermore, it abolished the colonial education system, introducing instead the same programmes and diplomas as in France. Though this legislation came up against several severe obstacles, the colonial assimilation policy did finally bring an end to the original system (Mouralis, 2001).

Moreover, the colonial system was not homogeneous in time and space. African colonial history can be divided into two eras that differ in their mode of exploitation and administration. The first period, running through the 16$^{th}$ century to the middle of 19th century, was of a system of domination founded on the slave trade and presupposing the institution of slavery and a plantation economy on the North American continent and in the West Indies. The second period, which started around 1880 (earlier, however, in Algeria and South Africa) and ended with the independence movements of the 1960s, saw a much more elaborate territorial domination and political and administrative organisation of the African countries[4]. Here, a comparative study of French, Belgian, English and possibly Portuguese modes of colonisation would not be satisfactory for our analytical approach. We would miss out on important knowledge and insight if we neglected to include the specific histories of the colonised

---

[4] For archival references, see Delavignette, 1950 (1946) and Mbembe, 1996.

territories in our range of observation. A different option is to formulate two groups of countries, one in which the coloniser took the land from the Africans (Algeria, South Africa, Kenya...) and imposed a form of administration that deprived the inhabitants of their former rights of property, and another where property rights were sustained but controlled by the colonial tutelage (AOF – *Afrique Occidentale Française*) (Mbembe 1996).

This distinction remains of the utmost significance for our present research, referring as it does to historical and structural facts that can help elucidate some of the problems that followed independence. African authors thus write from different historical backgrounds, and their attitudes to and modes of perceiving their own countries and the history they share with the colonial powers are also different. Their narration of the national space is in each case marked by its history as a geographical territory as well as an 'imagined community'. The existential question which tacitly underlies all formulations of collective identities, namely 'what is my/ our place in life?' is present in the literature and in the various administrative, discursive and historical modes of representing both 'space' and 'place' in Africa.

We must also be aware that territorial colonisation operated on two levels. On the one hand, colonial conquest resulted in military, administrative, economic and often cultural control of the colonised space. On the other, it set up a specific understanding of this space in order to explore its geography, natural resources, societies, history, and languages. The epistemology of colonial authority was as effective a means of power as was the military, and it is thus not surprising that this knowledge, and the mode of representing it, was met with suspicion in much African literature. However, the historical concomitance of these scientific disciplines and colonial rule is not enough to dismiss all that these modes of knowledge may induce. A significant part of 'Africanist' research developed largely independently of colonial power and enjoyed evident academic recognition from scholars such as Marcel Mauss, who always had deep esteem for Maurice Delafosse and Marcel Griaule, two eminent anthropologists. In fact, African writers and scholars have drawn largely on the work of European Africanists to elaborate their own vision of Africa. A striking instance of this is the fascinating relationship between Hampâté Bâ and Griaule, whose vigorous dialogue conveyed both respect for and profound criticism of the colonial representation of knowledge. Hampâté Bâ's *Kaidara, récit initiatique peul* (1968) is one example of this dialogue. Another classic example is the way in which the works of Delafosse became a central source of inspiration for both Cheikh Anta Diop's Afrocentrism and for the *Négritude*-movement as it was formulated by Léopold S. Senghor and Aimé Césaire. If Afrocentrism and the *Négritude* movement reproduced, at least to some extent, the same received ideas of categorizing peoples, races and territories as the ethnography of the time, Césaire's *Discours sur le colonialisme* (1955) and the critique formulated by Hambâté Bâ present convincing arguments for going beyond these divisions. Likewise, the *Chants d'ombre* (1956) by Senghor exposes the theme of antifascism, and his discourse on *Négritude* has always been closely connected with a universal poetry and thinking whose relevance goes beyond the issue of 'black people'.

In our attempt to explain the different modes of representing national identity in the literature in Africa, we cannot ignore the question of the colonial state. The second era of colonialism in Africa entailed the construction of a state as a centralising administrative institution that did not necessarily respect the triptych division between the legislative, executive and jurisdictional powers within the colonial territories. This state apparatus usually remained unchanged even after independence was achieved. In certain cases, the installation of the state completely altered local 'governmentalities' and the conceptualisation of public life, whilst in other cases the result was a combination of new and pre-existing governing systems. Such vestiges of the colonial administrative system may be seen as proof of an incomplete decolonisation, often defined by the term 'neo-colonialism', as expressed in Frantz Fanon's *The Wretched of the Earth* (*Les damnés de la terre*, 1961) or in Mongo Beti's essay, *Main basse sur le Cameroun* (1972). Yet this choice of word may again lead to an unnecessary simplification of the heterogeneous colonial experience. In fact the various advocates of African nationalism are far from unanimous in their critique of the state administration. Some present an essentialising and fundamental critique and dismissal of the State administration because of its colonial nature; others take a more analytical (and constructivist) approach and direct their criticism at the specific modes of exercising control and power used by different state administrations. In *Remember Ruben* (1974), Beti attempts to develop the idea that strong state leaders did not exist in pre-colonial Africa. He claims that instead there were clan democracies in which conflicts were resolved by means of discussion, and that this system ended when the colonisers appointed leaders in the belief that they were conforming to African 'tradition'. However, both Anta Diop (*Nations nègres et cultures*, 1954) and Delafosse, (*Haut Sénégal Niger*, 1912) argue for the existence of African pre-colonial states.

### Reading the texts

These reflections on the colonial experience and the impact it might have had on literary production constitute a necessary first stage of our analysis of literature in Africa. Acknowledging the fact that we are thus also complicit in the previously mentioned obsession with reading African literature within the scope of political and historical contexts, we nevertheless hope to add to the utility of this theoretical approach (which is also justified by the thematic choices and references in many of the volumes) by stressing how this literature opens the way for a renegotiation of the epistemological assumptions implicit in such a reading.

There is however a number of other methodological considerations connected with literary analysis, and here the concept of intertextuality can be seen as especially rewarding. The reception of African literature seems to focus largely on biographical circumstances while neglecting, to a large extent, the importance of the intertextuality in which the authors work[5]. This textual context, which may be regarded as part of the authors' literary resources, includes written literature both in the main European languages and in African languages, and also the very sophisticated African oral literature, which is mediated through the narrations of the local *griot*. Consequently, the author finds his place and creates a space for himself (in life and literature) within this network of texts. As critics we need to ask ourselves both how the writers respond to all these texts and employ them in their creative work, and also how the various systems of representation generated in the texts give shape to the concept of the African author. One element in this intertextuality is the stereotyping discourse of especially colonialist fiction, whose vocabulary and views were largely rejected by African writers. However, as illustrated by the *Négritude* movement, other concepts have readily been appropriated and inserted into an African mode of conceptualising African space. This has been the case with the notion of primitivism, which was established as a long European tradition from Montaigne to Lucien Lévy-Bruhl[6]; Lévy-Bruhl's thinking was an inspiration to the surrealists and to such influential writers as Senghor, Césaire and J.-P. Sartre, as well as to the Caribbean writer Jules Monnerot, in their criticism of Western rationalism.

To a greater extent than writers from any other part of the world, African writers are compelled to produce their fiction while at the same time elaborating a discourse on literature. The function of this discourse is mainly to proclaim what African literature *should be*; it does not usually seek to define an existing literature from a purely critical perspective, as is seen in Boniface Mongo-Mboussa's collection of interviews and essays by African writers (Mongo-Mboussa 2002). This prospective and voluntarist discourse emerges from a number of events, such as the First Congress of Black Writers and Artists (Paris, 1956), the Second Congress (Rome, 1959), and the role of journals such as *Présence Africaine*.

---

[5] For an example see Sainville 1963, 31.

[6] For detailed documentation see Montaigne 1987, I, chapter 31, "Des cannibales" (1580) and 1987, III, chapter 6 "Des coches" (1588); Diderot 1798; Lévy-Bruhl, 1910 and 1922.

However, a closer analysis of the actual texts will reveal that the writers do not necessarily adhere to the dictates of this discourse. Beti's novels, for instance, have given brilliant accounts of the social and institutional contexts that writers had to engage with during the colonial period and after independence was achieved. When we read his novels (*Le pauvre Christ de Bomba* (1956), *Mission terminée* (1957), *Remember Ruben* (1974)), we are reminded of Balzac's description of the novelist as '*un docteur ès sciences sociales*' (a social science specialist), as he said in *La cousine Bette* (1846). But this is only one aspect of the art of the fiction. Parallel themes run through Beti's work: the question of alliance, a protest against the roles that society imposes on the individual, and the special relation between brother and sister. The theme of incestuous desires has not been shown to be linked with the situation of Africa at any particular moment of its history: it merely expresses the specific universe of one individual, and can be characterised as what Charles Mauron calls a 'personal myth' (Mauron 1963).

This reflection leads to the question of the autonomy of the writer. Does the writer only translate a culture and the literary forms that exist before him, the elements given to him by society? This point of view has been propagated by a number of critics who have stressed the opposition between a European and an African conception of literature. However, in quite a number of texts African writers insist on asserting themselves as subjects of their own writing, not as translators of an already existing culture. They resist being completely determined by their historical past and present context, though they do not deny the influence of those dimensions, as is apparent in such texts as *L'écart* (1979) by Mudimbe, *La reproduction* (1986) by Thomas Mpoyi-Buatu, *The Interpreters* (1965) by Soyinka, and *Ce fruit si doux de l'arbre à pain* (1987) by Tchicaya U Tam'Si. And in this respect we must remember the last sentence of Fanon's *Peau noire, masques blancs* (1952) (*Black Skin, White masks*): 'My final prayer: Oh my body, make of me always a man who questions!' ("*O mon corps, fais de moi toujours un homme qui interroge*"). Those very significant words are not merely an appropriate epigraph both for the texts mentioned above and for Fanon's own œuvre, but constitute a (body)language which the critic can only benefit from mimicking. This *clin d'oeil* to Homi Bhabha's reading of Fanon in his essay on mimicry serves to underline how his use of the concept is consistent with our stand, in the sense that the habitual polarisation between the African novelist and European culture and critique is shown to be inadequate[7]. The failure to notice this aspect has too often led to a reductionist reading of the works of African writers because their creative and existential endeavour to

---

[7] See Bhabha's essay on mimicry 'Of mimicry and man: The ambivalence of colonial discourse' (Bhabha 1994, 85-92)

formulate paradoxes and subjectivity has not been fully understood, nor has its pertinence for literary analysis in general been fully recognised: The answers to the questions they pose, such as how ideas and thoughts are produced in a colonial context, and how the subject may carve out a place of his or her own, do not only relate to African history and culture. In fact, these answers are as much intertwined with aesthetic concerns and narrative complexity as is the case in any other literature.

At this crossroad between textual analysis and the institutional approach, the notion of the literary field as defined by Bourdieu, especially in *Les règles de l'art* (1992) (*The Rules of Art*), can be particularly profitable in the analysis of literary works from Africa. For a long time, critics tended to consider the literary production of African writers as a homogeneous entity and situated it in a binary opposition to European literary production. Reality, however, is more complex, and the notion of the literary field helps us to examine it more clearly. In his reading of Gustave Flaubert, Charles Baudelaire and Stéphane Mallarmé, Bourdieu argues that in France in the second half of the 19th century the literary field was or tended to become autonomous in relation to the field of economic and political power. Moreover, the literary field is a space of competition, "[...] a network of objective relations (of domination or subordination), of complementarity or antagonism, etc. between positions [...]. Each position is objectively defined by its objective relation to the other positions [...]. To the different *positions* [...] correspond equivalent *dispositions*, literary and artistic works, of course, but also political acts and discourses, manifestos and debates, etc. – thereby challenging the alternative between the internal reading of the work and the explanation of its production and utilisation through the social context" (Bourdieu 1996, 321-322).

It is in the study of situations including many heterogeneous elements that the notion of the literary field can be useful. These elements may include the choice of language (European or African), the genre (poetry, novel, drama, essay), the mode of distribution, the readership, and the writers' cultural resources, professional skills, level of education and experience with European lifestyles. Taking these factors into account, our analysis shows that the *dispositions* and *positions* in the literary field of writers like Romuald Hazoumé, Senghor, Sembène Ousmane, Soyinka, Amos Tutuola, Hampâté Bâ, Calixthe Beyala, Mariama Bâ, Abdourahman Waberi, Aminata Sow Fall, and Ken Bugul lead to very different aesthetic creative processes, testifying to the use of very different literary strategies for the development of symbolic capital.

In his reading of French 19th century literature, Bourdieu has theorised the different uses of such capital as aspects of power struggles where one literary field often comes to dominate another, and similar struggles for symbolic and manifest influence can be detected in Africa. The case of

*Négritude* is significant in the analysis of these struggles. Between 1930 and 1950, this literary movement constructed the paradigm of 'Africanity' by developing three main themes: the valorisation of African civilisations, the definition of black people's specific relationship to the world, and a reminder of the violence suffered by black people throughout their history. But the work accomplished by the *Négritude* writers is not limited to this thematic approach. What they wanted was not to be perceived as 'African writers', but to join forces with the literary avant-garde of the time and thereby attain fully-fledged authorial status. This is indicated in several ways. First of all, the writers of the *Négritude* movement had a strong interest in positioning the black struggle within the more general framework of the fight against racism and fascism. In this respect, the image of Ethiopia plays a significant role in Senghor's work. Other facts that add to the picture are the links with surrealism (especially the close relationship between André Breton and Aimé Césaire) and the role played by prefaces, such as that written by Robert Desnos for *Pigments* (1937) by Léon-Gontran Damas, by Breton for the second edition of *Cahier d'un retour au pays natal* (1947) by Césaire, and Sartre's famous *Orphée noir*, the *Préface* to *Anthologie de la nouvelle poésie nègre et malgache de langue française* (1948) by Senghor. Their need for recognition as writers who should be evaluated and appreciated on the grounds of their work rather than their place of origin made publication in France even more desirable to African writers, and a journal like *Présence Africaine* soon became a significant platform for their publications[8]. All these facts indicate a will to give African literature international status, and not to present it as a regional or peripheral literature dealing with local problems. Another instance of the complex rapport between African writers and their European readers is the fact that colonial officials provided prefaces for other African books: Georges Hardy for *Doguicimi* (1937) by Hazoumé, and Delavignette for the second edition of *Karim, roman sénégalais* (1948) by Ousmane Socé.

**Concluding remarks.**
The specific historical and contextual circumstances described above reveal what is in fact a forgotten common-place in the human sciences: our subject matter does not exist as such, but is the product of the epistemological questions we choose to ask. This requires, of course, a self-critical gaze at our own point of view. How far are our choices determined

---

[8] Of course, the urge to publish in France was also determined by very earthbound practical reasons such as the lack of a readership in the African countries, where a high rate of illiteracy and low incomes prevented African publishing houses from establishing themselves. This problem is still felt by many African writers, even though some countries, such as Senegal, Nigeria and South Africa, are now able to sustain publishing houses.

by the selected text? To what extent do our own histories and conceptual methods determine which texts we select?

At least during the first phase of research, for reasons linked to the context of its development the reading of literature from Africa requires an acute awareness of the inextricable ties between the aesthetic value of the literary production and its social context. Colonisation is a complex phenomenon, and reactions to its practices are also complex. It is commonly believed that there are two ways to escape domination: assimilation and independence. But when we scrutinize the concrete histories of the postcolonial spaces, can we conclude that independence alone always entails freedom? (Even Fanon did not believe this). And does assimilation always translate into submission, alienation and 'loss of authenticity'? In fact, the histories and literature from the African continent show how the practices and coincidences of real life often bear a disturbing and disseminating effect on the meaning of those concepts that we considered to be so well defined.[9]

The study of literature in Africa, as anywhere else in the world, requires the identification of the specific features that appear in the text. However, the results of our literary research will be of limited validity if we fail to recognise issues which might be universally at stake in any literature, written in Africa or elsewhere. It is perhaps most vital to bear in mind the opposition between what society wants and what authors perform in their works, as the critic is indeed a complicit agent in this problematic.

The notion of the literary field is useful as it permits one to theorise the constant circulation of individuals and texts between the European and the African worlds. Moreover, though it is true that knowledge of the histories and literature of France or Great Britain can contribute to a better understanding of the histories and literature of Africa, it is equally true that knowledge of the histories and literature of Africa can be a very effective tool for reading European texts in a different light. An acquaintance with the work of Mongo Beti deepens our reading of Honoré de Balzac.

Finally, because of the institutional framework from which they speak, it is important for scholars working on the literature of the 'periphery' to be aware of the appropriateness of their theoretical contributions. They must consider themselves specialists in the field of literature in general and not only in the field of 'African literature'. In particular, scholars should be able to formulate innovative and critical stands with regard to the traditional divisions of disciplines (and departments!) imposed by research insti-

---

[9] Such disturbance of habitual understanding of concepts pertaining to existential questions is particularly clear in Ahmadou Kourouma, *Allah n'est pas oblige...* (2000) and in Mongo Beti, *Trop de soleil tue l'amour* (1999).

tutions and universities. Firstly, we might want to demand the implementation of university policies in which these disciplines are at the service of knowledge and science, and not vice versa. Secondly, however, we know the extent to which the histories of literature departments are interconnected with the formation of national philological departments; and this reminds us that even the concepts of 'knowledge' and 'science' are historically and discursively constructed, and that our very epistemologies may thus be at stake as we work in the process of changing philologies.

## References

Aggarwal, Kusum: 1999. *Amadou Hampâté Bâ et l'africanisme. De la recherche anthropologique à l'exercice de la fonction auctoriale.* Paris, L'Harmattan.

Amselle, Jean-Loup & Emmanuelle Sibeud (eds.): 1998. *Maurice Delafosse. Entre orientalisme et ethnographie : l'itinéraire d'un africaniste (1870-1926).* Paris, Maisonneuve et Larose.

Bâ, Amadou Hampâté: 1968. *Kaidara, récit initiatique peul,* in co-operation with L. Kesteloot. Paris, Julliard, coll. Les Classiques Africains.

Bâ, Hampâté Amadou: 1973. *L'étrange destin de Wangrin ou les roueries d'un interprète africain.* Paris, UGE, coll. 10-18.

Bernal, Martin: 1996. *Black Athena : les racines afro-asiatiques de la civilisation classique*, Vol. I : *L'invention de la Grèce antique (1785-1985),* translated by Maryvonne Menget & Nicole Genaille. Paris, PUF, (1987).

Beti, Mongo: 1972. *Main basse sur le Cameroun. Autopsie d'une décolonisation.* Paris, Maspero.

Beti, Mongo: 1974. *Perpétue et l'habitude du malheur.* Paris, Buchet Chastel.

Beti, Mongo: 1974. *Remember Ruben.* Paris, UGE, coll. 10-18.

Bhabha, Homi: 1994. *The Location of Culture.* London, Routledge.

Bourdieu, Pierre: 1996. *The Rules of Art,* translated from *Les règles de l'art. Genèse et structure du champ littéraire* (1992) by Susan Emanuel. Oxford, Polity.

Bourdieu, Pierre: 1998. *Practical Reason: On the Theory of Action,* translated by Polity Press from *Raisons pratiques: sur la théorie de l'action* (1994). Cambridge, Polity Press.

Delafosse, Maurice: 1972. *Haut-Sénégal Niger.* Paris, Maisonneuve et Larose, (1912).

Delavignette, Robert: 1950. *Freedom and Authority in French West Africa,* translated by M. Fortes, Daphne Trevor & M. Manoukian. London, Oxford University Press (Translated from *Service Africain,* Paris, Gallimard, 1946).

Diderot, Dénis: 1798. *Supplément au voyage de Bougainville* (written in 1778-1779).

Durand, Jean-François and Jean Sevry (eds.) 2003: *Littérature et colonies.* Paris/Pondicherry, Kailash et Montpellier, SIELEC (Société Internationale d'Etude des Littératures de l'Ere Coloniale).

Durand, Jean-François (ed.): 1999. *Regards sur les littératures coloniales,* vol.I-III. Paris, L'Harmattan/Montréal, L'Harmattan Inc.

Fanon, Frantz: 1961. *Les damnés de la terre*. Paris, Maspero.
Fanon, Frantz: 1952. *Peau noire, masque blanc*. Paris, Seuil.
Fonkoua, Romuald & Pierre Halen: 2001. *Les champs littéraires africains*. Paris, Karthala.
Griaule, Marcel: 1948. *Dieu d'eau, entretiens avec Ogotémmêli*. Editions du Chêne.
Gueye, Lamine: 1955. *Etapes et perspectives de l'Union française*. Paris, Editions de l'Union française.
Lévy-Bruhl, Lucien: 1910. *Les fonctions mentales dans les sociétés inférieures*. Paris, Alcan.
Lévy-Bruhl, Lucien: 1922. *La mentalité primitive*. Paris, Alcan.
Mauron, Charles: 1963. *Des métaphores obsédantes au mythe personnel. Introduction à la psychocritique (Baudelaire, Nerval, Mallarmé, Valéry, Corneille, Molière)*. Paris, José Corti.
Mbembe, Achille: 1966. *La naissance du maquis dans le Sud-Camerounais (1920-1960), histoire des usages de la raison en colonie*. Paris, Karthala.
M'Bokolo, Elikia (in cooperation with Thierno Bah, Jean Copans, Sophie Le Callenec, Locha Mateso & Lelo Nzuzi): 1992. *Afrique noire, histoire et civilisations*, vol. II, XIX$^e$-XX$^e$ siècles. Paris, Hatier/AUPELF.
Meyer, Jean, Rey-Goldzeiguer Tarrade, Meynier Thobie, Ageron Coquery-Vidrovitch: 1991. *Histoire de la France coloniale*, vol. I-III. Paris, Pocket, coll. Agora.
Midiohouan, Guy Ossito: 2002. *Ecrire pays colonisé. Plaidoyer pour une nouvelle approche des rapports entre la littérature négro-africaine d'expression française et le pouvoir colonial*. Paris, L'Harmattan.
Mongo-Mboussa, Boniface: 2002. *Désir d'Afrique*, foreword by Ahmadou Kourouma. Paris, Gallimard, coll. Continents Noirs.
Montaigne, Michel de: 1987. *Essais*, 3 vol. Genève, Slatkine. (1580-1588).
Mouralis, Bernard: 1984. *Littérature et développement. Essai sur le statut, la fonction et la représentation de la littérature négro-africaine d'expression française*. Paris, Silex.
Mouralis, Bernard, Anne Piriou, Romuald Fonkoua (eds.): 2003. *Robert Delavignette (1897-1976), savant et politique*. Paris, Karthala.
Mouralis, Bernard: 2001. *République et colonies. Entre histoire et mémoire : la République française et l'Afrique*. Paris/Dakar, Présence Africaine.
Mudimbe, V. Y.: 1979. *L'écart*. Paris, Présence Africaine.
Mudimbe, V. Y: 1991. *Parables and Fables, Exegesis, Textuality, and Politics in Central Africa*. Madison, University of Wisconsin Press.
Mudimbe, V. Y: 1994. *The Idea of Africa*. Bloomington, Indiana University Press.
Mudimbe, V. Y: 1988. *The Invention of Africa: Gnosis, Philosophy, and the Order of Knowledge*. Bloomington, Indiana University Press.
Ngal, Georges: 1994. *Création et rupture en littérature africaine*. Paris, L'Harmattan.
Sainville, Léonard: 1963. *Anthologie de la littérature négro-africaine*; Tome I: *Romanciers et conteurs*. Paris, Présence Africaine.
Van Sertima, Ivan: 1976. *They were before Columbus*, New York, Random House.

# List of authors

**Hanne Leth Andersen**, Ph.D., is Senior Lecturer at the University of Aarhus. Recent publications:
"La politesse véhiculée par le vague : l'exemple d'*un peu*, de *presque* et de *peut-être* en français parlé". In: Pusch & Raible (eds): *Romanistische Korpuslinguistik: Korpora und gesprochene Sprache, ScriptOralia* 126. Tübingen, Narr. 2002.
"Modern Language Studies in Current Educational Planning". In: Hansen (ed.), *Changing Philologies*. Copenhagen, Museum Tusculanum Press, 2002.
With Christa Thomsen (eds), *Sept approches à un corpus. Analyses du français parlé*. Genève, Lang (forthcoming).

**Merete Birkelund**, Ph.D., is Senior Lecturer at the University of Southern Denmark. Recent publications:
*Modalité et temporalité dans les contrats commerciaux rédigés en français. Une analyse des temps verbaux dans les énoncés performatifs*. University of Southern Denmark, 2000.
With Boysen & Kjærsgaard (eds.), *Aspects de la modalité*. Tübingen, Max Niemeyer 2003.
With Bache & Nørgaard (eds.), *Ny Forskning i Grammatik*. Christiansminde, University of Southern Denmark, 2003.

**Jørn Boisen**, Ph.D., is Senior Lecturer at the University of Copenhagen.
He is the author of studies on 20th century French fiction, focusing in particular on the relationship between philosophy and the novel, and of two books, on Romain Gary, *Un picaro métaphysique*, Odense, Odense University Press, 1996, and on Milan Kundera, *Milan Kundera - En introduction*, Copenhagen, Gyldendal, 2001.

**Heidi Bojsen**, Ph.D. student at the University of Copenhagen. Recent publications:
"Le leurre théorique du multiculturalisme." *Portulan* 4, 2002.
"Entretien avec Patrick Chamoiseau". In: Degn (ed.), *Actes de colloque*. Romansk Institut, AU, 2001.
"L'hybridation comme tactique de "résistance" chez Patrick Chamoiseau : Un espace comparatiste : La Caraïbe". *Revue de Littérature Comparée* 2, 2002.
"Flash-Backs of an Orchid: Rhizomic Narration and Identity in Patrick Chamoiseau's *Biblique des derniers gestes*". In: Handley, *Caribbean Literature and the Environment: Between Nature and Culture*. Ithaca, University Press of Virginia (forthcoming).

*List of Authors*

**Teresa Cadierno**, Ph.D., is Senior Lecturer at the University of Southern Denmark. Recent publications:
"Expressing motion events in a second language: A cognitive typological approach". In: Achard & Neimeier (eds.), *Cognitive Linguistics, Second Language Acquisition and Language Pedagogy*. Berlin, Mouton de Gruyter, 2004.
"The acquisition of Spanish preterite and imperfect by Danish language learners". *Spanish Applied Linguistics* 4 (1), 2000.
"Formal instruction from a processing perspective: An investigation into the Spanish past tense". *The Modern Language Journal* 79 (2), 1995.

**Francesco Caviglia**, Ph.D., teaches Italian language, culture and history as Foreign Lecturer at the University of Aarhus. Recent publications:
*Tools for Advanced Literacy: Functional Approaches to Reading, Writing and Storytelling* (Ph.D. Thesis). University of Aarhus 2003.
"Lie Detecting as a Step Towards Critical Literacy". *L1-Educational Studies in Language and Literature*, 2, 2003.

**Edmond Cros** is Professor Emeritus of Spanish and Latin American Literature at the Université Paul Valéry, Montpellier, and Director of Institut International de Sociocritique. Recent publications:
*La sociocritique*. Paris, L'Harmattan, 2003.
*El sujeto cultural, sociocrítica y psicoanálisis*. Medellín Colombia, Fondo editorial, Universidad EAFIT, 2003.

**Inge Degn**, Dr. phil., is Senior Lecturer at the University of Aalborg. Principal publications:
*Her og Andetsteds. En introduktion til Henri Michaux's værk*. Arkona og Silkeborg Kunstmuseum, 1983.
*L'Encre du savant et le sang des martyrs. Mythes et fantasmes dans les romans de Michel Tournier*. Dissertation, Odense Universitetsforlag, 1995.
(ed.), *Frankofoni. Sprog, historie, litteratur og kultur*. Sprog og kulturmøde 33, Aalborg Universitetsforlag, 2003.

**Jan Gustavsson**, Ph.D., is Senior Lecturer at Copenhagen Business School. Recent publications:
"El salvaje y nosotros - signos del latinoamericano. Una hermenéutica del otro". Copenhagen Working Papers, 1999-2000.
"La semiosis limitada y la confección del Otro". In: *Semiosis Ilimitada 1: 'El otro'*. Río Gallegos, Argentina 2002.
"Textual Boundary Explorations: Positing Self and Other as Actors in global charity". In: Blasco & Gustafsson (eds.), *Intercultural Alternatives*. CBS Press, Copenhagen, 2004 (forthcoming).

**Hans Lauge Hansen**, Ph.D., is Senior Lecturer at the University of Copenhagen and Head Manager of the *Language and Culture Network*. Recent publications: (ed.), *Changing Philologies*. Museum Tusculanum Press, 2002.
"Towards a New Philology of Culture". In: Jensen (ed), *The Object of Study of the Humanities*. Copenhagen, Museum Tusculanum Press, 2003.
"Globalization of the Semiosfere". In: Ashley & Finke (eds), *Geolinguistics*. New York, (Forthcoming).

**Lisbeth Verstraete Hansen**, Ph.D., holds a postdoctoral position at the University of Copenhagen. Latest publication:
"Charles Paron, Les Chiens de la Senne". In: Bertrand & Gauvin (eds), *Littératures mineures en langue majeure*. Québec/Wallonie-Bruxelles, P.I.E. Peter Lang S.A. et Les Presses de l'Université de Montréal, Bruxelles-Montréal, 2003.

**Ken Henriksen** received his Ph.D. from the Faculty of Modern Languages, Copenhagen Business School in 2003.
His thesis, *The Construction of Ethnic and Spatial Identities. Everyday Forms of State mutation on Nicaragua's Atlantic Coast*, focuses on ethnicity and minority politics. He is Extra-Mural Lecturer at the Department of Intercultural Communication and Management, Copenhagen Business School, where he teaches Latin American Studies.

**Anne Marie Ejdesgaard Jeppesen**, Ph.D., is Senior Lecturer at the University of Copenhagen. Recent publications:
"Reading the Bolivian Landscape of Exclusion and Inclusion: the Law of Popular Participation". In: Engberg-Pedersen & Webster (eds.), *Political space for Poverty Alleviation*. ZED Books, 2002.
"Language as Intercultural Comunication". In: Hansen (ed.), *Changing Philologies*. Copenhagen, Museum Tusculanum Press, 2002.
"Using the past to construct present identities: Memories of Bolivian ex-miners". In: *Estudios Interdisciplinarios de America Latina y el Caribe*. Vol.15, 1, 2004 (forthcoming).

**Helge Jordheim**, Cand. Philol., Research Scholar at the University of Oslo. Recent publications:
*Lesningens vitenskap - utkast til en ny filology*. Oslo 2001.
"Die Hypokrisie der Aufklärer – oder: War Wieland ein Lügner. Eine Untersuchung zu Kosellecks *Kritik und Krise*". In: Palonen & Kurunmäki (eds.), *Time, History and Politics/ Zeit, Geschichte und Politik. Zum achtzigsten Geburtstag von Reinhart Koselleck*. Jyväskylä 2003.
"Teksthistorie i lys av en ny filologi". In Berge (ed.), *Teksthistorie - tekstvitenskapelige bidrag*, Oslo, 2003.

List of Authors 245

**Ingemai Larsen**, Ph.D., is Senior Lecturer at the University of Copenhagen.
Recent publications:
"Portugal and the Second World War, or the modification of an invented tradition". *Bulletin of Hispanic Studies*, Vol. LXXX, 3, 2003.
"O império Português responde por escrito ou: estamos numa nice – sobre a situação luso-africana na perspectiva dos estudos de pós-colonialismo". *Folha de Linguística e Literatura* 5, Maputo, 2003.

**Pia Schwarz Lausten**, Ph.D., is Extra-Mural Lecturer in Italian literature at the University of Copenhagen. She is at present Research Fellow at the *Danish Institute for Advanced Studies in the Humanities,* researching subjectivity in the Italian Renaissance with special reference to Boiardo's *Orlando innamorato*. Principal publications:
Articles on Pirandello, Tabucchi, Celati, Vassalli, Capriolo in literary reviews and in Petersen & Grundtvig: *Rejsen og blikket*. Copenhagen, 1999.
*Identità e alterità nell'opera di Antonio Tabucchi*. Etudes Romanes 57, Museum Tusculanum Press, 2004 (forthcoming).

**Anne Magnussen**, Ph.D., is Senior Lecturer at the University of Southern Denmark. Recent publications:
"Spanish Comics and Family". *International Journal of Comic Art.* Fall, 2003.
"Spanske tegneserier i 1970erne og 1980erne – fra politiske budskaber til europæisk integration". In: *Er Spanien anderledes?* Den Jyske Historiker 91/92, 2001.

**Bernard Mouralis** is Professor at the University of Cergy-Pontoise, France and Director of the research centre "Texte / Histoire". Area of research: African literature, the relationship between France and Africa, and literary theory. Principal recent publications:
*L'Europe, l'Afrique et la folie*. Présence Africaine, 1993.
With E. Fraisse (eds): *République et colonies*. Présence Africaine, 1999.
*Questions générales de littérature*. Seuil, 2001.

**Sofie Nielsen** is Ph.D. student at the University of Roskilde, researching the possibilities for a cultural orientation of literary studies on the premise of an understanding of functional changes of the aesthetic and of processes of aestheticization (i.e. 'aisthesis' as an opening out of the concept of aesthetics beyond the realm of art).

**Nina Nørgaard**, Ph.D., is Lecturer at the University of Southern Denmark. Principal publications:
*Systemic Functional Linguistics and Literary Analysis. A Hallidayan Approach to Joyce - A Joycean Approach to Halliday*. Odense, University Press of Southern Denmark, 2003.
"Halliday og Hasans kohæsionsbegreb i en litterær kontekst." In: Bache, Birkelund & Nørgaard (eds.), *Ny Forskning i Grammatik 10*. Odense, University Press of Southern Denmark, 2003.

**Johan Pedersen**, Ph.D., is Lecturer at the University of Copenhagen. Recent publications:
"La base discursiva de la oración compuesta". In: Delbecque (ed.): *Aproximaciones cognoscitivo-funcionales al español*. Ámsterdam/New York, Rodopi, 2003.
"Reflexive intensification in Spanish. Toward a complex reflexive?" In: Fortescue et al (eds.), *Selected Papers from the XVIth International Conference on Historical Linguistics*. Amsterdam, John Benjamins (Forthcoming).

**Jens Rahbek Rasmussen**, Ph.D., is Senior Lecturer at the University of Copenhagen. Recent publications:
*Modernitet eller åndsdannelse: Engelsk i skole og samfund 1800-1935*. Museum Tusculanum Press, 2003.
"'No Proper Taste for the English Way of Life': Danish Perceptions of Britain 1870-1940". In: Sevaldsen (ed.), *Britain and Denmark*. Museum Tusculanum Press, 2003.
"Love and Hate Between Nations: Britain in the Scandinavian Mirror". *European Journal of English Studies* (Forthcoming).

**Karen Risager**, Dr.Phil., is Senior Lecturer at Roskilde University where she is Director of the Cultural Encounters programme. Recent publications:
With Michael Byram: *Language Teachers, Politics and Cultures*. Multilingual Matters, 1999.
*Det nationale dilemma i sprog- og kulturpaedagogikken. Et studie i forholdet mellem sprog og kultur*. Akademisk Forlag, 2003.

**Mette Steenberg** is Ph.D. student and Extra-Mural Lecturer at the University of Aarhus. Recent publications:
"The Emotive Function of Poetic Imagery". *Odense Working Papers in Language and Communication*, no. 23, 2002.
"Carpe Diem: The study of periods within Cognitive Poetics". In: *Linguagem, cultura e cognicão: Estudios de Linguística Cognitiva*. Universidade Católica Portuguesa, Braga (Forthcoming).

**Thora Vinther** is Senior Lecturer at the University of Copenhagen. Recent publications:
"Exact repetition as input enhancement in second language acquisition". In: E.D.Jensen & Vinther (eds), *Language Learning* 53, 3, 2003.
"Den spanske konstruktion ir + a + infinitiv i grammatikaliseringsperspektiv". In: Heltoft, Nørgaard-Sørensen & Schøsler (eds): *Grammatikalisering og struktur*. Museum Tusculanum Press, 2004 (forthcoming).

## Changing Philologies
*Contributions to the Redefinition
of Foreign Language Studies
in the Age of Globalisation*

Edited by Hans Lauge Hansen, University of Copenhagen

Museum Tusculanum Press, 2002
160 pages, pb., ISBN 87-7289-790-2
Prices Dkr. 175, £16, $22, € 25

This book contains the proceedings from the conference *Changing Philologies* together with other contributions on the same topic. The conference was organised by the Danish Institute for Advanced Studies in the Humanities and was held on 8-9 February 2002 in Copenhagen.

The contributors to this book question whether the traditional paradigm of national philology, which dominated Foreign Language Studies for more than a century, is appropriate for meeting the challenge posed by the economic and political globalisation of today. They argue that the relation between languages and cultures will become an important field of investigation in the future, and that Foreign Language Studies must provide linguistically skilled candidates trained in cultural translation and intercultural communication. In order to do so, the departments of Foreign Language Studies must strengthen their interdisciplinary activities and engage in theoretical reflections upon the relation between such entities as language, culture, identity, and history, and the self-knowledge and imaginary world pictures represented in art and literature.

Contributors:
Susan Bassnett, University of Warwick, England
Gert Sørensen, University of Copenhagen, Denmark
Anne Marie Jeppesen, University of Copenhagen, Denmark
Hanne Leth Andersen, University of Aarhus, Denmark
Herbert Grabes, University of Giessen, Germany
Hans Lauge Hansen, University of Copenhagen, Denmark
Jostein Børtnes, University of Bergen, Norway
Jacob Mey, University of Southern Denmark
Nigel Fabb, University of Strathclyde, Scotland
Hanne Jansen, University of Copenhagen, Denmark
Lene Waage Petersen, University of Copenhagen, Denmark
Ingemai Larsen, University of Copenhagen, Denmark